US National Security

US NATIONAL SECURITY

New Threats, Old Realities

Paul R. Viotti

Rapid Communications in Conflict and Security Series
General Editor: Geoffrey R.H. Burn

CAMBRIA
PRESS

Amherst, New York

Requests for permission should be directed to:
permissions@cambriapress.com, or mailed to:
Cambria Press
University Corporate Centre,
100 Corporate Parkway, Suite 128
Amherst, New York 14226, U.S.A.

Front cover image: U.S. Soldiers with the 44th Chemical Company,
2nd Chemical Battalion, 48th Chemical Brigade, based out of Fort
Hood, Texas. (U.S. Army photo by Spc. Robert Farrell/Released).

Library of Congress Cataloging-in-Publication Data

Names: Viotti, Paul R., author.
Title: US national security : new threats, old realities / Paul R. Viotti.
Description: Amherst, New York : Cambria Press, [2016] |
Series: Cambria rapid communications in conflict and security series |
Includes bibliographical references and index.

Identifiers: LCCN 2016021832 |

ISBN 9781604979305 (alk. paper)

Subjects: LCSH: National security--United States. |
United States--Military policy.

Classification: LCC UA23 .V56 2016 |
DDC 355/.033073--dc23
LC record available at https://lccn.loc.gov/2016021832

TABLE OF CONTENTS

List of Tables

LIST OF FIGURES

PREFACE

This book sees national security as a highly subjective enterprise. This is a constructivist account in which ideas and their institutional carriers matter. What are presented as objective facts in security (as in other) discourses are really understandings distilled through interpretive filters that are themselves constructed from experiences and ideas embedded, often idiosyncratically, in the minds of those with authority or in a position to make national security decisions. What it means to be secure and what is a threat or opportunity to be pursued are not objectively clear. Decision-making processes are facilitated or constrained, illuminated or prejudiced by prior, internalized understandings.

Conceptual understandings about security-related matters—what we mean by war and peace, deterrence and war fighting, power and balance of power, arms control and conflict management, coercive diplomacy and other concepts examined in this volume—are social constructions internalized by decision makers and those who advise them. What is a threat (much less an existential threat), for example, is always subject to multiple interpretations.

The decision to impose a naval blockade on Cuba in October 1962 is a case in point. The idea of Soviet missiles with nuclear weapons in Cuba just ninety miles from Florida's shores was an existential threat to some, particularly the generals and admirals on the Joint Chiefs of Staff (JCS), joined as they were initially by secretary of state Dean Rusk, secretary of treasury Douglas Dillon, and Central Intelligence Agency (CIA) director John McCone—all part of the inner circle advising President John F. Kennedy. The president's brother, Attorney General Robert Kennedy, presidential adviser Theodore Sorensen, and Secretary of Defense Robert McNamara had different views, as did Undersecretary of State George Ball and UN Ambassador Adlai Stevenson.

The parties did not necessarily alter their understandings of the threat, but as the president's preferences on options became clearer—his brother the principal interlocutor—the Kennedy team finally came together in the consensus the president wanted. Coupled with diplomacy, members of the president's team favored the naval-blockade option, itself an act of war, but markedly less provocative than air strikes or a full-scale invasion. Only JCS Chairman, General Maxwell Taylor, and CIA Director McCone were not part of this consensus, preferring air strikes followed by invasion, if necessary. For his part, President Kennedy kept the latter two options open should the naval blockade and diplomacy not result in Soviet withdrawal of the missiles.

What this case illustrates clearly is the essential subjectivity of national security decision making. It was not merely perception of threat, as if that were an objective condition easily determined. No, it was subject to diverse interpretations apparently based on deeply embedded prior understandings that influenced how decision makers individually or collectively interpreted the degree of threat posed by the Soviet placement of nuclear-armed missiles in Cuba well within range of Washington, New York, and other cities on the East Coast and Midwest. However the degree of threat was seen, the efficacy of different options—doing nothing, diplomacy, naval blockade, air strikes, or full-scale invasion— was disputed between those favoring a robust response (air strikes or invasion) and those preferring a more measured or moderate approach (diplomacy alone or combined with naval blockade).

The Cuban missile crisis is by no means unique. Differences of views are more commonplace whether in crises or in less pressing circumstances. Different understandings, preferences, and exchanges of points of view among decision makers and those advising them become central in what is essentially an intersubjective process. Routines, procedures, and the frames of reference bureaucratic or other agents use to understand what is at issue also matter. The politics of pulling and hauling, coalition and countercoalition formation, and compromise typically influence the final decision-making outcomes.[1] It is not as if decisions are made rationally in an ivory tower or vacuum bereft of social constructions, intersubjectivity, and political interactions.

NETWORKS AND INSTITUTIONS—GROUNDING IDEAS IN INTERESTS

Ideas matter in the making and implementation of national security policy. Whether these ideas about national security are good, bad, or somewhere in between, they go nowhere in the absence of advocates who successfully ground them in the interests of the relevant players. Indeed, *ideas grounded in interests are the motive forces of politics.*[2] This is the case not just in domestic politics on the Potomac and elsewhere in the country, but also in US efforts with allies, coalition partners, and others abroad.

Ideas of primary concern to us in this volume, of course, are ideas related to US national security. Advocates carry them not just as individuals but also in the socially constructed networks and institutions to which they belong or use to advance their policy-related agendas. Neoconservatives were part of a network of likeminded individuals who saw an opportunity in the George W. Bush administration to advance their understandings of US national security interests in the Middle East. They saw effecting regime change in Iraq through armed intervention not only as preventing

Iraq from acquiring nuclear weapons or employing chemical or other weapons of mass destruction, but also removing a threat to Israel and establishing a US presence in a very strategically located country. Added to that was rhetoric—believed by some—that Iraq could become a model democracy for all of Araby to emulate.

Many disagreed with this neoconservative formulation, but their ideas mattered less, their voices less influential among those in positions with authority to make final decisions—the president, vice president, and secretary of defense who proved to be the decisive players. The secretary of state, secretary of the army, and army chief of staff all had reservations about the venture, but could not counter the consensus that formed within the inner circle, influenced as they were at the time by neoconservative (or militant internationalist) understandings of national interest.

These understandings or ideas—good or bad—in the minds of decision makers drive policy with substantial, sometimes adverse, consequences. The US-led invasion of Iraq destabilized further an already unstable region. Saddam Hussein's regime was overthrown, but insufficient numbers of ground forces were deployed to secure order and establish a new regime that would accommodate the interests of diverse ethnic groups—Kurds, both Sunni and Shia Arabs, and other minorities. Worse, the Sunni-dominated Iraqi military was disbanded and civil servants associated with Saddam's Baathist Party were dismissed. An insurgency of disenfranchised Sunni quickly formed. The seeds had been sown for what germinated as the Islamic State in Iraq and Syria (ISIS) or Iraq and the Levant (ISIL)—the Levant referring to the area encompassing Syria, Jordan, Lebanon, Israel, and the eastern Mediterranean. The equivalent Arabic acronym *Da'esh* has a decidedly negative connotation in Arabic, which is why Arabs and others opposed to the Islamic State prefer to use that term.

Networks matter, as do ideas grounded in interests and carried by these socially constructed networks and institutions that have influenced national security policy throughout the American experience. Accordingly, this volume frequently takes an historical approach to the subject, identifying networks and social constructions often overlooked in other accounts.

How We See and Understand National Security Policy Choices

Recent developments in neuroscience and new findings about how the human brain functions dovetail with long-term social science inquiries related to cognition—the way we perceive, process, understand, and make choices or decisions. Not just related to the sciences, the implications of these findings have also been the basis for a number of books in popular culture, bestseller, and trade-book markets. Taking this subjectivity into account and identifying the social constructions that influence the making and implementation of national security policy are the focus throughout this volume.

Threats, Opportunities, and the Use of Force

Part 1 takes up *threats, opportunities,* and the *use of force.* We begin in chapter 1 with the *"brave new world" of US national security*—such issues as cyber warfare, terrorism, global climate change, threats in outer space, and the proliferation of weapons of mass destruction. These are in addition to more conventional challenges dealt with in subsequent chapters.

Thus, *war and armed interventions*—the organized use of force by states against other state or nonstate actors—are the subjects of chapters 2 and 3 respectively. Related to the nonstate actor challenge are *insurgencies, terrorism,* and other forms of political violence that have increased dramatically over the decades since the 1980s, which are addressed in chapters 4 and 5. Chapter 6 on *intelligence* is important in both war and peace to include countering global or regional insurgents prone to use one form or another of politically motivated violence—insurrection, terrorism, assassination, guerrilla warfare, and even combat with regular military units.

Force Maximization—Human and Material Resources

Part Two deals with *force maximization—the human and material resources* that are core to implementing US national security policy. *Civil-military relations* under the US Constitution and traditions dating from the earliest days of the republic are the focus of chapters 7 and 8 that take up constructing and sustaining civilian supremacy over the armed forces and integrating ethnic or racial minorities, women, and persons of diverse sexual orientation or identity within the armed services. Chapter 9 delves into the *organization* of the Defense Department and its *budget*—allocating dollars to organizing, training, and equipping the armed forces—particularly outlays for personnel; procurement; operations and maintenance (O&M); and research, development, test and evaluation (RDT&E). Finally, in the conclusion we weave the threads of national security sewn in previous chapters into a new cloth of a reconstructed realism that embraces multilateralism and finds both cooperative and collaborative bases of security in this *brave new world* that is before us in the opening decades of the twenty-first century.

NOTES

1. See Graham Allison and Phillip Zelikow, *Essence of Decision: Explaining the Cuban Missile Crisis*, 2nd ed. (New York: Pearson, 1999).
2. I owe this insight to the late Ernst B. Haas, University of California, Berkeley.

ACKNOWLEDGEMENTS

I am indebted to professors who in the mid-1960s set me on the path to the study of American national security at the US Air Force Academy—Erik Ronhovde, Curtis Cook, John C. Ries, and Richard Rosser; Georgetown University—William V. O'Brien; and, in the mid-1970s at the University of California, Berkeley—Kenneth Waltz and Ernst B. Haas. The late Fred Sondermann at Colorado College, Klaus Knorr of Princeton University, and Laurence Martin of Kings College (UK) joined forces in the 1970s to conduct summer seminars on security that also brought me into contact in the early stage of our careers with Richard Betts, Dan Caldwell, Robin Dorff, Dennis Ross, and others. Catherine Kelleher was an early supporter who encouraged me to pursue security studies, nominating me for membership in the International Institute of Strategic Studies, which I still value highly for its ongoing work in this extraordinarily important field. I also acknowledge the security-related insights and encouragement of my friends and colleagues at the University of Denver's Korbel School of International Studies—David Goldfischer in the Institute on Globalization and Security and the curriculum we organized under his direction, Arthur Gilbert, Joseph Szyliowicz, Karen Feste, Jonathan Adelman, and Tom Farer, my former Dean. Thanks to critical reads of the intelligence chapter by Mark Kauppi, the two civil-military relations chapters by John A. (Jay) Williams, and the one on war by Tim Perry. Finally, most helpful in bringing this project to fruition are my graduate research associates—Eric de Campos, Daniel (Tyler) Brooks, Daniel Green, Trevor Jones (particularly for his graphic artistry on figures), Robert Shelala, and Frank Talbert. Thanks are also due to my reviewers for their comments and to my editor, Geoffrey Burn, for his suggestions and encouragement throughout.

US National Security

Chapter 1

A Brave New World

"Ferizi, it said, 'is accused of passing the data to Islamic State member Junaid Hussain, a British citizen who in August posted links on Twitter to the names, email addresses, passwords, locations and phone numbers of 1,351 US military and other government personnel. He included a warning that Islamic State 'soldiers ... will strike at your necks in your own lands!' F.B.I. agents tracked Ferizi 'to a computer with an Internet address in Malaysia,' where he was arrested. Meanwhile, Hussain was killed by a US drone in Syria. **Wow:** An Albanian hacker in Malaysia collaborating with an ISIS jihadist on Twitter to intimidate US soldiers online — before we killed the jihadist with a drone!"

—Thomas L. Freedman[1]

In Aldous Huxley's *Brave New World* (1932), the author satirizes the impact of technology on daily life. Although the advance of technology has had positive impact, Huxley gives us a glimpse at its dark side. Bravery is indeed a prerequisite of security in this new world.

In addition to concerns about war, armed interventions, insurgencies, terrorism, and other forms of political violence addressed in subsequent chapters, we take up briefly here the new challenges facing American decision makers operating within this brave new world: cyber threats and cyber warfare; climate change; water and resource competition; pollution and resource depletion; food production and distribution shortfalls; health crises, particularly epidemics and pandemics; increasingly globalized crime; weaponization of space; and the consequent prospects for armed conflict there—the science fictional "star wars" made real; and the proliferation of weapons of mass destruction across the globe—not only among states, but also potentially among terrorist groups or other nonstate actors. Finally, there is also the devastation of natural events like hurricanes and tornados, floods and droughts, earthquakes and tsunami, volcano eruptions, and even asteroids impacting planet Earth.

THE GREAT DIVIDE

A great divide separates those who see security as dealing exclusively with threats from state and nonstate actors and those who see security more broadly as including challenges to the welfare of people. Indeed, the classical lines drawn between security and welfare become blurred when we take into account criminal or terrorist threats to individuals, inequality and poverty, unequal access to health care, poor nutrition, and other human-security issues. As noted earlier, American national security in this increasingly globalized world also faces a new set of technological, environmental, and arms control challenges.

On top of these are wars and "rumors of wars"—using force, the threat of force, and other forms of military influence to achieve objectives (as, for example, Russia has done in Georgia, the Ukraine, and Syria); insurgencies like the Islamic State in Syria and Iraq as well as al Qaeda and their affiliates; intercommunal strife in deeply divided societies; terrorism and other forms of political violence. These diverse forms of violence adversely affect people, leading many to seek safer havens— migrations of refugees that challenge the societies to which they flee. Finally, international crime, well established in the twentieth century, not only will persist but also likely will expand substantially—its predatory actions an ongoing threat to human security.

Complicating approaches to many of these challenges is lack of policy consensus on desired ends and the means to achieve them. If that were not enough, policy choice is confounded further by scientific uncertainties on both cause-and-effect and the efficacy of proposed remedies for dealing with the complex set of issues on the US national security agenda. Nicely capturing this policy challenge is an adaptation in Table 1 of J.D. Thompson's policy matrix[2] that arrays cause-effect considerations against uncertainty on desired ends and the means to achieve them.

Table 1. Causal Understandings and Policy Options.

	Policy Options: How Means Relate to Ends	
	Certain	Uncertain
Relation Between Cause & Effect — Certain		
Relation Between Cause & Effect — Uncertain		

Source. Adapted from J.D. Thompson, *Organizations in Action.*

Applying this matrix to a particular issue like climate change is instructive. There is scientific consensus that global warming is occurring and that hydrocarbon emissions are the major (but not only) cause of greenhouse gases in the upper atmosphere. There is substantial disagreement, however, on the speed of climate change and relative contribution of different sources of this atmospheric pollution which, in turn, adds to uncertainty on policy options; that is, proposed remedies. Adding noise to the issue are those politically motivated individuals and groups who dispute scientifically based claims that they deem adverse to oil, gas, and other industries or capital interests.

Cyber Threats and Cyberwarfare

Hacking into electronic data systems with intent to do damage is the stuff of cyberwarfare. Perpetrators include agents acting for states as well as nongovernmental hackers. Their targets include the Internet itself as well as the networks, computers, and data banks of both state and nonstate actors—military and other government agencies, businesses—particularly the securities and financial sectors, electric grids, other infrastructure, and individuals.

Increasing dependence on the web for day-to-day transactions means increasing vulnerability to disruptions of any kind, particularly those perpetrated with malicious intent. Indeed, cyber and the rest of societal infrastructure have become increasingly integrated and thus highly vulnerable to attack—as are military command-and-control communications, reconnaissance, and other intelligence operations upon which national security depends.

Old ideas from an earlier era still hold sway. How can we deter, how can we dissuade attacks on the infrastructure upon which daily life has come to depend?[3] Do we plan and threaten attacks on the infrastructures of adversaries to deter them from attacking us? When they develop nuclear or other weapons systems of mass destruction that are threatening to us, do we go on the offensive, searching for and destroying the cyber or telecommunications technologies that, in Clausewitzian terms, define the adversary's center of gravity? Even if we could deter or dissuade states from cyber or nuclear attacks, what means will curb nonstate actors from engaging in such conduct?

In addition to military preparations, is there a place for arms control? Can countries reach consensus on rules of the road—at the very least to keep conflicts contained? Can the International Telecommunications Union (ITU) or other international organizations play a constructive role in helping keep cyber conflicts from spinning out of control?

Whatever these future prospects, by executive order the Obama administration, seeking a balance between security needs and civil-liberties concerns, framed the American national response to cyber threats as follows:

> It is the policy of the United States to enhance the security and resilience of the Nation's critical infrastructure and to maintain a cyber environment that encourages efficiency, innovation, and economic prosperity while promoting safety, security, business confidentiality, privacy, and civil liberties. We can achieve these goals through a partnership with the owners and operators of critical infrastructure to improve cybersecurity information sharing and collaboratively develop and implement risk-based standards.[4]

Establishing government-corporate partnership has not been easy, particularly because corporations have a business interest in keeping the promise of protecting the privacy of its customers. Relinquishing their own access, Apple, Google, and other private-sector providers increasingly encrypt the phone or message data of their customers, thereby effectively denying government access as well. Whether for counterterrorism or other law-enforcement purposes, the Federal Bureau of Investigation (FBI) and other government agencies engaged in law enforcement, counter-terrorist, and other activities cannot readily get access if the service providers do not retain the keys to decoding data encrypted individually for each customer.

For its part, the Department of Homeland Security (DHS) has the cybersecurity task of protecting the country's critical infrastructure,[5] but it also depends on the cyberwarfare capabilities of the Department of Defense (DoD). A part of the US Strategic Command, the US Cyber Command (CYBERCOM) is conveniently also located at Fort Meade in Maryland with the DoD's National Security Agency (NSA). Consolidating access to long-established national communications-security (COMSEC) assets at NSA facilitates identification of cyber threats and formulation of effective responses. Army, air force, navy, and marine corps components of CYBERCOM round out the DoD effort in cybersecurity.[6]

It is a three-pronged approach with both offensive and defensive components: *combat mission forces* tasked with attacks on the cyber and other capabilities of adversaries; *national mission forces* that defend computer systems linked to government, the power grid, dams, water, wastewater, air traffic control, and other transportation systems, financial networks, and other critical infrastructure; and *cyber protection forces* focused on protecting DoD's own computer systems.[7]

By presidential directive,[8] other key governmental participants in cybersecurity matters include the Directorate of National Intelligence (DNI) and the intelligence community it oversees, the Nuclear Regulatory Commission (NRC), the Federal Communications Commission (FCC), and the Departments of State, Justice (particularly the FBI), Interior, and Commerce. Beyond this interagency cybersecurity effort coordinated by the Department of Homeland Security, the presidential directive provides for public-private partnerships.

Google, Microsoft, Apple, and other firms have the cyber capabilities to augment US government capabilities it offers to protect as part of national infrastructure. These technologies give greater capacity for probing the vast "deep web" well beneath the surface of (and much larger than) the worldwide web—information of intelligence and cyberwarfare value—pages not normally reachable through the usual search engines.

Indeed, the challenges of cyberwarfare are deep in this brave new world. How can we avoid the disruption of military command and control, financial systems, air traffic control, and telecommunications? It is a conundrum that challenges the finest minds, real and artificial! On the other hand, to what extent can the United States use cyber tools effectively against adversaries—disrupting nuclear and other weapons development programs, blocking their command-and-control communications, and attacking selected infrastructure? Put another way, cyber security has both its defensive and offensive sides.

GLOBAL CRIME

Centuries-old "brotherhoods" in crime remain on the global scene, now engaged in ever more sophisticated operations that draw on advanced technologies. Moreover, the ranks of Italian and American mafias, Japanese yakuza, Chinese triads, Russian mafia, and Mexican or other Latin American drug cartels have been joined by other criminally oriented networks that have global reach.

Given their oftentimes separate national or ethnic identities, these networks tend not to form coalitions with each other. Competition within and among them for greater criminal "market share" reduces to some extent the collective, adverse impact they otherwise might have on the global stage. Nevertheless, corporations, banks, and other financial institutions—not to mention individuals—are vulnerable to their predatory conduct, their adverse impact enhanced by cybercrime.

Use of the Internet for cyber theft of financial assets, contract details, trade secrets, customer files, and other documents has already redefined the face of organized crime. Not just confined to these well-established networks, individuals and groups with cyber skills can access the same sources. Moreover, cyber espionage has become one of the covert action tools governments directly or indirectly ("outsourcing" through inter-mediaries) have employed against adversaries.

Of course, cybercrime is only part of the action. Narcotics and human trafficking for prostitution, slave labor, child labor, and other human rights and human security abuses continue, aided as they are by the transportation and telecommunications modalities so integral to an increasingly globalized world.

Countering these threats to human security means having to enhance law-enforcement capacity to identify and apprehend perpetrators of criminal activities. Technologies for doing so—intercepting communications and tracking the movements of suspects raise substantial privacy concerns as those innocent of any wrongdoing may fall under the spotlight of criminal surveillance by state authorities. Where the lines are drawn for such surveillance within the United States and abroad is an ongoing concern. Security of individuals is not only about protecting them from criminal predators, but also allowing them to live in their own spaces not violated by undue intrusions of law enforcement and other government or private-sector agencies, firms, and individuals.

Climate Change, Resource Competition, and Food Security

Global climate change and its adverse implications for the population make it a national security issue in this brave new world. The scientific consensus on human-caused climate change is clear. We ignore evidence of global warming at our peril. We explore this phenomenon here and briefly assess its implications for human security. To burdening the atmosphere with excessive carbon emissions, add resource depletion and other forms of atmospheric, land, and water pollution.

Climate change directly affects food distribution (e.g., production on land and fish stocks at sea). Access to food is thus becoming an even greater human security concern than it already is in so many densely and increasingly populated parts of the world. Scarcity of fresh water is another result of climate change; this impact is happening in many countries, including the United States where some parts of the country that had ample water supplies in the past now suffer from long-term droughts. Depletion of aquifers and decreased river flow also deprive agriculture and populations downstream of adequate water access.

Before us in this brave new world is the increasing displacement of people not just because of wars, insurgencies, and intercommunal strife, but also migrations forced by adverse circumstances related to climate change. Moreover, wars and other forms of domestic violence may break out in regions around the world as states and other groups compete for water, food, and other increasingly scarce resources.

These are not just environmental issues that somehow can be set aside as having no bearing on the lives of the citizenry. Many are in denial when it comes to concerns about the environment. Because the lives and wellbeing of human beings are at stake, these are indeed national security matters that cannot be so easily dismissed.

One of the curious phenomena of the late twentieth and early twenty-first centuries is the rejection of science in certain circles. Unpleasant "truths" are conveniently set aside.[9] The routine skepticism and disputes in scientific communities about any truth claim are turned against them. Although uncertainties are inherent within the scientific enterprise (e.g., atmospheric scientists differing on the rate of change or severity of effects), critics prefer to ignore the consensus in this same scientific community that global climate change is in fact occurring. Particularly troubling to decision makers is when opposition to scientific findings takes the form of moral or religious absolutism.[10]

The great increases in productivity spawned by the nineteenth-century industrial revolution and the vast improvement in the human condition resulting from applications of science and technology in the decades that followed have come at an enormous environmental price. In addition to ongoing resource depletion, the pollution of land, the atmosphere, lakes, rivers, streams, oceans and seas continues to have adverse effects on the health and welfare of human beings globally as well as on the animal and plant life that also make up the human habitat.

Burning of fossil fuels adds to "greenhouse gases" in the relatively thin atmosphere that blankets the earth. To grasp just how thin is the space in which humankind live, look some two miles down the road and, in your mind's eye, rotate this relatively short distance upward toward the sky.[11] In this part of the troposphere where human beings live and in the upper atmosphere are the greenhouse gases like carbon dioxide, methane, nitrous oxide, and ozone that, in addition to natural phenomena, come directly from the combustion of carbon fuels. Through increased evaporation from oceans and other bodies of water, increasing global temperatures also add more water vapor—another greenhouse gas that helps retain heat from the sun.

The net effects of adding greenhouse gases are increasing temperatures and, given the climatic transformation underway, extreme and irregular weather patterns. The United Nations' Intergovernmental Panel on Climate Change (IPCC) finds a one-degree Celsius increase in global temperature during the past 100 years, predicting a further increase of 1.5 to 4.5 degrees Celsius (2.7–8.1 degrees Fahrenheit) by the end of the twenty-first century. The sea level already has risen about 7.5 inches (19cm) since the nineteenth century and likely will rise an additional 10–32 inches (26–82 cm) by 2100.

IPCC reports consistently underscore how curbing carbon emissions is the core policy challenge. The effects of increased greenhouse gases already put into the atmosphere since the dawn of the industrial revolution will continue to be felt in the decades to come. The modest goal of stabilizing climate change to allow more time for human, animal, and plant life to adapt is likely the best that can be achieved. The IPCC call to policy makers is strong—that we cannot lose yet another decade due to inaction if we are to slow or stabilize the rate of climate change.

A few atmospheric scientists—dubbed "radicals" among mainstream environmentalists—go well beyond these more conservative IPCC predictions. They see a real threat of rapid runaway, catastrophic climate change if we continue current patterns of energy consumption with the resulting carbon emissions. One of these scientists warns: "If we burn all reserves of oil, gas, and coal, there is a substantial chance we will initiate the runaway greenhouse." Even worse, if we add oil from tar sands to the other reserves, he sees as "a dead certainty" the Earth becoming overheated like Venus—the so-called "Venus syndrome" that will extinguish life on the planet.[12]

Table 2a. The Risks to Human Security of Global Climate Change.

Reasons for Concern (RFC)* are specified for each of the following risks listed:

- Death, injury, ill health, or disrupted livelihoods in low-lying coastal zones and small island developing states and other small islands, due to storm surges, coastal flooding, and sea level rise. [RFC 1-5]
- Severe ill health and disrupted livelihoods for large urban populations due to inland flooding in some regions. [RFC 2 and 3]
- Extreme weather events leading to breakdown of infrastructure networks and critical services such as electricity, water supply, and health and emergency services. [RFC 2-4]
- Mortality and morbidity during periods of extreme heat, particularly for vulnerable urban populations and those working outdoors in urban or rural areas. [RFC 2 and 3]
- Food insecurity and the breakdown of food systems linked to warming, drought, flooding, and precipitation variability and extremes, particularly for poorer populations in urban and rural settings. [RFC 2-4]
- Loss of rural livelihoods and income due to insufficient access to drinking and irrigation water and reduced agricultural productivity, particularly for farmers and pastoralists with minimal capital in semi-arid regions. [RFC 2 and 3]
- Loss of marine and coastal ecosystems, biodiversity, and the ecosystem goods, functions, and services they provide for coastal livelihoods, especially for fishing communities in the tropics and the Arctic. [RFC 1, 2, and 4]
- Loss of terrestrial and inland water ecosystems, biodiversity, and the ecosystem goods, functions, and services they provide for livelihoods. [RFC 1, 3, and 4]

Source. IPCC, Climate Change 2014: Impacts, Adaptation, and Vulnerability.

Table 2b. The Risks to Human Security of Global Climate Change (*Cont'd*).

* The reasons for concern (RFC):

RFC 1. Unique and threatened systems;

RFC 2. Extreme weather events;

RFC 3. Uneven distribution of impacts, generally greater for disadvantaged people and communities;

RFC 4. Global aggregate impacts on biodiversity and the global economy;

RFC 5. Large-scale singular events that cause abrupt and irreversible changes to some physical systems or ecosystems

As a practical matter, however, such dire predictions have had relatively little effect in a world more focused on the here and now. In the six years between the 2007 and 2013 IPCC meetings, for example, some 200 billion tons of carbon dioxide were added to the atmosphere. For its part: "The United States consumes 25 per cent of global energy each year and generates over 20 per cent of the world's carbon emissions!"[13] Not only do advanced industrial economies continue to add carbon emissions at high levels, but now they also are joined by developing economies, many of them claiming a right to continue to do so in much the same way as advanced industrial countries have done in the last century and a half. So much for protecting the global commons!

Attempts to update and expand international limits on carbon emissions have been fraught with difficulties. The United States signed but never ratified the 1997 Kyoto Protocol to the United Nations Framework Convention on Climate Change (UNFCCC),[14] which set carbon emissions targets. The modest aim was merely to slow down and stabilize the rate of global climate change—buying time to allow for adaptation to the new environmental circumstances.

Short-term economic stakes are high, driving the parties to the UNFCCC apart as so many pursue a less-than-enlightened understanding of national interest. For its part, the Obama administration put global climate change in its National Security Strategy (NSS) document, identifying it explicitly as a significant national security concern:

> The present day effects of climate change are being felt from the Arctic to the Midwest. Increased sea levels and storm surges threaten coastal regions, infrastructure, and property. In turn, the global economy suffers, compounding the growing costs of preparing and restoring infrastructure.[15]

Given this concern, the NSS includes a national commitment to reduce "greenhouse gas emissions by 26 to 28 percent of 2005 levels by 2025" while participating in global efforts with China and other countries to the same end.

Building on a draft agreement reached in Bonn (October 2015), 196 countries agreed in Paris in December 2015 that "climate change represents an urgent and potentially irreversible threat to human societies and the planet and thus requires the widest possible cooperation by all countries, and their participation in an effective and appropriate international response, with a view to: [1] accelerating the reduction of global greenhouse gas emission; [2] holding the increase in the global average temperature to well below 2°C above preindustrial levels; [3] pursuing efforts to limit the temperature increase to 1.5 °C." Critics observe that the precise ways and means to achieving these goals include "preparation of nationally determined contributions" to carbon reduction are not yet agreed, left to follow-up discussions and a "facilitative dialogue" beginning in 2018.

The longer-term human security implications of climate change are clear. Compared to many other countries, the United States already experiences more than its share of violent storms—mainly tornados and hurricanes that devastate towns and cities, primarily in the midwest, south, and northward along the east coast. Rising sea levels raise questions about which seacoasts are to be saved by dikes or other barrier walls and which are to be surrendered to the encroaching ocean.

Persistent droughts in some areas and floods in others not only impact agricultural production adversely but, as noted earlier, also displace populations, if not immediately, then over time as people must migrate to more habitable regions. To where and how are these peoples to move? How are the masses of displaced persons to have the necessary food, clothing, and shelter to sustain life? Human security quickly becomes national security.

Resource depletion, coupled with pollution of both surface and underground water systems, could result in a struggle for access to fresh water, timber, minerals, and fuels—a competition that some say may lead to interstate war. Change in climate also impacts access to resources, exacerbated by disruptions in transportation networks. If not managed carefully, this struggle for resources—fresh water, timber, minerals, and fuels—increases the likelihood of both civil strife and interstate conflicts. Among these conflict areas abroad are the Nile, Jordan, Tigris-Euphrates, and Indus river basins. Competition over oil drilling rights (access as well as oil) in the Persian Gulf, South China Sea, the Caspian Sea basin, and now, with the increasing ice melt off due to global warming, even the Arctic Ocean.

Canada, Denmark, Finland, Iceland, Norway, Russia, Sweden, and the United States are part of the Arctic Council, an international organization that seeks cooperative security measures to deal with potential conflicts as polar ice continues to melt. The Arctic region is resource rich—oil reserves difficult to access until now due to layers of ice and extreme cold as well as ample fish stocks of halibut, cod, herring, and salmon in the Bering Sea. Seen as a resource in itself, specialists note how sea ice—now being depleted—contains life forms and also serves as the "world's air conditioner."

Melt off opens the Arctic to more maritime use, but it also adds to the problem—accelerating the warming effect as open oceans continue to absorb rather than reflect heat as ice does. Seaside Alaskan villages are already in jeopardy as walruses increasingly come ashore because of reduced access to sea ice. Sovereignty disputes of lesser importance when the area was iced over become more of an issue as the Arctic becomes increasingly open to naval and merchant ships, fishing boats, oil rigs, and other commercial activities pursued by one country or another. How the 12- and 200-mile limits of the law of the sea apply to these activities in addition to navigation, fishing, and resource exploitation on the high seas are important security-related questions. In their division of labor, the US Coast Guard is a "governing force" along Alaska's coastline, the US Navy a war-fighting or deterrence force there and in the Bering Sea and Arctic waters north of Canada.[16]

Regional conflicts may affect US sources of water supply as well as the interests of American allies or coalition partners. Closer to home, resource allocation, including water distribution with Canada to the north and Mexico to the south, will require substantial diplomatic efforts to manage conflicts as they arise. Distribution of water from the Colorado River basin, for example, pits states in the American southwest against each other as well as with Mexico further south.

HEALTH: EPIDEMICS AND PANDEMICS

Human security in this brave new world includes global health and disease control. Epidemics that spread or are endemic within a community are common enough. Diseases that become pandemics—spreading over a wide area—have also plagued humankind over the millennia. History is replete with examples. Prominent among them are the fourteenth-century "Black Death" plague that scourged Europe during which at least 75 million people died and, more recently, the 1918 influenza virus pandemic that took some 50 million lives.

Globalization and the worldwide communications and transportation technologies that bring people together across national boundaries make it ever more difficult to contain outbreaks of contagious diseases to the smaller communities or areas where they first occur. Outbreaks of disease can occur anywhere but the living conditions associated with poverty, particularly in densely populated urban areas, can be a breeding ground for bacterial or viral infections that spread throughout a region and even become global.

It is not just capital-poor areas that are affected. One of the negative externalities of globalization is the way human interactions across countries and regions spread sexually transmitted infections (STI) and diseases (STD) globally, infecting the rich and poor, educated and uneducated. Access to remedies—more prevalent among those in capital-rich, better educated than in capital-poor, less-educated areas—is key, of course, to containing these diseases.

Prominent among these STI is the human immunodeficiency virus (HIV). More than 35 million people worldwide are infected, although access to antiretroviral medications now reduces its progression to acquired immune deficiency syndrome (AIDS). Prevention of the spread of this disease depends on education on modes of transmission, promotion of condom use, and, more recently, selective use of pre- and post-exposure prophylaxis pills (PrEP and PEP respectively). Efforts to contain or eliminate these and other diseases require substantial allocations of capital to programmatic education and distribution of what is needed for disease prevention—a worldwide cooperative effort that brings together efforts by international and both governmental and nongovernmental organizations.

Longer-term remedies for viruses include developing and providing vaccines for particular viruses for populations not just in the United States but also abroad where the diseases may have started. To reduce the likelihood of diseases spreading this way requires economic development, particularly of the health infrastructure in capital-poor countries.

The Ebola virus outbreaks in 2014 are a case in point. Although a worldwide effort finally scored success, initially the ways and means for treating the disease were woefully inadequate. In addition to the aid provided by the World Health Organization (WHO) and nongovernmental organizations, strengthening the capacity of local governments to respond is essential to managing future disease outbreaks.

Unhealthy living conditions are breeding grounds for disease—the recent mosquito-borne Zika virus a case in point. The threat of such diseases breaking out and, in some cases, becoming pandemics likely will remain with us. Poverty, the absence of a determined and sustained effort to improve levels of living, and the absence of adequate health facilities in densely populated areas in Africa, South Asia, and in other capital-poor countries are at the root of the problem. Given transportation and worldwide movement of people in an increasingly globalized world, it is difficult to contain diseases to the areas in which they first emerge.

Both HIV and Ebola are not communicable by air, but are spread by exchange of body fluids or, in the case of Ebola, by physical contact. If a serious virus like either one emerges that is contagious by air, devastation to a population and its global spread can be truly catastrophic.

Arms Control Challenges: Space, Weapons of Mass Destruction, Targeted and Mass Murders, and the Proliferation of Private Weaponry

Arms control and disarmament issues pursued aggressively after World War II during the Cold War and in the 1990s, the immediate postwar years, no longer have the attention arms control advocates wish it still had. In its heyday, arms controllers put together agreements on both weapons of mass destruction as well as conventional, nonnuclear weapons and weapons systems. These agreements typically took one or more of three forms—quantitative reductions or limitations and qualitative restrictions on armaments; spatial or regional, geographic restrictions on military deployments (or operations) and weapons or weapons systems; and functional measures like maintaining hotlines—

communications between adversaries—and such confidence-and-security-building measures (CSBMs) as notifications of military exercises, allowing observers, and having representatives at each other's headquarters.[17]

One of two major twenty-first-century arms-control challenges is keeping the ongoing military use (or militarization) of space for reconnaissance, telecommunications, and geopositional or targeting purposes while simultaneously avoiding weaponization—preventing space from becoming a combat zone. Precluding any "weaponization" of space means prohibiting deployment or operational use of weapons systems in space, on the moon, or on other "celestial bodies." The other ongoing arms control challenge is eliminating, if possible, or at least stopping, the spread of weapons of mass destruction—nuclear, biological, chemical, and radiological weapons.

Space

In what was once a US-Soviet Cold War duopoly reserved almost entirely to the superpowers, both state and private-sector satellites now orbit the earth primarily for telecommunications, photography and other forms of imagery. These satellites and other space objects have become ever more densely concentrated and diverse. Just keeping track of them has become a national security matter, the prospect of attacks by state actors moderated somewhat by understandings of mutual vulnerabilities. Attacking another state's assets or those owned by their private-sector interests likely would invite counterattacks either in space or on Earth.

Probing more deeply into space, we can anticipate installations on the moon one day for scientific, exploratory, or commercial purposes. The Outer Space Treaty (1967)—well ahead of its time—prohibits weaponization of the moon and other celestial bodies that are to be used "exclusively for peaceful purposes." The treaty also explicitly prohibits weapons of mass destruction in orbit or elsewhere in outer space. Space does remain a place for telecommunications, reconnaissance, and locational or geopositional functions, all of which are essential to both civilian and military activities on Earth.

Lest the domain of space becomes a place for the "star wars" of science fiction, the treaty did put in place important foundation stones of national and international security. Little progress has been made since then, however, on expanding the scope or specifying further operational details of the basic agreement. The Moon Treaty (1979), for example, sought an international regime for space similar to what is used for dealing with territorial waters and the high seas on earth, but to date only sixteen countries have ratified its provisions. Mechanisms for resolving space-related conflicts also remain decidedly underdeveloped.

Finally, space is the place of comets and asteroids, the latter particularly threatening because, given their number and the difficulty of their detection (identifying dark objects against the blackness of space), there is very little, if any, warning time. In the United States, efforts by National Aeronautics and Space Administration (NASA) and nongovernmental groups are underway to improve detection, but the problem is mammoth. For its part, the US-Canadian North American Air Defense Command (NORAD) tracks space objects, mainly those in orbit around the Earth, but its mission is principally a military one that does not focus on comets and asteroids.

Although most smaller asteroids disintegrate in the earth's atmosphere, should an extremely large asteroid impact the earth the consequence could be devastating for cities or, in the extreme, even continents—not to mention climatic effects. Such concerns are customarily dismissed as rare events (such as the extinction of the dinosaurs some 65 million years ago). Accordingly, neither NASA nor DoD have received much funding either for detection or for development of technologies to intercept and divert or alter the course of asteroids that may threaten the planet. Nevertheless, in 2013 the impact of an asteroid at Chelyabinsk, east of the Ural Mountains, in Russia was a wakeup call that more needs to be done in the interest of national security to detect and, if necessary, deflect asteroids, comets, or other space objects.[18]

WEAPONS OF MASS DESTRUCTION

The 1925 Geneva Protocol proscribed any use of "asphyxiating, poisonous or other gases" and "bacteriological methods of warfare." Building on this foundation, the Biological Weapons Convention (drafted in 1972, in force three years later) added prohibitions on the development, production, and stockpiling of such weapons. A score of years later, the Chemical Weapons Convention (signed in 1992, in force five years later) prohibited the development, production, stockpiling, and use of chemical weapons and established the Organization for the Prohibition of Chemical Weapons (OPCW) at The Hague to monitor the agreement.

There is consensus among policy makers that radiation weapons have little value for use in state-to-state warfare. Perhaps because of this, there are no agreements reached to date prohibiting the development, production, and stockpiling of such weapons. The greater concern is terrorist or other nongovernmental fabrication of radiation devices. Materials for such weapons can be found in stocks used routinely for medical purposes.

Nuclear weapons are another matter. Proliferation of them takes two forms—vertical and horizontal. The first is the stockpiling of such weapons. During the Cold War the United States and the Soviet Union accumulated some 12,000 strategic nuclear weapons as well as thousands of tactical weapons designed for battlefield use. Although numbers of strategic nuclear weapons have declined by more than 85%, the United States and Russia still retain more than 1,500 strategic warheads each. When shorter range "tactical" or battlefield weapons are added to the mix, numbers reach some 6,970 and 7,300 respectively, worldwide total more than 15,000 (France 300, China 260, UK 215, Pakistan 130, India 120, Israel 80, and North Korea 15).[19]

Horizontal proliferation of nuclear weapons and weapons-related technologies—passing them to other, nonnuclear states—is prohibited by the Non-Proliferation Treaty (1968), Articles I and II. At the same time, countries possessing such weapons are committed under Article VI to reducing their stockpiles—working toward complete nuclear disarmament. In Article III, the agreement assigns the task of monitoring compliance with the agreement to the International Atomic Energy Agency (IAEA) in Vienna.

The twenty-first-century challenge is to keep the lid on both horizontal and vertical proliferation. Since coming into force and notwithstanding the treaty's prohibitions against horizontal proliferation, the five-country nuclear "club" in 1968 (the United States, United Kingdom, Russia, France, and China) has expanded now to include Israel, India, Pakistan, and North Korea. Successful multilateral negotiations with Iran give promise to ongoing diplomatic efforts to keep other countries in the Middle East and elsewhere from acquiring nuclear weapons.

TARGETED OR MASS MURDERS AND THE PROLIFERATION OF PRIVATE WEAPONRY

The massive proliferation of hand guns, assault and other rifles, and other weaponry in private hands globally and domestically poses an ongoing threat to citizens who may become the innocent victims of targeted or indiscriminate mass murders. It is a human security problem without an easy solution. The sheer volume of weapons of all kinds in private hands makes any effort to impose limits a formidable challenge. Given a deeply embedded gun-ownership culture in the United States with deep roots in its frontier past, even raising this as a subject for arms control is highly controversial. In this regard, the US Supreme Court has legitimated claims to gun ownership as a Constitutional right.

So deeply embedded are these norms that mass murders have not altered understandings about the sanctity of weapons among many, particularly those in rural areas. Hunting and target shooting have sport status, but a substantial minority also sees the right of gun ownership on extreme libertarian grounds—an ultimate defense held by the citizenry should government become oppressive at any future point in time. It is a position rooted historically in the American Revolution—an insurgency against British control in which private citizens took up arms against the Crown.

Given these embedded norms and the short shelf lives of hand gun and assault weapons bans, those who try to limit access to hand guns, automatic (and semiautomatic) weapons, assault rifles, or any other weaponry face formidable obstacles. The politically powerful National Rifle Association (NRA) and other opponents of such measures argue that guns do not kill people—that people do. If this is so, then the problem becomes one of keeping weaponry from falling into the wrong hands.

Quite apart from seemingly futile efforts to reduce the numbers and types of weaponry already in private hands domestically and globally, measures to reduce access in the United States to weapons by those with mental disorders, records of terrorist activity or other violent crime still face stiff opposition by the NRA and others who influence members of the Congress. Efforts to keep weaponry out of the hands of those who may use them for untoward purposes through extensive national agency checks and keeping a national data base of sales are measures falling just short of registering guns—the kind of "gun control" that gun rights advocates in the United States abhor.

If there were to be a feasible approach to reducing, if not eliminating, targeted and mass murders, arms control advocates will have to construct a sufficient consensus to prohibit possession or sales to persons of risk and to limit the kinds of weapons available on the open market. Even agreeing on these relatively modest measures will continue to be an uphill struggle for arms controllers.

AFTERWORD

The national security agenda in a still-anarchic, globalized world is daunting. It includes not just traditional threats posed to and by states and nonstate actors, but also the broader category of human security that includes the adverse implications of climate change, natural events, epidemics, and pandemics. In addition to interstate wars, armed interventions, insurgencies, terrorism, and other forms of political violence that continue in this brave new world, national security decision-makers also have to deal with cyber threats and cyber warfare in which states, criminal networks, or individuals are the perpetrators; natural threats from asteroids to climate change, water shortages, other resource competition, and food security; arms-control challenges—space and weapons of mass destruction; and health—epidemics and pandemics. These are not just matters for the Defense Department and the US armed forces. Security will require cooperative action across the US government and private sectors as well as with allies, coalition partners, other states as well as both international and nongovernmental organizations. Orchestrating this response in cooperative security efforts is in itself a daunting challenge for US leaders tasked with managing these issues in our brave new world.

NOTES

1. *New York Times*, October 21, 2015.
2. J.D. Thompson, *Organizations in Action* (Piscataway, NJ: Transaction Publishers, 1967, 2003).
3. See the discussion in Eric de Campos, "Robustness: A New U.S. Cyber Deterrence Strategy," M.A. Thesis, University of Denver, June 2013.
4. Executive Order 13636: "Improving Critical Infrastructure Cybersecurity" (February 12, 2013): Section 1.
5. Presidential Policy Directive-21: "Critical Infrastructure Security and Resilience" (February 12, 2013): Roles and Responsibilities; cf. the specification of tasks on www.dhs.gov/topic/cybersecurity.
6. For personal reflections by the former director of NSA and CIA on cyber security and its organizational aspects, see Michael V. Hayden, *Playing to the Edge: American Intelligence in the Age of Terror* (New York: Penguin Press, 2016), 127–152. See also Ted Koppel, *Lights Out* (New York: Penguin/Random House, 2015).
7. Elisabeth Bumiller, "Pentagon Expanding Cybersecurity Force to Protect Networks Against Attack," *New York Times*, February 12, 2013.
8. Presidential Policy Directive-21: Additional Federal Responsibilities
9. This, of course, is Al Gore's argument in *An Inconvenient Truth: The Crisis of Global Warming* (New York: Viking Books/Penguin, 2007).
10. It is as if the Enlightenment had not occurred more than three centuries ago. The nonproductive "wars" between religion and science are apparently not yet over, at least not in some absolutist circles.
11. Although the extraordinarily thin exosphere arguably goes out to more than 700 kilometers (some 420 miles), the troposphere to just 12 km (7.2 miles). With few exceptions, most human beings live their lives in breathable space well under 12,000 feet, just 2.3 miles (3.7 kilometers) up.
12. Anthony Giddens, *The Politics of Climate Change*, 2nd ed. (Cambridge, UK: Polity, 2011), 29.
13. Ibid., 87.
14. The UNFCCC emerged from the "Earth Summit" in Rio de Janeiro (1992) with the objective to "stabilize greenhouse gas concentrations in the atmosphere at a level that would prevent dangerous anthropogenic interference with the climate system."
15. *National Security Strategy*, February 2015, p. 12.

16. Comments by Margaret Williams (Managing Director, Arctic Program, World Wildlife Fund) and Vice Admiral Peter Neffenger (U.S. Coast Guard) at a meeting of the Pacific Council on International Policy in Santa Monica, California, October 17–18, 2014.
17. For details of these agreements, see Robert Williams and Paul R. Viotti, eds. *Arms Control: History, Theory, Policy*, 2 vols. (Santa Barbara, CA: Praeger/ABC-CLIO, 2012). For arms control documents, see Paul R. Viotti, ed. *Arms Control and Global Security*, 2 vols (Santa Barbara, CA: Praeger/ABC-CLIO, 2010).
18. For more on the threat of asteroid impacts, see Duncan Lunan, *Incoming Asteroid: What Could We Do About It?* (New York: Springer, 2014).
19. Hans M. Kristensen and Robert S. Norris, "Nuclear Notebook," *Bulletin of the Atomic Scientists*, Vol. 72, No.2 (2016): 63-73 and 125-134.

CHAPTER 2

WAR

In Flanders fields the poppies blow
Between the crosses, row on row,
That mark our place; and in the sky
The larks, still bravely singing, fly
Scarce heard amid the guns below.

We are the Dead. Short days ago
We lived, felt dawn, saw sunset glow,
Loved and were loved, and now we lie
In Flanders fields.

Take up our quarrel with the foe:
To you from failing hands we throw
The torch; be yours to hold it high.
If ye break faith with us who die
We shall not sleep, though poppies grow
In Flanders fields.

—John McRae, "In Flanders Fields"

As indicated in table 1, war has very much been part of the North American and European experience. Like Canadian Lt. Colonel John McRae, southern writer Mark Twain (Samuel Langhorne Clemens, 1835–

1910) often saw things through the dark lenses he wore, describing in great human detail the devastation of the Civil War—a war within one state, the United States of America (USA) from the northern point of view, a War Between the States (USA vs. CSA—Confederate States of America) from the southern perspective. War is war, but the label (the social construction) for a particular war seems always to belong to the victors.

Using force in interstate war or in armed interventions is fraught with high human and material costs. Yet it may be necessary to do so, given the human security and other national interests or objectives at stake. As Machiavelli (1469–1527) put it, the prince or leader has the obligation to assure security and thus acts from necessity (*necessità*), knowing the harm (*male*)[1] that accompanies the use of force.

However compelling the reason for using force, there is no ironclad guarantee that using force will successfully achieve the intended purposes. The wise leader weighs carefully the means needed to achieve the ends sought and acts with an enlightened boldness (*virtù*). He (or she) does not act impulsively, but does not hesitate to act when force is called for. It is the wise prince who decides when and how to use force, if at all. It is not indecisiveness when a leader chooses not to use force when the time or circumstances are not favorable, although at other times delaying the use of force may make matters worse. Such calculations are highly subjective, hence Machiavelli's call for leadership that acts with enlightened boldness in the interest of securing the state.

Even with this *virtù*, the leader may suffer malice of fortune (*Fortuna*) and lose even the best-played hand. Indeed, to Machiavelli *Fortuna* might decide at least half of the outcomes of even an ideal, enlightened prince who acts decisively in the exercise of his *virtù*. The world is a very uncertain place—much determined by chance. In this context, indecisive, weak-kneed or ill-advised princes would likely be thwarted or defeated easily by *Fortuna*.[2] Figure 1 captures the interactions of these three factors in Machiavelli's analysis.

Figure 1. Necessity, Enlightened Boldness, and Chance: Contextual Factors Affecting Security Decisions.

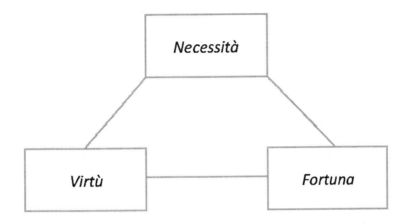

Thus, presidents—like princes—and (following Article II of the US Constitution as chief executives, chief diplomats, and military commanders-in-chief) face uncertainties in an anarchic world. Now, as in Machiavelli's time, there is no authority above a state in this anarchy of international relations and world politics—much less one with sufficient power to stop a state, alliance, or coalition of states from using force other than another state, alliance, or coalition of states. Given that political leaders may see armed intervention or other use of force as viable options in relation to the objectives they seek, efforts by others to blunt such moves result in the outbreak of interstate war.

Table 3. American Wars.

- **French and Indian War** (1754–1763)
- **War of Independence** (1776–1781, peace Treaty of Paris in 1783)
- **Barbary Wars**: North Africa: Tunis, Algeria, Tripoli (1801–1805 and 1815)
- **War of 1812** (1812–1815)
- **Mexican-American War** (1846–1848)
- **Civil War or War Between the States** (1860–1865)
- **Spanish-American War** (1898)
- **World War I** (1914–1918; US participation 1917–1918)
- **World War II** (1939–1945; US participation 1941–1945)
- **Korean War** (1950–1953; a peace treaty not agreed)
- **Vietnam War** (1956–1975; US participation formalized by 1964 Tonkin Gulf Resolution)
- **Gulf War** or **First Iraq War** (1990–1991)
- **Afghanistan War** (2001–)
- **Second Iraq War** (2003–2011)

The conduct of other states as well as the actions of nonstate actors like ISIL (or *Da'esh*, the Arabic acronym) and al Qaeda or al Qaeda in the Arabian Peninsula (AQAP) or elsewhere may lead American presidents to use force against them—perhaps troops on the ground, Special Forces units, fighter aircraft, or drones (remotely piloted vehicles). Although the term *war* is often used to label this kind of tactical response, I reserve the term primarily for *interstate* conflicts covered in this chapter—the use of force against other states, alliances, or coalitions of states. Armed interventions within states that fall short of interstate war are the subject of chapter 3.

MARK TWAIN'S WAR PRAYER

Mark Twain captures descriptively the horrific nature of warfare. He also plays on the religiously inspired moralism and patriotic expression that one finds in the American historical experience with combat. Indeed, evangelical Christianity—rooted as it is in biblical understandings of war —was particularly prominent on both sides in the American Civil War, perhaps more strongly in the South—the apparent setting of Twain's "War Prayer." In it he identifies the patriotic fervor one often finds at the outset of wars: "Daily the young volunteers marched down the wide avenue gay and fine in their new uniforms, the proud fathers and mothers and sisters and sweethearts cheering them with voices choked with happy emotion as they swung by." He adds:

> Nightly the packed mass meetings listened, panting, to patriot oratory which stirred the deepest deeps of their hearts, and which they interrupted at briefest intervals with cyclones of applause, the tears running down their cheeks the while; in the churches the pastors preached devotion to flag and country, and invoked the God of Battles beseeching His aid in our good cause in outpourings of fervid eloquence which moved every listener.

The minister at church invokes God's direct sponsorship:

> An ever-merciful and benignant Father of us all would watch over our noble young soldiers, and aid, comfort, and encourage them in their patriotic work; bless them, shield them in the day of battle and the hour of peril, bear them in His mighty hand, make them strong and confident, invincible in the bloody onset; help them crush the foe, grant to them and to their flag and country imperishable honor and glory.

The frequency by which God is invoked for human causes, then as now, makes one blanch. Indeed, Americans routinely use the name of God on behalf of the nation in war and peace. But this invocation, of course, is by no means unique to Americans. For the Germans in both twentieth-century world wars, it was *Gott mit uns* (God is with us), the slogan engraved on the soldier's belt buckle (accompanied by a swastika in World War II—the obvious contradiction apparently not understood or overlooked in patriotic fervor). Similarly, *Allahu Akbar* (God is great) is the epithet frequently used by Islamist insurgent groups wreaking violence upon other human beings.

Twain has compassion for the deity whose name is used in vain in prayers uttered in much the same way as one seeks a human ally for a personal cause. Twain obviously saw this in the practice of church and state in his time, both north and south. It is the religious understanding expressed politically by Abraham Lincoln that rescues us from this satire —his hope being only to be on God's side rather than to be soliciting God to be on his: "Sir, my concern is not whether God is on our side; my greatest concern is to be on God's side...."

So what happens in war that makes Twain such a skeptic about its utility? Countering the patriotic fervor expressed in the quest for victory on the battlefield (and the glory that comes with it) are the unspoken parts of the prayer calling for decimation of an enemy—the costly other side of the war coin. Calling for God's help in attaining victory amounts to a prayer for some six unspoken things that necessarily go with it.

Twain puts these into the words of a "messenger" from on high who speaks to the congregation. He expresses what they really are praying for is God's help to accomplish six tasks directed toward the enemy, which are to:

(a) tear their soldiers to bloody shreds with our shells;
(b) cover their smiling fields with the pale forms of their patriot dead;
(c) drown the thunder of the guns with the shrieks of their wounded, writhing in pain;
(d) lay waste their humble homes with a hurricane of fire;
(e) wring the hearts of their unoffending widows with unavailing grief; [and]

(f) turn them out roofless with their little children to wander unfriended in the wastes of their desolated land in rags and hunger and thirst, sports of the sun flames in summer and the icy winds of winter, broken in spirit, worn with travail, imploring thee [God] for the refuge of the grave and denied it....

Old Testament scriptures give ample biblical grounds for this legitimacy in warfare which church leaders have found. In what they represented as the word of God, biblical accounts chronicled the acts of patriarchs and other prominent figures who also were military commanders: Abraham (c. 1400 BCE), Moses (c. 1250 BCE), Joshua (c. 1230 BCE), Gideon and Deborah (c. 1100 BCE), King Saul (c. 1025 BCE), Saul's son, Jonathan, and his dear friend who would become King David (c. 1016 BCE).[3] They fought wars, sometimes brutally, in centuries-long campaigns against the foes of the Israelites—the Mesopotamians (present-day Iraq), Egyptians, Canaanites , Edomites, Moabites, Amalekites, and Philistines.

The legitimacy of war as a social construction was buttressed by this biblical record, particularly among those who believe the Bible is not just inspired by, but *is* the word of God—that the scriptures should be understood literally—that they say what they mean and mean what they say. For those seeking biblical bases for the legitimacy of using force, they need only point to the depiction of God serving as military advisor to Joshua in the battle of Jericho:

And the Lord said to Joshua: "See! I have given Jericho into your hand, its king, *and* the mighty men of valor. You shall march around the city, all *you* men of war; you shall go all around the city once. This you shall do six days.... But the seventh day you shall march around the city seven times, and the priests shall blow the trumpets. It shall come to pass, when they make a long *blast* with the ram's horn, *and* when you hear the sound of the trumpet, that all the people shall shout with a great shout; then the wall of the city will fall down flat...."[4]

We find in Twain a bitter satire of churchmen and their congregations so easily drawn to support warfare, as if it were a godly or God-inspired endeavor. Quite apart from claims by political and religious leaders to just cause, the irony of this religious connection to war is clear: "For our sakes who adore Thee, Lord, blast their [the enemy's] hopes, blight their lives, protract their bitter pilgrimage, make heavy their steps, water their way with their tears, stain the white snow with the blood of their wounded feet!"[5]

Given these calls for vanquishing the foe, the next (and final lines) of "The War Prayer" capture the essential contradiction in their thinking: "We ask it, in the spirit of love, of Him Who is the Source of Love, and Who is the ever-faithful refuge and friend of all that are sore beset and seek His aid with humble and contrite hearts. Amen." From a pacifist position, then, "war is not the answer" to problems affecting humankind. Yet, in the twenty-first century (as in previous centuries), the use of force by states against other state and nonstate actors remains the order of the day.

The horrific human and financial costs of wars may dissuade American presidents and most world leaders from engaging in war when diplomatic, economic, and other remedies to conflicts are present. Nevertheless, using force in fact remains part of the fabric that describes present-day conduct exhibited by states, insurgencies, and other nonstate actors in an anarchic world lacking central authority with the capabilities or power to stop such activities.

WAR, ARMED INTERVENTION, AND MORALISM

As Twain's "War Prayer" implies, there is an unmistakable, recurrent moralism[6] in American foreign and national security policy, usually accompanied by a strongly rooted liberal quest to make the world a better place. Americans often do not consider themselves ideological. In fact, most are so ideological in their classical liberal commitments that they tend to see commitments to free speech, a free press, freedom of assembly, freedom of religion, equality before (and due process of) law as self-evident truths, rather than ideological beliefs.

This American liberalism, a pluralist ideology, is grounded in individualism—not only that individuals (or groups of individuals) matter, but also what they do matters.[7] Notwithstanding substantial differences on social values and on the proper role of government in the economy and society, both social progressives and conservatives are all still liberals in the classic sense, committed as they are to individualism.

The American aim in promoting representative democracies or republics is to extend throughout the world American understandings of the gains to be had from this pluralist liberalism of individuals and groups. It is a familiar story grounded in religious or moral understandings. These values, deeply embedded as they are in the American culture, not surprisingly are also internalized by many among the policy elites. Failing to recognize that much of the world does not share precisely this set of liberal commitments is a source of great frustration to many American presidents and their advisers.

The puritan heritage—often clothed in secular garments—remains strong. The present-day understanding drawn from the eighteenth and nineteenth centuries that the U.S. is *exceptional* appears in presidential speeches. Like the shining city on the hill, the American self-image is of a moral force for good. Force even finds justification in the task of spreading democracy whether in nineteenth-century campaigns to advance democratic republics in Latin America, Woodrow Wilson's World War I quest to defeat dictatorship and make the entire world "safe" for democracy, Franklin Roosevelt's vision of the United States as the "arsenal" of democracy, or George W. Bush's effort to effect regime change in Iraq and use the occasion to transform the country into a model of democracy for all of Araby to emulate.

The exceptionalism sentiment dates back to at least 1630 when Massachusetts Governor John Winthrop put pen to paper, articulating what has become an article of even secular faith in American understandings of the country's purpose: "We entered into a covenant with Him for this work.... We shall find that the God of Israel is among us.... *For we shall be as a city upon a hill.* The eyes of the people are upon us." He adds how compliance with this exceptional mandate will "make light spring out in darkness" and we will see "light brake [*sic*] forth as the morning."[8]

The metaphor has been invoked historically by presidents such as John Adams and Abraham Lincoln, among others. Ronald Reagan spoke of a "divine plan that placed this great continent between two oceans to be sought out by those" with "an abiding love of freedom and a special kind of courage." Indeed, in his farewell address, Reagan recalled that

> I've spoken of the shining city all my political life ... a tall proud city built on rocks stronger than oceans, wind-swept, God-blessed, and teeming with people of all kinds living in harmony and peace, a city with free ports that hummed with commerce and creativity, and if there had to be city walls, the walls had doors and the doors were open to anyone with the will and the heart to get here....[9]

The "city of light" theme had become central in Republican Party circles and was core to the political campaign of Reagan's successor, George H. W. Bush, who observed that "the city on the hill shined so bright it became 'a thousand points of light.'"[10] His son, George W. Bush, campaigned on America being "chosen by God and commissioned by history to be a model to the world." On the 9/11 al Qaeda attack on New York and Washington, he commented that "America was targeted for attack because we're the brightest beacon for freedom and opportunity in the world." He added: "No one will keep that light from shining."[11]

On the Democratic side, Bill Clinton acknowledged a "new covenant"—a term that implied a scriptural basis for his progressive agenda in both domestic policy and world affairs—an echo of Winthrop's invocation of a godly purpose for the city on the hill and, for that matter, Woodrow Wilson's advocacy of a "covenant" for the League of Nations.[12] For his part, Barack Obama was challenged for earlier being critical of American exceptionalism due to its ethnocentrism. He had not yet internalized the term, which—like wearing an American flag pin on one's suitcoat—had become socially constructed as an ideological tenet and mark of patriotic commitment. President Obama subsequently spoke in these terms, but clarified more precisely what he means by American exceptionalism:

> Looking to the future instead of the past. Making sure we match our power with diplomacy, and use force wisely. Building coalitions to meet new challenges and opportunities. Leading—always—with the example of our values. That's what makes us exceptional. That's what keeps us strong. And that's why we must keep striving to hold ourselves to the highest of standards—our own.[13]

The connection between the use of force and a moralism born of religiosity is not unique to the United States—given its earlier prevalence in Europe and now in the Islamic world where it abounds. In the American experience, engagement in wars is almost always accompanied by strong arguments cast in these moral terms. It is not sufficient to state simply that using force is in the national interest or that doing so is the best means to accomplish agreed objectives.

When rallying public support, it is always more persuasive to represent armed intervention as driven by the obligation to stand up to such "evil" forces as national socialists, communists, or Islamists who have subverted their religion. Taking down demonic leaders—from Adolf Hitler, Saddam Hussein, or Osama bin Laden—is akin puritanically to putting a stake through the hearts of diabolical elements. The same moral suasion can be mustered, of course, to serve any cause that, without the use of force, would suffer defeat.

THE USE OF FORCE: STRATEGIC AND MORAL CONSIDERATIONS

The horrific nature of war makes it a blunt, barbaric instrument of national policy, not a tool that often can be used with the same precision of a surgeon employing a scalpel! At the same time, the use of force for just cause has substantial legitimacy in the American body politic as a whole, particularly in rural areas of the country from which the bulk of volunteers for military service still come.

If war is so barbaric, decision makers may regard it as such and yet, out of necessity, still resort to the use of force, then how can they at least reduce both the frequency and the degree of such barbarism? Fortunately, *military necessity* in warfare—narrowly construed as what one side needs to destroy the military capability (or substantially weaken this war-making capacity) of an enemy—*also provides a basis for a just war doctrine* that seeks to limit both human costs and material damage.

Jomini

The French-speaking Swiss strategist Baron Antoine-Henri de Jomini influenced American military thought, particularly in the nineteenth century. His use of geometry—references to bases, lines, and points —appealed to officers trained as engineers during their cadet years at the US Military Academy at West Point, New York. In particular, Sylvanus Thayer—"father" of the West Point curriculum that focused on engineering problem solving and the carrot-and-stick approach embodied in the daily quiz—was directly influenced by Jomini's strategic thinking during an 1815–1816 trip to France, after the defeat of Napoleon.[14]

Jomini's writings "emphasized physical features in his analyses, especially lines of communication and key positions such as fortified bases. The ideal strategic arrangement, Jomini, argued, was one where an army could use its own physical location and speed of movement to defeat individual components of an enemy force before they could unite." Dennis Hart Mahan, a student and later close friend of Thayer's at West Point (class of 1824) remained and taught engineering there for some four decades. Mahan passed the Jominian torch at West Point to Henry Wager Halleck ("Old Brains," as he was called) who influenced a generation of future generals who would see combat in the Mexican War and Civil War.[15]

Jomini's thinking also influenced Dennis Hart Mahan's son, Alfred Thayer Mahan, who became principal strategist at the US Naval War College. The younger Mahan, who had direct connection with Theodore Roosevelt, incorporated both Jomini's and his own understandings of the British Royal Navy's role—sea power core to Britain and its empire. As Tim Perry puts it, Mahan's strategic thinking emphasized "geography, technology, and linearity. Success in naval warfare, Mahan wrote in the best Jominian tradition, depended upon control of sea lanes and chokepoints through which trade flowed. To secure these, a navy must first destroy its opponent in a large-scale, decisive naval battle, just as Thayer and Mahan the elder had argued that Napoleon did on land."[16]

Clausewitz

In the twentieth century, Prussian general and writer Carl von Clausewitz (1780–1831) gradually displaced the prominent position Jomini had held in US military thinking about war.[17] It took a while. Two world wars against Germany made the Prussian inherently unpopular among many. Moreover, he was misrepresented as an advocate of violence and bloodshed. The increasing prominence of Clausewitz in US circles after World War II also paralleled the Soviet Red Army's adoption of Clausewitz's ideas that dominated its strategic writings during the Cold War years.

When US decision-makers think strategically about the use of force as an instrument of policy—linking military and other capabilities to the national purposes, objectives, or ends policymakers seek, they are following a path blazed by Clausewitz, a critic of Jomini. Beginning in 1818, he worked for some thirteen years on a theory of war that brought reflections on personal experiences in military service for both Prussia and Russia—France the common enemy until Napoleon's defeat in 1815.

Clausewitz put all of this together in *On War* (1832), the manuscript assembled by colleagues the year after his death. In these writings, he underscored his point that the military (or military action) is not an end

in itself, but rather *a means to ends specified by the political leadership.*
Put another way, he subordinates the military to the political purposes
of the state:

> War is an instrument of policy; it must necessarily bear its char-
> acter, it must measure with its scale: the conduct of War, in its
> great features, is therefore policy itself, which takes up the sword
> in place of the pen, but does not on that account cease to think
> according to its own laws.[18]

This Clausewitzian view of war is itself a construct that has become
embedded in the minds of American strategic thinkers, even as they
debate what he meant and assess the applicability of his work in a world
in which technology has transformed weapons and weapons systems and
the way wars are fought tactically. Still, the subordination of the military
to the political in Clausewitz is in accord with the long-established
American norm of civilian supremacy discussed in chapter 7 on civil-
military relations. Moreover, the Clausewitzian formula for winning
a battle (and, for that matter, an entire war) depends on destroying
an enemy's war-making capability, which remains core to present-day
American strategic thinking.

As Clausewitz scholar, Sir Michael Howard, observes:

> Clausewitz had described war as a "remarkable trinity" composed
> of its *political objective*, its *practical instruments* and of popular
> passions, [and] the *social forces* it expressed. It was the latter,
> he pointed out, that made the wars of the French Revolution so
> different in kind from those of Frederick the Great and which
> would probably so distinguish war in the future. In this he was
> right.[19]

Howard extends the argument by identifying four dimensions of strategy
that matter: the often-overlooked *social aspect*, the *technological, logistical,*
and *operational.*[20] Success in battlefield *operations* are aimed at destroying
or substantially weakening the enemy's war-making capability, which

depends on recruitment of educated and skilled personnel committed to the war effort and supported by the population as a whole (the *social* dimension). *Technology* brings effective weapons and weapons systems to the battlefield and enhances communications and transportation or *logistics* capabilities.

Seen as a schematic in figure 2, the relations among these four dimensions become clearer. Firepower matters in modern warfare, particularly in the American style of war fighting. Whether by aircraft, missiles, drones, artillery, rifles or other weaponry, continued advancement of weapons-related technologies has combined increased accuracy of delivery with greater precision in the assignment of explosive power needed to effect destruction of military targets.

Military necessity was defined narrowly by Clausewitz as what it takes to win any battle or win any war: *to destroy or substantially weaken an enemy's war-making capability.* To kill noncombatants—people not directly connected to the enemy's war effort—was not part of his game plan. Targets of military value—those that adversely impact war fighting, not population centers—were his focal point.

Victory in Europe in World War II was accomplished by destroying the German Wehrmacht's capability to continue the war. Losses to the Soviet Red Army on the Eastern Front were massive, American and allied efforts in the west (and earlier in the South) contributing to the final defeat. The same was true in the Pacific. Defeat of the Japanese navy at sea brought the war to the home islands. Nuclear attacks on Hiroshima and Nagasaki precipitated the surrender, but the war had already been lost at sea.

Figure 2. The Four Dimensions of Warfighting Strategy.

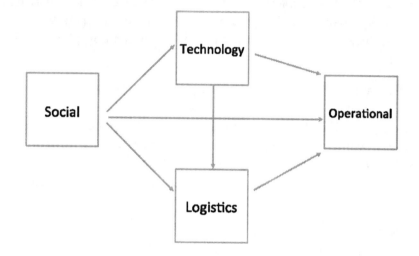

Directly or indirectly, then, these Clausewitzian understandings—that the way to win a war is to destroy or substantially weaken an enemy's war-making capabilities—gradually have become a bedrock in the American strategic culture, superseding the earlier understandings attributed to the Frenchman, Jomini. Only when US decision-makers stray from Clausewitz's canonical principles (as in obliteration bombing in World War II and fighting a war of attrition in Vietnam) do they encounter difficulties. In the last half of the twentieth and now in the twenty-first century, US decision-makers have taken great pains to avoid unnecessary civilian death and destruction, focusing instead on targets of military value to the enemy. Killing civilians does not win wars. It was defeat of the Wehrmacht, including its resources, logistics, and lines of communication to the battlefield, that spelled Allied victory in the European theater in World War II. Likewise, as noted earlier, it was destruction of the Japanese navy in the Pacific theater that accounted for US victory there.

Withdrawal and then defeat in Vietnam underscored how political limits placed on potential targets of military value in North Vietnam, coupled with an unwillingness to move the ground war there, made military victory elusive. The rationale for these limits was obvious—not to draw China or the Soviet Union into the conflict. The learning outcome for decision makers is, if one can avoid them, not to enter wars that put the military into unwinnable positions. As Clausewitz would have put it, to win, they need to use force that weakens substantially, if not destroying completely, an enemy's war-making capability.

This premise that the military objective in a particular war as a whole and on the battlefield (on land, at sea and in the aerospace) remains to destroy or substantially weaken an enemy's war-fighting or war-making capability is clear from the Clausewitzian text: "If War is an act of violence to compel the enemy to fulfill our will, then in every case all depends on our overthrowing the enemy, that is, disarming him, and on that alone." Put even more succinctly: "The *military power* [of an enemy] must be destroyed, that is, reduced to such a state as not to be able to prosecute the War."[21] Military necessity, so defined, is focused on actions taken in war only for this purpose—destroying or weakening an enemy's war-fighting or war-making capability.

Clausewitz differentiates *strategy* (connecting means to ends) and plans for fighting a war from *tactics* (methods of combat operations). *Tactics* are the "theory of the use of military forces in combat" and *strategy* is "the theory of the use of combats for the object of the War." Put another way: "Strategy forms the plan of the War" and "is the employment of the battle to gain the end [or objectives] of the War." He adds that "strategy has its "moral, physical, mathematical, geographical, and statistical elements."[22]

Still, Clausewitz warns of the uncertainty facing commanders and their political leaders. It is a distant echo of Machiavelli's *Fortuna*—the best-laid plans can go awry. There may be *friction* (a Clausewitzian mechanics metaphor) in the execution of even well-constructed war plans causing them to fail. There is a gap between the "conception" of war and its "execution." He elaborates: "Everything is very simple in War, but the simplest thing is difficult. These difficulties accumulate and produce a friction which no one can imagine exactly who has not seen war."[23]

One remedy to avoid this outcome is to exercise war plans before they have to be executed in warfare. Field and command-post exercises by US military forces are conducted precisely for this purpose. The *postmortem* review at the end of an exercise may lead to minor (or even major) revisions in the war plan aimed at reducing, if not eliminating, friction.

Even so, one still has to deal with other uncertainties in a "twilight" or *fog of war*—this time a meteorological metaphor that captures the uncertainties and unpredictable occurrences that happen rapidly in warfare:

> The great uncertainty of all data in War is a peculiar difficulty, because all action must, to a certain extent, be planned in a mere twilight, which in addition not infrequently—like the effect of fog or moonshine—gives to things exaggerated dimensions and an unnatural appearance. What this feeble light leaves indistinct to the sight, talent must discover, or must be left to chance. It is therefore again talent, or the favor of fortune, on which reliance must be placed, for want of objective knowledge.[24]

The commander confronts the confusion of fast-paced events on the battlefield, but still needs to act and react skillfully, albeit with much less knowledge than desired of what is happening. Although there is no perfect remedy for this challenge, Clausewitz calls for commanders with strong mental "power of discrimination" and "good judgment"—decidedly not automatons, but rather officers who can think critically and creatively in such circumstances.[25]

Clausewitz has also put forth important guidelines or principles to be followed when waging war.[26] Victory can come from mass or concentration of forces—"the greatest possible number of troops . . . brought into action at the decisive point," coupled with surprise—"secrecy and rapidity." The principle of *economy of force*—making the most out of resources that are by their nature finite or limited—is corollary to military necessity. To Clausewitz, "waste of forces . . . is even worse than their employment to no purpose."

Just as he would concentrate bombardment (by artillery in his day) on military targets, he would not "waste" bombs on population centers lacking military value. Because one's own soldiers are part of the country's military capability, he also would not "waste" them in wars of attrition. Clausewitz observes how defeating an enemy requires us to direct and "proportion our efforts to his powers of resistance."

An efficient way to do so is to attack the adversary's *center of gravity* (another mechanical engineering metaphor used by Clausewitz) that, if successfully taken out, will cause the enemy's forces to collapse. Searching for, finding, and attacking the enemy's *center of gravity* or focal point—"the hub of all power and movement,"[27] as he put it—is a core military objective. It could be the enemy's command-and-control centers or, perhaps, the way the enemy's forces are configured—"where the mass is concentrated most densely."[28] If successful, this approach facilitates destruction or, at least, disruption of enemy forces.

Moreover, a center of gravity is not just confined to an adversary's military:

> In countries subject to domestic strife, the center of gravity is generally the capital. In small countries that rely on large ones, it is usually the army of the protector. Among alliances, it lies in the community of interest, and in popular uprisings it is the personalities of the leaders and public opinion. It is against these that our energies should be directed.[29]

This leads him to three policy prescriptions toward an enemy, contingent on circumstances:

1. Destruction of his army, if it is at all significant;
2. Seizure of his capital if it is not only the center of administration but also that of social, professional, and political activity; [and]

3. Delivery of an effective blow against his principal ally if that ally is more powerful than he.

Clausewitz's concept of how war in the extreme can become absolute has been misinterpreted by some as a prescription for total war. There are no bases in his thought, however, to sustain "counter-value" targeting against essentially civilian targets. Nor should one put troops unnecessarily in harm's way against other soldiers as if, at the end of the day, relative casualties (or body counts) were what decided who won a particular battle, much less an entire war.

As Clausewitz repeats time and again, what constitutes victory in warfare is destroying war-making capability. As noted earlier, the US victory over Japan in World War II was not decided by bombing Hiroshima and Nagasaki, but rather by the United States defeating the Japanese navy in the Pacific. Nuclear-weapons bombings only precipitated the surrender and thus avoided any need to invade the Japanese home islands, but the defeat of Japan was already sealed by the loss of its fleet—its principal means for projection of national power throughout the region. Similarly, in Europe it was defeat of enemy military forces (the Wehrmacht) in the East by the Soviet Red Army and in the West by the United States and its allies that produced victory.

Military Necessity and Moral Understandings

Although Clausewitz was a military strategist (not an ethicist or moral thinker), defining military necessity narrowly (as Clausewitz did) solely in terms of what it takes to defeat an enemy does provide a foundation for developing moral limits or boundaries on the use of force that resonate with present-day American thinking. Constructed as it was in Western thought over the millennia, the just war doctrine seems compatible with Clausewitzian thought. It seeks to avoid unnecessary resort to the barbarism of war while, at the same time, limiting resort to this barbarity in the conduct of war itself. The set of rules seeking to limit the barbarism of war is a social construction that Michael Walzer labels the *war convention*: the "articulated norms, customs, professional codes, legal precepts, religious and philosophical principles, and reciprocal arrangements that shape our judgments of military conduct."[30]

Not only does one need a just *casus belli*, but resort to war must also be proportional to this provocation. Only with legitimate authority does one wage war—thus subordinating the military to the political. War is a last resort that has some possibility of success. As Clausewitz warned, one ought not to take the first step into war until knowing where the last steps likely will lead.[31]

Beyond these stringent conditions for any right to wage war (*jus ad bellum*) are additional requirements related to right conduct in war (*jus in bello*). One should concentrate on military targets and thus spare noncombatants. Weapons used should be proportionate (or scaled) to the legitimate targets of military value to the enemy. Thus, one ought not put a 10,000-pound bomb on a helicopter pad used by enemy forces when a 300-pound bomb is enough to take it out, particularly because excessive force likely would cause undue collateral death and destruction.

Table 4. The Right to Go to War and Right Conduct in War: Moral Criteria (when acting with right intention).

Right to Wage War	Right Conduct in War
(*Jus ad Bellum*)	(*Jus in Bello*)
1. Just Cause	1. Spare Noncombatants
2. Legitimate Authority	2. Means Proportional to Legitimate
3. War as a Proportionate	(Militarily Necessary) Targets
Response to Provocation	3. Military Necessity Narrowly
4. Chance of Success	Construed (What is Necessary to
5. Exhaust Peaceful Remedies	Destroy or Weaken Military
	Capability)
	4. Means not immoral in themselves
	(i.e., indiscriminate or causing
	needless human suffering)

In addition to the obvious moral considerations, avoiding use of excessive force also conserves such weapons for legitimate use against other targets —an *economy of force* that one also finds in Clausewitz's teachings. Finally, one ought not use weapons immoral in themselves due either to (1) their indiscriminate quality (thus not sparing noncombatants or, as in chemical or biological weapons use, exposing one's own troops to life-threatening effects) or (2) their causing needless human suffering. Consistent with Clausewitzian military-necessity understandings, then, employment of such weapons achieves no useful military purpose and may even be dysfunctional militarily, causing harm to the party using them.

Right intention is an underlying moral assumption in both the *jus ad bellum* and *jus in bello*. Of course, these principles can be manipulated easily by those acting without right intention and contrary to the spirit embedded in them, but still seeking to *appear* compliant with the doctrine's morally based imperatives. Rationalizing conduct, for example, by invoking just cause—trumping up or exaggerating the case for war when doing so is really a stretch—is abuse of just war doctrine—not, as is often alleged, a flaw in the doctrine itself. Indeed, the doctrinal principles are consistent with the Clausewitzian understanding of military necessity—not destroying every man, woman, child, and all things of material value, but rather waging war that is focused only on what an enemy needs to engage in warfighting.

In the following section, we move to a discussion of deterrence based on nuclear weapons. Although the purpose of deterrence is to avoid war—to keep the peace—an admirable thought, the *means* used to achieve that end raise serious moral questions. Were deterrence to fail and nuclear war to break out, we have no basis of assurance that it could be kept limited to targets of military value, particularly given the collateral effects of blast, heat, and radiation.

Nuclear Weapons, Deterrence, and Warfighting

Proponents of the efficacy of nuclear weapons have designs that customize the amount of blast to particular targets and minimize radiation or, conversely, maximize radiation and minimize blast[32] as in battlefield use against massive tank or other formations. The ability to vary the yield of a particular nuclear weapon (as some have said, rather casually, "dial a yield") is not particularly reassuring given that such limiting decisions would be made in the heat of battle under the stress of uncertainties of which Clausewitz was so aware. The battlefield more likely would become extreme rather quickly—the domain of absolute war in which notions of proportionality and sparing noncombatants seemingly have no place. Once Pandora's nuclear box is open, the idea of imposing limits, much less closing the lid, seems farfetched.

Few today would disagree that the Armageddon quality of fighting such a war with nuclear weapons is at odds with the Clausewitzian concept of war as an instrument of policy—merely diplomacy by other means—intended to achieve political objectives. Nor is it consistent with the just war doctrine, grounded as it is in the limiting principles of military necessity, proportionality, the obligation to spare noncombatants, and the prohibition of weapons immoral in themselves—those that are indiscriminate or cause needless suffering.

Michael Walzer's *Just and Unjust Wars*, an otherwise admirable volume that underscores the importance of moral considerations in relation to warfare, makes "supreme emergency" one exception to the set of limiting principles in just war thinking:[33]

> If we are to adopt or defend the adoption of extreme measures, the danger must be of an unusual and horrifying kind.... Faced with some ultimate horror, their options exhausted, they will do what they must to save their own people....
>
> It is not usually said of individuals in domestic society that they necessarily will or that they morally can strike out at innocent people, even in the supreme emergency of self-defense. They can

> only attack their attackers. But communities, in emergencies, seem
> to have different and larger prerogatives....[34]

Saying what people likely will do in extreme emergency, of course, is not to say that such conduct is right. What Walzer has done is open a door that allows escape from the stipulations of the war convention without legitimating the departure in terms of military necessity or other legitimate criterion. Just because there is a "supreme emergency" is not to say that departures from the war convention are a viable remedy, much less an approach with moral legitimacy. By allowing this seemingly unfettered exception, Walzer has put us on a very slippery slope.

Finally, if war fighting with nuclear weapons (or other biological, chemical or radiological weapons of mass destruction) is morally bankrupt—"supreme emergency" or not, we are still left with the question of whether deterrence with weapons of mass destruction has any moral content when it is based on the credible threat of their use. Can these means be used legitimately to achieve peace or stability? Does the end justify the means? The road to hell is oftentimes paved with the best of intentions. Even Machiavelli warned "*si guarda al fine*"—focus on the objective and be mindful of outcomes from the actions we take. Consistent with this understanding, we conclude with Clausewitz:

> Theory demands . . . that at the commencement of every War its character and main outline shall be defined according to what the political conditions and relations lead us to anticipate as probable. The more that, according to this probability, its character approaches the form of absolute War; the more its outline embraces the mass of the belligerent States and draws them into the vortex —so much the more complete will be the relation of events to one another and the whole, but so much the more necessary will it also be *not to take the first step without thinking what may be the last*.[35] [emphasis added]

Deterrence and Compellence or Coercive Diplomacy

Clausewitz rationalizes the use of force. It is for political purposes—diplomacy by other means. In present-day understandings, force (or the threat of force) is used not just in warfighting, but also in both *deterrence* (keeping an adversary from attacking or doing something else untoward) and *coercive diplomacy* or *compellence*[36] (moving an adversary to do what it would not otherwise do—like Soviet withdrawal of nuclear capabilities from Cuba in 1962, which is discussed in the preface to this volume).

In present-day usage, deterrence (D) of an enemy is a function of enemy understandings of one's *capabilities* as well as the *will* to carry out threats related to the use of force—perceived capabilities (C) and credibility (W). Expressed algebraically: $D = (C)(W)$. If either capabilities or credibility decline (or if either approach zero), deterrence may fail. Similarly, the success of coercive diplomacy or compellence depends upon a similar calculus of perceived capabilities and credibility of threats.

Although Clausewitz does not deal explicitly with deterrence (much less compellence or coercive diplomacy), these present-day concepts do follow the Clausewitzian text on battlefield effectiveness (E). In this regard, Clausewitz specifies a physical (or material) factor—military capabilities (C)—and a moral factor—the will to use these means (W)—as instrumental to battlefield effectiveness. He concludes that winning (battlefield effectiveness) is the "product of two factors which cannot be separated, namely, *the sum of available means* [or capabilities] and the *strength of the Will*."[37] Expressed algebraically, then: $E = (C)(W)$. If either capabilities or will decrease, so will battlefield effectiveness. If either approaches zero, defeat will be the expected outcome.

Credible threats are constructions not only in the minds of decision makers who make them, but also on the interpretations made by those to whom they are directed. The deterrence discourse is a highly masculinist one. It is cold and rationally analytical, allowing one, bereft of emotions, to think about the unthinkable.[38] Threats of massive death and destruction are dealt with often casually, certainly abstractly, and apparently for peaceful purposes—maintaining the stability of nuclear deterrence relations.

US decision-makers moved in the late 1940s from a relatively small number of nuclear weapons systems at the outset (a so-called finite- or minimum-deterrence posture) to a more robust offensive posture during succeeding decades of the Cold War. The aim was to prevent war with the Soviet Union or other adversaries through fear—threatening retaliation with an unacceptable level of destruction should they attack first. In the 1980s, however, American understandings of deterrence began to take a different form. Instead of its basis in fear of retaliatory death and destruction, it was to become a deterrence based on denial. By developing capabilities to win or "prevail" in a nuclear war, the Soviets (or any other state or alliance) could not achieve any sought-after objective should war break out and fighting escalate to a nuclear level. War no longer would be a viable Soviet option, hence sustaining a nuclear peace.

To guide the discussion that follows, table 5 relates the kinds of force postures required for (1) finite or minimum deterrence (relatively few weapons or weapons systems—often vulnerable to an enemy's first strike and thus a less-stable basis for deterrence),[39] (2) deterrence based on assured (or mutual, assured) destruction, (3) some "damage-limitation" defenses should deterrence fail and war break out, and (4) deterrence by denial that relies on robust offensive and defensive capabilities, which tends to make it the least stable form of deterrence. The massive strategic offensive and defensive buildup in deterrence by denial also makes it as unstable or more than the minimum-deterrence force posture.

Minimum deterrence required a smaller number of "survivable" nuclear weapons systems that would be left in the US arsenal for retaliation should the enemy (principally the Soviet Union) strike first. Given that the survival of a few was always in doubt, the United States and the USSR dramatically increased the numbers of bombers and missiles in the 1950s and 1960s to be sure that enough would survive to enable retaliation should either be attacked first.

Table 5. Relating Strategic Nuclear Deterrence Doctrines to Force Posture.

	Minimum Deterrence	Assured Destruction (AD)	AD + Damage Limitation	Deterrence by Denial
Forces Required				
Offense (bombers & missiles)	perhaps 100 or fewer nuclear weapons	large numbers of nuclear weapons	large numbers of nuclear weapons	very large numbers of nuclear weapons
Defense				
Active (fighter-interceptor aircraft, surface-to-air missiles, anti-aircraft artillery, anti-ballistic missiles, space-based systems	none required	none required	some	robust, fully developed
Passive (radars, command & control communications)	some for early warning	some for early warning	substantial need	robust, fully developed
Stability of Deterrence Relations	potentially unstable	usually the most stable	potentially unstable	usually the most unstable

This "second-strike" capability depended on an enemy not only knowing that the United States possessed these capabilities, but also that the United States would have the will to use them. Hence, US threats to adversaries would have to be credible to sustain the deterrent effect. Survivability of weapons systems depended on making them less vulnerable to attack: (a) enabling weapons delivery to targets by multiple platforms—long-range bombers, intercontinental land-based and submarine-launched ballistic missiles (ICBMs and SLBMs)—the "triad" as they came to be called; (b) opting for greater mobility, as in bombers once airborne and submarines moving underwater to avoid enemy detection,;(c) hardening, as in putting land-based missiles in underground "silos," thus making them more difficult to destroy; (d) assuring "penetration" by aircraft and cruise missiles either by reducing enemy detection of a strike by flying under (or outside of) their radar coverage or by employing "stealth" technologies—use of less radar-detectable materials or geometries (reducing substantially the radar image of aircraft); (e) developing the greater accuracy needed to destroy enemy missiles before launch lest they be used to take out American strategic weapons systems; and (f) taking measures to assure the command-and-control communications necessary to put bombers in the air or launch land- or submarine-based ballistic missiles.

This was deterrence through fear of *punishment* that held sway from the Truman-Eisenhower period through the Kennedy-Johnson, Nixon-Ford, and Carter administrations. It was a period in which defenses were minimized lest either side suspect the other of preparing to fight a war, particularly a nuclear one that would require robust defenses in addition to offensive weapons systems. There was consideration in the late 1960s and early 1970s of some anti-aircraft and antiballistic missile defenses for "damage limitation" should an attack occur, but even these modest steps —particularly when coupled with civil defense preparations—were seen by many as potentially provocative. The Soviets might interpret such *active* measures as preparation for war, much as US decision-makers would tend to see Soviet defensive measures in the same light. In the minds of American decision-makers, only *passive* defenses like radar-based early warning systems deployed by both sides and minimal *active* defenses (fighter-interceptor aircraft, surface to air missiles, anti-aircraft artillery, and a small number of antiballistic missiles—later none) had legitimacy in this period.

Soon after taking office in January 1981, the new Reagan administration raised the ante substantially. Not only were strategic-offense capabilities to be expanded, but also strategic defenses. Deterrence—war prevention based on fear of an unacceptable level of retaliatory destruction or *punishment*—was to be replaced by a deterrence based on *denial* of gains from attacking.[40] By the United States developing capabilities to win or "prevail" in fighting a nuclear war with the Soviet Union, the aim was to *deny* the enemy any likelihood of achieving whatever sought-after objectives were at issue should fighting escalate to a nuclear level.

The intent was to take nuclear war off the table as a Soviet option. Peaceful rhetoric aside (and quite apart from technological challenges and the massive cost of adding a strategic defense component), the United States was planning to acquire a nuclear war-fighting capability. Soviet military writings often presented nuclear weapons as just another category in their arsenal that could be used should war break out in Europe, but now the United States was to have a strategic posture with robust space-based defenses added to offensive weapons systems.

Concern that the United States might consider launching a first strike and fear in Moscow that their second-strike capabilities were being undermined led the Soviets to consider moving to a launch-on-warning position (rather than the more stable launch under- or after-attack criteria). Launch-on-warning leaves no time to correct for false indications of attack, miscalculations, or other accidents. Put another way, going forward on the president's Strategic Defense Initiative (SDI) was destabilizing deterrence relations between the superpowers.[41] We now know from Politburo minutes that Soviet leaders at the time saw SDI deployment as antecedent to a US first strike—very unstable deterrence relations indeed.

The MAD "Balance of Terror"

The World War II Manhattan Project had resulted in nuclear fission weapons (at the time dubbed atomic- or "A-bombs" for short), first tested on July 16, 1945, and dropped by B-29 bombers on the Japanese cities of Hiroshima and Nagasaki less than a month later on August 6 and 9 respectively—to date the only detonations of nuclear weapons in warfare. Next in this competitive arms race, the Soviets detonated their first fission weapon in August 1949.

By 1951 the United States had developed a thermonuclear- or hydrogen-fusion weapon (then popularly called a hydrogen bomb or H-bomb) that was a hundred or more times as powerful as a fission weapon, and detonated it on November 1, 1952. The United Kingdom, which had collaborated with the United States on nuclear technologies, had tested its own weapon in October 1952. In August 1953 (four years after its first nuclear test), the USSR successfully tested a thermonuclear or fusion weapon. Following suit, France demonstrated a nuclear weapons capability in 1960; China in 1964.

A nuclear "balance of terror" had emerged.[42] As Winston Churchill put it with his customary eloquence: "It may well be that we shall, by a process of sublime irony, have reached a stage in this story where safety will be the sturdy child of terror, and survival the twin brother of annihilation."[43] He was correct—by the 1960s and into the 1970s, the United States (and its British and French allies on one side) and the Soviet Union on the other were locked into deterrence based on mutual assured destruction (MAD).[44]

It amounted to a mutual suicide pact that was to preserve the peace given that it was hoped that neither side rationally would opt for going to war in these circumstances.[45] It was a horrific social construction—world peace resting on the hope that rationality would drive both sides to avoid armed conflicts or wars that could escalate to the nuclear level. So much faith was placed on the hope that the intersubjectivity of both sides would produce a "rational" outcome. To say the least, it was a dangerous time that, with ebbs and flows in degrees of tension, would last some four decades.

It was a nuclear peace dependent on the stability of deterrence relations. The Americans and the Soviets each developed their own triad of bombers, land-based intercontinental ballistic missiles (ICBMs), and submarine-launched ballistic missiles (SLBMs). This was in addition to "theater" (mainly European-based) nuclear weapons and weapons systems that were for both battlefield use ("tactical" weapons) and for strategic purposes (US targeting the USSR and its Warsaw Pact allies in Eastern Europe, the USSR targeting US forces and its NATO allies). In the minds of most decision makers in Washington, US and NATO nuclear and conventional forces in Europe, as well as supporting allies in East Asia, were linked to the US-Soviet deterrence relation—all part of a global construction in which the United States gave its allies assurance under the extended-deterrence, nuclear umbrella of the United States.

Were armed conflict between the United States and USSR to break out, the "battlefield" could be a conventional or nuclear one in Europe, a nuclear exchange between the two superpowers or, more likely, both. *Angst* felt by Europeans, particularly in Germany that was *the* central front in any such confrontation, produced a nightmare that the superpowers would somehow conduct their war in central Europe, leaving their homelands unscathed. As unrealistic as that nightmare was, the converse "dream" that, if such a dreadful conflict occurred, the superpowers would conduct nuclear attacks back and forth over the North Pole, leaving Europe intact. Most frustrating to European leaders and their populations, of course, was their understanding that such decisions were entirely out of their direct control—solely in the hands (and minds) of decision makers in Washington and Moscow.

A massive nuclear-arms race—deploying ever-larger numbers and technologically ever-more-sophisticated weapons systems—resulted in very robust strategic offenses. Efforts were made to develop strategic defenses against bombers (mainly surface-to-air missiles and fighter interceptor aircraft). Effective missile defenses were the larger techno-logical challenge, but developing an antiballistic missile (ABM) system was also part of the US plan that mirrored Soviet development of strategic defenses.

In part due to frustrations (and the high cost of such defense programs), both parties agreed in the 1972 ABM Treaty to limit further development and deployment of strategic defenses. Caps also were placed on offensive systems by executive agreement in the same year between Richard Nixon and Leonid Brezhnev in the Strategic Arms Limitations Talks (SALT). In the minds of US decision-makers, it was enough to maintain a second-strike capability and thus put its hope on diplomacy—moving toward the more relaxed tensions of *détente*, albeit coupled with the success of nuclear-deterrence relations based on fear, specifically the threat of mutual punishment should either side opt for war.

Toward the end of the Cold War and after, strategic arsenals have been reduced on both sides, the process underwritten by Strategic Arms Reductions Treaties (START). From some 12,000 strategic nuclear warheads in their strategic arsenals at the end of the Cold War, each side retains close to 1,500—an 87.5% reduction! Although alert levels are not what they once were, when political tensions rise between Russia and the West, one becomes mindful that both effectively are still part of an assured-destruction, nuclear-deterrence relation.

WHY THE USE OF FORCE? WHY WAR?

As zoologist Konrad Lorenz once observed, war is very much a human construction.[46] To him its social construction made possible its elim-ination—what people create, they also can terminate. Lorenz looked to the animal kingdom, identifying innate behavior patterns that kept animals from aggression within their own species. By contrast, human beings do not have natural obstacles to intraspecific aggression. They are drawn to using force against one another when they perceive net gains from doing so.

Because the organized use of force or violence is usually for political or other purposes, engaging in it is a rational choice. It is also a phenomenon with deep historical roots in the human experience—the stuff of tribal (and clan) conflicts, empires and, in the present period, both state and nonstate actors.

As a rational or purposive enterprise designed to achieve particular objectives, one can try to dissuade those with such capabilities that war is not the answer. As a practical matter, of course, the pacifist argument—however defensible philosophically—does not persuade those who pragmatically see war as a means to the ends they seek. In the lead up to war or other uses of force, there typically is a weighing of expected human and material costs, oftentimes underestimated. The operative, highly subjective question at issue is whether the use of force is worth the cost relative to expected gains from going to war.

Following Kenneth Waltz, the underlying or *permissive* cause—what allows wars to occur—is the anarchy of international politics.[47] Although Waltz deals exclusively with interstate war, his identification of anarchy among states as a causal condition also describes the environment within which nonstate actors operate. There is nothing in an anarchic world to block or try to stop a state or nonstate actor from using force except another state, alliance or coalition of states. There is no superordinate authority, much less one with requisite power, to stop state or nonstate actors from using force against each other. The resulting clash between or among states, alliances, coalitions of states, or nonstate actors is a state of war.

If anarchy is the underlying condition that allows wars to occur, then one explains the outbreak of a particular war by combining *efficient* causes or factors found at different levels of analysis: (1) individual and small groups (the domain of psychology and social psychology respectively) the first image as Waltz calls it; (2) state and society (the domain of sociology) or "second" image, and (3) the *system* of states or "third" image. Causal explanation of World War I in 1914, for example, would combine the following: *first image* perceptions, personality, and other characteristics of leaders and leadership elites; *second image* focus on the types of states involved—whether more authoritarian regimes (as in Germany at the time) were more prone to war than democracies like Britain and France; and *third image* factors such as whether arms races (Germany contesting the French on land and the British at sea) or secret and other automatic commitments in alliances (Germany in central Europe, Britain and France in the West and Russia in the East respectively) contributed causally to the outbreak of war.

International anarchy thus permits the use of force—the principal obstacle posed by other states or alliances willing and able to use force as a counter, which is a prescription for war. Given this underlying condition of international relations, we take account of factors in all three images or levels of analysis, but it is a first-image focus on decision makers that fits our purposes in this volume. To explain decisions and actions taken, we look first to the understandings of threats, opportunities, and the costs and benefits of pursuing military and nonmilitary approaches to the ends they seek.

Afterword

As documented in this chapter, the United States is no stranger when it comes to war and other armed interventions—the latter the subject of chapter 3. The United States in a typical year spends substantially more than a third of what the entire world allocates to defense—clear indication of consensus among policy elites in both political parties that the use of force will continue to be an important dimension of American national security policy. Administrations differ on when and how to use force, but there are relatively few inhibitions against doing so when judging it to be justified in accordance with one or more of the criteria detailed in the next chapter.

NOTES

1. *Male* (\mah-leh\)—a word with more than twenty meanings or shades of meaning in an unabridged Italian dictionary—is often mistranslated simply as "evil." From the context of Machiavelli's usage, however, "harm" captures the intended meaning. After all, princes (and presidents) put troops in harm's way when they send them into combat. Their duty to maintain security is the justification they use for such state action (raison d'état).

2. Machiavelli feminizes *Fortuna* (Lady Luck) and casts her as more powerful than any prince. She does not respect princes lacking in *virtù*, which takes masculine form. On the power of the feminine in Machiavelli's writings, see Hanna Fenichel Pitkin, *Fortune Is a Woman: Gender and Politics in the Thought of Niccolò Machiavelli*, 2nd ed. (Chicago, IL: University of Chicago Press, 1984, 1999).

3. For a documentary that brings this military dimension into focus, see *Bible Battles*, History Channel DVD, 2005.

4. Joshua 6: 2–5.

5. Mark Twain, "The War Prayer."

6. For a longer, more detailed discussion of this moralist component, see Paul R. Viotti, *American Foreign Policy* (Cambridge, UK: Polity Press, 2010), chapter 4, esp. pp. 111–113.

7. Citizens are free to express themselves, to aggregate, to travel, to act socially or politically, to buy and sell, to form businesses or invest and realize gains (or suffer losses), and to engage in other work or leisure activities. They also have a right to due process of law.

8. John Winthrop," A Model of Christian Charity." On the Manichaean dark-light contrast in biblical passages, see Matthew 5:14–16, John 1:4–5, and 19–21, and Revelation (or Apocalypse) 21:23–6.

9. "The Shining City upon a Hill" speech, January 25, 1974, and his "Farewell Address to the Nation," January 11, 1989. This also underscored President Reagan's views that were more positive toward immigration than most of his followers, then as now.

10. See his inaugural speech on January 20, 1989, in which he defined these "points" as "all the community organizations that are spread like stars throughout the Nation, doing good."

11. Speech to the nation by President George W. Bush on September 11, 2001, 8:30 PM EDT.
12. "Acceptance Speech," Democratic National Convention, New York, July 16, 1992.
13. "State of the Union Address," January 20, 2015.
14. Tim Perry, "Grey Eminence: The Influence of Sylvanus Thayer on American Military Education," paper presented to the Red River Valley Historical Conference and University of North Dakota, March 2009.
15. See Daniel T. Rean, "Shifting Strategies: Military Theory in the American War," http://www.militaryhistoryonline.com/civilwar/articles/militarytheory.aspx, accessed January 27, 2015.
16. Perry, *op. cit.*
17. Clausewitz, Book II, chapter 2. Clausewitz's own critique of Jomini can be found in this chapter.
18. Carl von Clausewitz, *On War*, Book V, chapter 6. Translations used in the citations here and later are from three sources: Michael Howard and Peter Paret (ed. and trans), *On War* (Princeton, NJ: Princeton University Press, 1976); Caleb Carr (ed.), *The Book of War* (New York: Random House/Modern Library, 2000); and Anatol Rapoport (ed.), *On War* (New York: Penguin Books, 1968).
19. Michael Howard, *The Causes of Wars and Other Essays*, 2nd ed. (Cambridge, Mass.: Harvard University Press, 1984), 103.
20. "The Forgotten Dimensions of Strategy," *Foreign Affairs* (Summer 1979). The full article is available at http://www.foreignaffairs.com/articles/32623/michael-howard/the-forgotten-dimensions-of-strategy.
21. Ibid., Book I, chapter 2.
22. Ibid., Book I, chapter 1 and Book III, chapters 1 and 2.
23. Ibid., Book I, chapters 6–8.
24. Ibid., Book II, chapter 11.
25. Ibid., Book I, chapter 6.
26. Ibid., Book III, chapters 8, 9, 11, and 14.
27. Ibid., Book VIII, chapter 4.
28. Ibid., Book VI, chapter 27.
29. Ibid., Book VIII, chapter 4.
30. Michael Walzer, *Just and Unjust Wars: A Moral Argument with Historical Illustrations* (New York: Perseus, 1977), esp. 44–47.
31. Ibid., Book V, chapter 3.
32. Enhanced radiation weapons (ERW), dubbed "neutron bombs," were developed by the late 1970s to blunt any Soviet-Warsaw Pact attack

against the central front between West and East Germany (to include the latter's Czechoslovak Warsaw Pact ally).

33. See Walzer, *Just and Unjust Wars*, chapter 16, 251–268.
34. Ibid., 253–254.
35. Clausewitz, *On War*, Book V, chapter 3.
36. The former was developed by Alexander George. See, for example his *Forceful Persuasion: Coercive Diplomacy as an Alternative to War* (Washington, DC: United States Institute of Peace, 1991) and George *et al.* (eds.), *The Limits of Coercive Diplomacy* (Boston: Little Brown, 1971 and, in second edition, Boulder, CO: Westview Press, 1994). On compellence, see Thomas Schelling, *Arms and Influence* (New Haven, CT: Yale University Press, 1966, 2008); cf. Schelling's *Strategy of Conflict* (Cambridge, MA: Harvard University Press, 1960, 1981).
37. *On War*, Book I, chapter 1, section 5. See also Book V, chapter 3.
38. Herman Kahn, *Thinking About the Unthinkable* (New York: Simon & Schuster/Touchstone, 1962, 1985).
39. Dan Caldwell, Pepperdine University, prefers either the term *basic deterrence* used by Bernard Brodie or *fundamental deterrence* because, as he puts it, there's nothing "minimal" about nuclear weapons.
40. Rather than call this *deterrence*, to some it is a form of defense based on war-fighting capabilities that *dissuade* an enemy from engaging in armed conflict. See Glenn H. Snyder, *Deterrence and Defense* (Princeton, NJ: Princeton University Press, 1961); cf. the review article by Glenn H. Snyder, "Deterrence, Defense, and Disengagement," *World Politics* 14, no. 2 (January 1962) and B.H. Liddell Hart, *Deterrent or Defense* (New York: Frederick A. Praeger, 1960).
41. Given its cost (some estimates at the time putting the program cost from beginning to deployment at a trillion dollars) and technical problems with such a space-based and ground, multilayered deployment, President Reagan's National Security Adviser Robert McFarlane saw SDI more as a bargaining chip in US-Soviet arms control negotiations. The president remained adamant, however, that SDI be pursued. Members of the Joint Chiefs of Staff were not enthusiastic because funds for SDI likely would have reduced their budgets for personnel, ships, tanks, aircraft, and other Earth-based equipment and weapons systems. To accommodate the president, however, an SDI office (SDIO) was set up in the Pentagon, but its director wore only three stars, a clear signal of the relative importance of SDI within DoD.

42. The phrase, apparently used first in San Francisco on June 24, 1955, by Lester Pearson (then Canadian secretary of state for foreign affairs, later prime minister) built on Churchill's earlier (March 1, 1955) reference to "sturdy child of terror" cited in this paragraph of the text (see the following note). For an assessment, see Albert Wohlstetter, "The Delicate Balance of Terror," (Santa Monica, CA: RAND Corporation Paper P-1472, November 6, 1958).

43. Churchill's "Never Despair" (or farewell) speech to the House of Commons on March 1, 1955.

44. During the Cold War, China did not have the long-range (ICBM) capability to hit targets in the United States, although it did pose a threat to US allies in the region, especially Japan and South Korea, that are under the extended-deterrence, US nuclear "umbrella"—a commitment that, in principle, makes it unnecessary for them to acquire their own nuclear weapons capabilities.

45. Michael Howard and others on the British side of the Atlantic preferred to call it mutually assured destruction—not just a grammatical correction of American English, but also because this wording underscores that both parties were in tandem in making this peace-oriented, mutual-suicide pact work.

46. Konrad Lorenz, *On Aggression*, 6th ed. (New York: Bantam Books/Random House, 1967).

47. Kenneth N. Waltz, *Man, the State and War* (New York, Columbia University Press, 1959), 234.

Chapter 3

Armed Intervention

Epitaph for an Enemy

What led us here, could it be fate
That brings us face to face?
I don't know you, you don't know me
And yet we're full of hate.
We know that one of us must die,
But which one will it be?
Will it be you that falls today?
Or will your mark find me?

I think of things that might have been
If you and I had met
Some other time, some other place,
Some other circumstance.
But we are here and time is now,
This we cannot alter.
I aim for you, you aim for me.
Neither one can falter.

Twas you young man that fell today
Your face now pale and still.
You were like me so full of fear

When you came up that hill.
Your mark missed but mine was true,
I saw you fall in pain.
I breathed a sigh of sad relief,
I lived it once again.

How much longer must I go?
Or how long will I last
Until your comrade faces me
And I will be a past?
I'll live from day to day, young man,
With hope that war will end,
When men like you and men like me
Can be the best of friends.

—Anonymous

As in the late nineteenth and early twentieth centuries, the entire post–World War II period has been marked by frequent armed interventions. To answer why the use of force, we explore understandings in the heads of most policy makers on the factors that lead them to engage the country in wars or armed interventions. Prior understandings internalized by decision makers color the interpretations they make and the actions they decide in relation to the use of force. Among internationalists, *neoconservatives* (or *militant internationalists*) are the most prone to use force or contain adversaries, the least likely to find diplomacy as the answer to national challenges. Both *conservative* and *liberal internationalists* are willing to engage in armed intervention or merely contain adversaries (and their records in office document this in practice), but the former tend to prefer containment and the latter diplomatic engagement, before deciding to use military force. Finally, *nationalists* historically have been less prone to intervene abroad outside of the Western Hemisphere.[1] We take this up in regard to the development over time of the Monroe Doctrine—a social construction that has profoundly influenced the way American decision-makers historically have thought and, to varying degrees, still think about Latin America—Mexico and Central America, the Caribbean, and South America.

THE TAKING OF HAWAII

In 1893 American and other businessmen objected to Hawaiian Queen Liliuokalani's efforts to trim their position of economic and political dominance in Honolulu and throughout the kingdom. Seeking eventual annexation by the United States as an interim step, business elites mustered some 1,500 armed men (dubbed "The Rifles") and overthrew the monarchy, placing the queen under house arrest in her Iolani Palace. Responding to alleged concerns about the safety of Americans and their property, Minister John L. Stevens, the senior US diplomat in Honolulu, called for an armed intervention. More than 160 US marines and sailors then came ashore in a show of strength for the insurgents. After all, the US Navy had its own interests in Pearl Harbor as a base for its Pacific operations. His pineapple plantation commercial interests well served by the coup, Sanford Dole became president of the new Hawaiian Republic.

If there were any doubts, the defeat of Spain in the Spanish-American War (1898) made clear the prominence of US interests in East Asia and the western Pacific in general, the Philippines in particular. On July 7, 1898, the McKinley administration annexed Hawaii, making it a US territory until 1959 when both Alaska and Hawaii became the 49th and 50th states respectively. The self-image held by US policy elites of inherently being an anticolonial power led them to use the term *territory* as a euphemism for the term *colony*. Given the historical precedent set by American colonies—breaking away from Britain—how could the United States acquire colonies in the nineteenth-century European pattern? In this self-serving social construction, territories are one thing, colonies quite another.

Five years after this rather modest armed intervention by some 160 men, the United States annexed Hawaii and also displaced Spain from Cuba, Puerto Rico, and the Philippines—the latter three "prizes" from winning the Spanish-American War. Events were on a roll. In October and November 1903, American officials—wanting finally to build a canal across the isthmus of Panama (then still part of Colombia), actively supported the Panamanian separatist movement. The US Navy's presence patrolling offshore—a show of US strength and resolve—bolstered the separatists. Colombian resistance crumbled, and President Theodore Roosevelt recognized the new government of Panama on November 3. It was the opening to three decades of frequent armed interventions in Mexico, Central America, and the Caribbean.

Using Force

Armed interventions are plentiful in the American experience against nonstate actors or for other purposes that are not resisted by force of another state, alliance, or coalition of states.[2] See the list of US armed interventions compiled in table 6. In chapter 4 we focus on both the underlying causes of insurgencies and the terrorism, assassination, and other forms of political violence they employ to advance their purposes. Following that we take up in chapter 5, measures taken by the United States and its state partners to counter insurgencies, terrorism, and other forms of organized political violence.

Table 6a. Armed Interventions Abroad by the United States: A Partial List.

Afghanistan	1998 (missile attack on Islamist sites), 2001
Albania	1997 (evacuation of US and other foreigners)
Angola	1976–1992
Argentina	1833, 1852–1853, 1890
Bolivia	1986
Bosnia	1993–1995
Cambodia	1969–1975
Chile	1891
China	1843, 1859, 1866, 1894–1995 (Sino-Japanese War), 1898–1900 (Boxer Rebellion), 1911–1941(various), 1946–1949
Colombia	1870, 1895, 2003 (support government's anti-drug efforts)
Croatia	1995
Cuba	1898–1902, 1906–1909, 1912, 1917–1933, 1961 (Bay of Pigs invasion), 1962 (naval blockade)
Dominican Republic	1903–1904, 1914, 1916–1924, 1965–1966
Egypt	1882 (British Egypt), 1956
El Salvador	1932, 1981–1992
Falkland (Malvinas) Islands	1831
Fiji	1840–1841, 1858
France	1798–1800 (Undeclared Naval Warfare), 1806–1810 (against French shipping in Caribbean)

Source. Adapted from Global Policy Forum data; cf. Barry M. Blechman and Stephen S. Kaplan, *Force without War: United States Armed Forces as a Political Instrument* (Washington, DC: Brookings Institution, 1978.

Note. The focus here is on international uses of force. For this reason, excluded from this list are dark chapters in the American experience—the use of force against Native American tribes and to quell slave revolts by African Americans. Covert actions (espionage) are covered in chapter 6 on Intelligence and not included here unless Special Forces or other military units were involved.

Table 6b. Armed Interventions Abroad by the United States: A Partial List (*Cont'd*).

Germany	1948
Greece	1827 (marines invade islands of Argentiere, Miconi, and Andross), 1947–1949
Grenada	1983–1884
Guam	1898, 1903
Guatemala	1920, 1966–1967, 1983–1989
Haiti	1888, 1891, 1914–1934, 1959, 1991, 1994–1996, 2004–2005
Hawaii	1874, 1893
Honduras	1903, 1907, 1911, 1912, 1919, 1924–1925, 1983–1990
Iran	1946, 1980 (failed hostage rescue), 1984 (2 Iranian military aircraft shot down), 1987–1988 (US military actions supporting Iraq in war with Iran)
Iraq	1991–2003 (no fly zone, air strikes, navy-enforced sanctions), 2014–
Ivory Coast	1843
Japan	1854, 1863, 1864, 1868
Korea	1871, 1894–1996 (during Sino-Japanese War), 1904–1905
Laos	1962, 1965–1973 (bombing campaign)
Lebanon	1958, 1982–1984
Liberia	1990, 1997, 2003
Libya	1981 (Libyan aircraft shot down), 1986 (air strikes), 1989 (Libyan aircraft shot down), 2011
Macedonia	2001

Table 6c. Armed Interventions Abroad by the United States: A Partial List (*Cont'd*).

Marquesa Island	1813 (seizure and establishment of first US naval base in Pacific)
Mexico	1836, 1842, 1859–1860 and 1861 (Cortina Wars), 1876, 1913, 1914–1918, 1923
Midway Island	1867
Nicaragua	1850, 1853, 1854, 1857, 1867, 1894, 1896, 1898, 1899, 1907, 1910, 1912–1933, 1981–1990
Pakistan	2005–
Panama	1856, 1860, 1865, 1866, 1873, 1885, 1895, 1901-14, 1918-20, 1925, 1958, 1964, 1989–1990
Paraguay	1859
Peru	1835–1936
Philippines	1898–1910, 1989 (air cover to support government in coup attempt), 2002 (anti-insurgent actions)
Portugal	1860 (West Africa colony)
Puerto Rico	1898
Russia	1918–1922 (Russian Civil War)
Samoa	1841, 1885, 1888, 1889, 1898–1899 (Samoa becomes US territory)
Somalia	1992–1994, 2006–
Spain	1806–1810 (against French shipping in Caribbean), 1806 (Spanish Mexico), 1810, 1812, 1814 (taking of Spanish west Florida, east Florida, and Pensacola, respectively), 1816–1819 (attacks on remaining Spanish positions, Spain finally ceding east Florida), 1822–1825 (marine landings in Cuba and Puerto Rico)
Sudan	1998 (attack on alleged chemical weapons plant)
Sumatra	1832, 1838

Table 6d. Armed Interventions Abroad by the United States: A Partial List (*Cont'd*).

Taiwan (Formosa)	1867
Syria	2008, 2014–
Turkey	1849, 1922
Uruguay	1855, 1868
Vietnam	1960–1964 (military advisors and Special Forces), war: 1965–1975
Yemen	2002 (strikes on *al Qaeda*), 2009
Yugoslavia	1919, 1946, 1992–1994, 1999 (air strikes)
Zaire (Congo)	1996–1997

PRIOR UNDERSTANDINGS AND THE AMERICAN PROPENSITY TO INTERVENE MILITARILY

If the understandings decision makers hold are that using force or going to war is in the national interest or serves particular objectives, there likely will be relatively few inhibitions or constraints against taking such actions. Still, the weighing of costs and benefits related to any decision to use force is highly subjective.

What is a *threat* (and how serious it is) or *opportunity* (and how viable or worthwhile it is to pursue), then, are subjective calls informed by current perceptions and prior understandings held by individual decision-makers who also interact with one another as they render advice or make authoritative choices. The benefits or costs of one alternative or another are highly subjective calculations.

Those with authority to advise or make foreign-policy choices construct the decision-making context. It may be "rational choice" among alternatives, but one that is subjectively filtered through both present and prior understandings that decision makers hold of what is at hand. Given this subjectivity, *who* is deciding matters. It is not rationality in the abstract apart from those engaged in what are essentially subjective and intersubjective processes. Sometimes the decision to intervene militarily seems unavoidable or, as Kenneth Waltz put it: "The balance of power is not so much imposed by statesmen on events as it is imposed by events on statesmen."[3]

American presidents often find themselves in this reactive mode as, for example, when the Royal Navy challenged American independence in the run up to the War of 1812 (James Madison), the South attacked Fort Sumter in 1860 (Abraham Lincoln), what appeared (or was made to appear) to be an attack in Havana Harbor by Spain on the USS Maine in 1898 (William McKinley),[4] the sinking of the *Lusitania* in World War I by German submarine attack (Woodrow Wilson), the bombing of Pearl Harbor and elsewhere by the Japanese in December 1941 (Franklin Roosevelt), the 1950 attack by North Korea across the 38th parallel (Harry Truman), the perceived attack in 1964 by North Vietnam against US Navy ships in the Gulf of Tonkin (Lyndon Johnson),[5] Iraq's invasion of Kuwait in 1990 (George H. W. Bush), and the attack by al Qaeda on September 11, 2001 (George W. Bush).

A review of these cases reveals a number of criteria present to a greater or lesser degree in the thinking of presidents and their advisers. They typically construct objectives in relation to what they see as the national interest, some saying, more restrictively, that force should only be used if core values or *vital* national interests are at stake. Consensus—much less unanimity—on such subjective considerations is often very elusive.

CRITERIA FOR INTERVENING (OR NOT INTERVENING)

Threats and opportunities are constructions in the minds of decision makers. They do not all agree on these subjective calculations or on the weight or utility to be placed on diverse criteria for deciding to use force. The criteria that decision makers tend to consider to a greater or lesser degree, depending on who is participating in (or influencing) the decision-making process, are listed next. Their rank order in importance often varies significantly among members of the decision-making group. Thus, these eight criteria are by no means a rank-ordered list:

1. *objectives in relation to calculations of national interest*: Next to defining the meaning of national security, nothing is more subjective than understandings of what is or is not in the national interest—not to mention specifying *core* or *vital interests*.

2. *expected cost in lives and treasure*: Difficult to estimate, the more typical error is understating both human and financial costs;

3. *likelihood of winning* (or risk of losing or not attaining objectives): Dangers in confronting other great powers and the complexity of trying to counter insurgencies effectively have made expectations of "winning" difficult to substantiate;

4. *legal and moral bases for armed intervention*: How much stock a given president and advisers put in the prohibition against intervening in the domestic affairs of another sovereign state affects the range of options they select. Governmental authorities frequently refer to the sovereign rights of the states they govern. Constructed and sustained as principles over the last half millennium, the domestic or *internal* claim is a *right* to exercise complete jurisdiction within the territorial boundaries of the state. Other states are prohibited from intervening in what are purely domestic matters. The *external* claim is to a *right* to be autonomous or independent of other states in the formulation of its foreign policy, the decisions and actions taken abroad. However much they may try to influence the foreign policy or international conduct pursued by the governing officials of a particular state, leaders of other states have no *right* under international law to dictate what these leaders choose to say and do.

Nevertheless, certain legal exceptions may allow armed intervention: if (a) the legitimate government of a state invites the intervention, (b) the United Nations Security Council authorizes it under Article 42 of the UN Charter in efforts to maintain or restore international peace and security, (c) an alliance like NATO, consistent with Article 51 of the UN Charter, authorizes it under Article 5 of the North Atlantic Treaty for collective-defense purposes, (d) a legal claim of a national right only to rescue citizens caught in harm's way due to natural disasters or political unrest, and (e) a customary international claim to intervene for human rights, as in stopping genocide.[6]

5. *readiness of military forces for deployment:* Are military forces ready for deployment in sufficient numbers to carry out assigned tasks? Even if they are technically *ready,* have they been taxed by prior deployments with sacrifices that undermine morale so important to combat effectiveness? Is public and congressional support substantial enough to warrant calling up reserve forces or committing air and army National Guard units for overseas deployments? For major contingencies, is there public and congressional support for activating the selective service system, reinstituting the draft?

6. *support from allies or coalition partners:* Going it alone means imposing the entire human and financial cost of the intervention on the American citizenry. By contrast, enlisting allies and coalition partners not only shares costs, but also tends to legitimate an intervention as having international support—a multilateral action, not just an American event.

7. *expected net effect on the human condition:* Often difficult to estimate accurately, armed interventions gain in legitimacy when the net effect is expected to be positive. By contrast, when the net effect on the country and its people (as well as the sacrifices made by the intervening party) are judged to be negative, the proposed intervention may not be warranted.

8. *degree of public support for armed intervention:* In some ways, this factor may become the most important if the intervention is to be sustained over a long period of time—measured in years, not just months or days. The following paragraphs address this conundrum in greater detail.

Is there public support for armed intervention that may lead to war with state or nonstate actors? If so, how long is that support likely to last? What education steps need to be taken to garner and sustain public backing for the war effort? Precipitating events, like the bombing of Pearl Harbor (1941) and the terrorist attack on 9/11 (2001), galvanize public commitment to taking action but, as a practical matter, public support for armed interventions or wars has a relatively short shelf life in the US experience—limited to a few years at most.

Even in World Wars I and II, American involvement amounted only to some two years in the former, four years in the latter. Erosion of public support occurs even in wars of relatively short duration, support for fighting in Korea (1950–1953) diminishing significantly as casualties (killed and wounded) continued to mount. Escalation of the war in Vietnam from about 35,000 troops in 1965 to some 550,000 by 1968 became a decade-long commitment with declining public support that tore apart the national fabric into pro- and antiwar factions.

American troop strengths in Vietnam were drawn down in the first half of the 1970s in a failed attempt at "Vietnamization" of the conflict (replacing American with Vietnamese ground forces) that ended with the fall of Saigon in 1975. It was the first war in the American experience that the United States had lost. Shattering the myth of American invincibility, the country descended into a period of collective amnesia about the war that lasted at least until the mid-1980s when courses on the Vietnam War began to emerge on college campuses.

Although casualties in the Afghan and Iraq interventions (2001 and 2003 respectively) were far fewer than had occurred in the world wars, Korea, and Vietnam, public support still waned substantially as these contingencies continued seemingly unabated. The drawdown of forces began in the outgoing Bush administration, leaving the final act to the incoming Obama administration that took office in 2009 and pledged to end the substantial ground force commitment in both countries. Even when this "final act" was followed by the breakdown of governance in

Iraq, there was insufficient public support to return substantial numbers of ground forces to the country. The same has been the case in Afghanistan. Smaller numbers of advisers and special forces troops have had to suffice.

Answering these questions requires judgments by decision makers who typically look to inputs by civilian and military leaders in the Department of Defense, Congressional leaders and others on Capitol Hill, and the public as a whole. As commander-in-chief, the president has constitutional authority to commit the armed forces to combat, but in any decision to use force he or she is facilitated or constrained by these understandings.

INTERNATIONALIST AND NATIONALIST ORIENTATIONS

Underlying all of these subjective calculations, of course, is the decision maker's relative propensity to use force or go to war—informed as that is by prior experiences or understandings embedded in his or her mind. Although we need not construct a rigid, airtight taxonomy of thought, American decision-makers do tend to fall historically into one or another pattern of *internationalist* or *nationalist* modes or orientations— the former referred to in the following section as liberal, conservative, and neoconservative or militant internationalist understandings of how foreign and national security policy should be conducted.

Liberal-Internationalist Orientations. While willing to use force more as a last resort, those of *liberal-internationalist* persuasion tend to put a premium on diplomatic and other means short of armed intervention to include deterring or containing adversaries. The liberal-internationalist presidencies of Woodrow Wilson, later Franklin Roosevelt and Harry Truman, are twentieth-century examples of administrations diplomatically focused but willing, if deemed necessary, to engage even in world war. Diplomacy took its place with allies during these wars, but also played a central role in reconstructing the order of relations among states when these wars ended—Wilson's 14 points and the establishment of the

League of Nations after World War I and the Yalta, Potsdam, and San Francisco Conferences as World War II was ending. The last of these led to replacement of the League with a new United Nations organization and "system" or network of affiliated international organizations.

Theirs was a liberal vision of national and international security resting first on diplomacy with both allies and adversaries. The use of force was not removed, but put in second position or as backdrop designed to make diplomatic efforts more effective. Thus, Chapter Six of the UN Charter describes diplomatic and various peaceful (or less warlike) remedies for maintaining international peace and security. In principle, only when these peaceful remedies have been exhausted, does one get to Chapter Seven, particularly Article 42, which authorizes the use of force as a collective security remedy consistent with the international law-enforcement understandings of the earlier League of Nations Covenant. In the absence of a majority in the Security Council (or if one of the five permanent members exercises its veto), states may take individual or collective action with allies consistent with international law—their inherent sovereign right of self-defense explicitly recognized in Articles 2 and 51. Although the term *alliance* does not appear, they have legal standing when one reads Articles 51 and 52 that provide legal legitimacy for such international "defensive" arrangements. Consistent with these liberal-internationalist understandings in the Roosevelt-Truman administrations, the *War* Department (army) was combined with the navy department and a new Department of the Air Force came into being in a newly constructed Department of *Defense.* When the Truman Administration went to war in Korea (1950), it was initially referred to not as a "war," but rather as a "police action" under legal auspices of the Security Council.[7]

Conservative and Neoconservative (or Militant) Internationalist Orientations. Though willing to engage in diplomacy as far as it will go, *conservative internationalists* tend to have relatively less faith in the diplomatic instrument of policy, preferring to rely for the most part on deterrence or containment before intervening militarily. Nevertheless, conservative internationalists like Richard Nixon did use diplomacy vis-à-vis normalization of relations with China (1971–1972). For their part, beginning in the mid-1980s the Ronald Reagan and George H. W. Bush administrations established a new framework for relations with the Soviet Union, which became the new Russian Federation that emerged in 1993.

By contrast, the more assertive *neo-conservatives* or *militant internationalists* tend to be highly skeptical about the efficacy of diplomacy as remedy and thus not only rely primarily on deterrence or containment, but also have relatively fewer inhibitions about using force when they see it in the national interest to do so. Neoconservatives drove US policy toward invasion of Iraq in 2003—the announced aims being to prevent proliferation of weapons of mass destruction (WMD), to overthrow a dictatorship, and help establish a democracy that would be a model for all of Araby.

Such militant internationalism is not without its historical antecedents in the American experience—examples including the "war hawk" faction leading to the war with Britain in 1812, those pushing for war with Mexico in 1845 and Spain in 1898, and advocacy following the defeat of Germany in World War II of "finishing the job" (as in liberating Eastern Europe from the Soviet yoke with force, if necessary, or even invading the Soviet Union itself). Failing to move American policy toward that end, their refrain at the time and in the 1950s was that the United States had surrendered US and other countries' interests to the Soviet Union at the 1945 Yalta and Potsdam Conferences ("sold them down the river" the popular colloquial phrase used by Congressman Richard Nixon and other conservatives at the time). So much for the efficacy of diplomacy![8] And, on top of that, the United States (to partisan Republicans, the Democrats) had "lost" China—the communist takeover there in 1949.[9]

Even John Foster Dulles, secretary of state for the more moderate Eisenhower administration, favored "roll back" of Soviet gains in Eastern Europe. Rhetoric aside, the administration was careful to avoid a confrontation with the Soviet Union when Hungarians rose up in 1956 against their communist leaders. The same was true, of course, more than a decade later when the Soviets crushed an uprising in Czechoslovakia in 1968.

Nationalist Orientations. Although those of *nationalist* orientation who decidedly avoid foreign entanglements are fewer in numbers today, they were the mainstream from the late eighteenth to the early twentieth centuries, particularly in relation to European wars. At the same time, however, this nationalist (or noninterventionist) view did not extend to the Caribbean or elsewhere in Latin America that many saw as being within the US sphere of interest.

Thus, references to the "Americas" in the Pan-American Union and, later, the Organization of American States (OAS) were more than casual designations. The Monroe Doctrine (1823) that closed the region to further colonization was an early expression of this view. With *rapprochement* and normalization of relations with Britain accomplished, President James Monroe was clearly opposed to any effort by Spain and Portugal to reestablish themselves in colonies lost to liberal revolutionary movements in which fellow Freemason liberals had played so instrumental a role.[10] Following the Spanish-American War (1898), the American sphere had become particularly strong in Central America and the Caribbean (especially in Cuba and Puerto Rico), but also extended further west to Hawaii and the Philippines, the former annexed and the latter taken from Spain.

That the Americas are a US sphere of influence was a nineteenth-century social construction that developed and has taken different forms over almost two centuries. This essentially nationalist doctrine was (and remains) a lens through which American decision-makers have interpreted events in the Western Hemisphere as somehow different from Europe, European colonies, and other states in Africa, Asia, and the Pacific. Ideas about spheres of influence that legitimate intervention and become embedded in the minds of decision makers influence the way they interpret threats and opportunities and consider the diverse policy options before them. In this regard, the Monroe Doctrine became a policy basis for legitimating in American minds closing the hemisphere to direct Portuguese and Spanish power and influence—a nineteenth-century American project that was not completed until victory over Spain at the end of the century in the Spanish-American War.

Underlying the doctrine was a widespread nineteenth-century American understanding of "manifest destiny"—a widespread religious belief that the Creator not only had favored the United States with the territory it possessed (or came to possess in its westward expansion), but also had given the country a geopolitical mandate to spread its republican form of governance throughout the North American continent, by extension to the Western Hemisphere as a whole and, later, the entire world.

The Monroe Doctrine is a case in point which is chronicled in greater detail in the next section, its social construction traced over almost 200 years since it was first articulated. In the years since the Monroe Doctrine was formally stated in 1823, its meaning evolved over time, taking diverse twists and turns. It remains a backdrop for American thinking on Latin America, however, and decision makers in Washington still tend to see the region subjectively as in the US sphere of influence. It is a lens that influences how decision makers interpret what is going on and affects what they choose to do south of the border. More often than in other regions of the world, armed intervention historically has been the preferred remedy when decision makers see threats adverse to their understandings of US interests.

Internationalists of all stripes—liberal, conservative, and neoconservative or militant—dominate the foreign policy discourse in Washington. Nevertheless, deep pockets of nationalist sentiment still reside in the countryside, tapped by diverse political movements from time to time—among them trade protectionists, some libertarians, "Tea Party" activists, antiwar and anti-interventionist groups. Present-day echoes of earlier nationalist sentiments can be heard in relation to anti-immigration policy debates—keep foreigners out, whether they be Mexicans and others from south of the border or Muslims from one country or another. Some nationalists also argue against US intervention abroad unless vital or core national interests are at stake. To them, the United States should not see itself (much less be) the world's policeman. At the same time, other nationalists are prone to join with militant internationalists to advocate massive armed interventions (as in the Middle East) they see as clearing out safe havens used by terrorist movements wishing to bring harm directly upon the United States.

Nineteenth- and twentieth-century interventions in Latin America were justified in the minds of American decision-makers as being within the US sphere of influence. In their view, it was the God-given "manifest destiny" that gave the United States the responsibility and authority to intervene in hemispheric affairs. Support for efforts to oust Catholic and authoritarian Spain and Portugal from the hemisphere—efforts pursued by Latin American "liberators"; Simón Bolívar, José de San Martín, and Bernardo O'Higgins prominent among them—was apparent in the Monroe Doctrine. Indeed, President James Monroe, referred to them in his doctrine as "southern brethren."

It was a liberal ideology these liberators were advancing in the republics they were establishing south of the US border. Closing the hemisphere to further colonization, the statement pragmatically allowed the British, French, and Dutch to retain their colonial domains. On its own, the US Navy was not able to keep the Iberian powers from retaking their lost colonies; enforcement of the Monroe Doctrine depended upon the Royal Navy—Britain sharing the US interest in keeping the Iberian powers from returning to retake lost territories.

The Monroe Doctrine as an Interventionist Social Construction

As it developed over time, the Monroe Doctrine gave legitimacy in the minds of American policy makers for armed interventions in Latin

America. It was in his seventh annual message to Congress (December 2, 1823) that President James Monroe laid the cornerstone of his policy that closed the new world to further colonization, particularly by Spain and Portugal that had lost their colonies to successful insurgencies led by freemasonic liberal revolutionaries. Left intact, as noted earlier, were British, French, and Dutch residual colonies in Central America (British Honduras, now Belize), various Caribbean islands, and South America (the Guiana colonies). The still-fledgling US Navy was not yet able to enforce so expansive a doctrine, but the Royal Navy could be relied on because the doctrine also served anti-Iberian British interests.

Monroe's message captures the central claims of this new construction, which became embedded over time in American understandings:

> We ... declare that we should consider any attempt on their [i.e., European] part to extend their system to any portion of this hemisphere as dangerous to our peace and safety. With the existing colonies or dependencies of any European power we have not interfered and shall not interfere. But with the Governments who have declared their independence and maintain it, and whose independence we have, on great consideration and on just principles, acknowledged, we could not view any interposition for the purpose of oppressing them, or controlling in any other manner their destiny, by any European power in any other light than as the manifestation of an unfriendly disposition toward the United States....

> It is impossible that the allied powers [i.e., Spain and Portugal] should extend their political system to any portion of either continent without endangering our peace and happiness; nor can anyone believe that *our southern brethren* [emphasis added], if left to themselves, would adopt it of their own accord.....

The Platt Amendment (1901). By the end of the nineteenth century, the Monroe Doctrine had expanded beyond the original doctrine that prohibited the Iberian powers from reinserting themselves into the hemisphere. With victory in the Spanish-American War (1898), the United

States now asserted that it had a right to intervene in Latin American republics, using the Monroe Doctrine as justification. This was formalized in relation to Cuba in the Platt Amendment , passed by Congress on March 2, 1901, as an amendment to a US Army appropriations bill.

Theodore Roosevelt's Corollary to the Monroe Doctrine (1904). President Theodore Roosevelt extended to the whole of Latin America this newly established Monroe Doctrine–based right to intervene in Cuba. In his Annual Message to Congress (December 6, 1904), he carved out this newly claimed US right to intervene lest, contrary to his expansive interpretation of the Monroe Doctrine, European states intervene in Latin American countries to collect unpaid obligations or address other concerns or interests. Armed interventions to support US business interests in Central America and the Caribbean during the Theodore Roosevelt and William Howard Taft administrations reached a crescendo under Woodrow Wilson's very interventionist administration (1913–1921). Indeed, Wilson ordered more armed interventions in Latin America than any other president.

Franklin Roosevelt's Good Neighbor Policy (1933 and 1936). Theodore Roosevelt's corollary had opened the gates to US armed interventions in Latin America in the first three decades of the twentieth century—the Monroe Doctrine the underlying justification. As noted in the opening section of this chapter, in 1903 (just before Roosevelt formulated his corollary), the US Navy supported separatists favorable to the US canal project to secede from Colombia and establish Panama as a new republic.

By no means, of course, was American presence new to politics on the Isthmus of Panama. The Bidlack Treaty (1846) with Colombia gave the United States the right to transit the isthmus. A railway was built across the isthmus at the time of the California gold rush (construction underway, 1849–1856). The treaty also granted a right to US military intervention to quash anti-Colombian revolts or other social unrest in the isthmus, which the United States exercised on a number of occasions.

US military interventions also occurred in Nicaragua (1912–1933), Cuba (1898–1902, 1906–1909, 1912, and 1917–1922), Dominican Republic (1903, 1904, 1914, and 1916–1924), Haiti (1915–1934), Honduras (1903, 1907, 1911, 1912, 1919, 1924, and 1925), and Mexico (1910–1919).

The Pan-American Union (its origins in 1889) had focused on building cooperative relations in the hemisphere, but it was not until Franklin Roosevelt's presidency (1933–1945) that the United States reversed its policy on intervention in Latin American countries. In his first inaugural address on March 4, 1933, Roosevelt stated: "In the field of world policy I would dedicate this nation to the policy of the good neighbor—the neighbor who resolutely respects himself and, because he does so, respects the rights of others—the neighbor who respects his obligations and respects the sanctity of his agreements in and with a world of neighbors."

He amplified this general statement in 1936, specifying Latin America as a nonintervention zone. Later, the Charter of the Organization of American States (OAS, 1948)—successor to the Pan-American Union—institutionalized further in inter-American law prohibitions against such interventions. The Monroe Doctrine's tenet against further colonization (now interpreted more broadly as intrusions by any foreign power) remained in effect, but the doctrine was no longer to be used as a basis for US intervention in the domestic politics of Latin American states. Ultimately (some twenty years later), that would not be the case.

The Return to Armed Intervention. Breaking with this Rooseveltian "good neighbor" policy that had been sustained in the Roosevelt-Truman years (1933–1953), the Eisenhower administration authorized the CIA to intervene in Guatemala against the left-oriented Jacobo Árbenz regime (1954) that threatened American business interests, notably United Fruit. With the Eisenhower administration's concurrence, the CIA later planned a counter-revolutionary invasion against the Castro regime in Cuba that had come to power in 1959. The succeeding Kennedy administration authorized execution of the plan on April 17, 1961, at the Bay of Pigs; this was a colossal failure.

Three months before, the Monroe Doctrine was implicitly acknowledged as still being in force during John F. Kennedy's January 20, 1961,
inaugural address: "Let all our neighbors know that we shall join with
them to oppose aggression or subversion anywhere in the Americas. And
let every other power know that this hemisphere intends to remain the
master of its own house." These tenets were later invoked in Kennedy's
response to the Soviet placement of nuclear capabilities in Cuba (October
22, 1962):

> We are calling tonight for an immediate meeting of ... the Orga-
> nization of American States, to consider this threat to hemispheric
> security and to invoke articles 6 and 8 of the Rio Treaty in support
> of all necessary action. The United Nations Charter allows for
> regional security arrangements, and the nations of this hemisphere
> decided long ago against the military presence of outside powers.

The Johnson administration subsequently intervened in Panama (1964),
the Dominican Republic (1965–1966), and Guatemala (1966–1967). The
Reagan-Bush years saw various military operations, sometimes coupled
with CIA covert actions, in El Salvador (1981–1992), Nicaragua against
the Sandinistas (1981–1990), Honduras (1982–1990), Grenada (1983–
1984), Bolivia (1987), and Panama (1989). The Clinton administration
intervened in Haiti (1994–1995), and the George W. Bush administration
sent troops to Haiti (2004) but also supported covert actions against Hugo
Chavez regime in Venezuela.

Although direct references to the Monroe Doctrine are less frequent
today, it still defines a mental frame supporting those who see the Western
Hemisphere as an inherently US sphere of influence. Notwithstanding
various twists and turns in interpretation, it remains an influential social
construction that has enjoyed a very long shelf life both in mind and
practice.

AFTERWORD

The use of force to achieve national security objectives—whether by war or through armed interventions—is very much a part of the American experience. Understandings of national interest, cost-benefit calculations, sovereignty and interpretations of international law, positions of the UN and other international organizations of the proposed intervention, the willingness of coalition partners, and human-rights commitments are among the considerations that inform decisions to use force. Legitimating armed interventions as serving not just national but also international security interests is almost always part of the discourse. The Monroe Doctrine from the outset carved out Latin America as a US sphere of interest, later legitimating in the minds of US decision-makers their resort to armed interventions in countries south of the US border.

Notes

1. For a more detailed discussion of these four orientations (nationalists and liberal, conservative, and neoconservative internationalists) toward diplomacy, containment, and armed intervention or war, see the introduction and first three chapters of *American Foreign Policy* by Paul R. Viotti (Cambridge, UK: Polity Press, 2010), 1–95, especially Table 1.1 on 18.
2. We reserve the term *war* primarily to armed conflicts between states and alliances or coalitions of states. *Armed interventions* are war-like activities directed typically against actors *within* a state or that operate across national borders.
3. Kenneth N. Waltz, *Man, the State and War.* (New York: Columbia University Press, 1959), 209.
4. That the explosion of a steam engine below decks—not action taken by the Spaniards—appears to have been the cause of the sinking of the Maine was a conclusion drawn by a study conducted for Admiral Hyman Rickover in 1974, although others have disputed the finding. See Louis Fisher, "Destruction of the Maine (1898)," The Law Library of Congress, August 4, 2009, accessed at http://www.loc.gov/law/help/usconlaw/pdf/Maine.1898.pdf on June 20, 2016.
5. As likely with the sinking of the Maine in 1898, the Gulf of Tonkin incident was not as originally reported. North Vietnamese torpedo boats were accused of firing upon the destroyer *USS Maddox* on August 2, 1964 when, in fact, the *Maddox* had fired warning shots against the boats first, thus provoking the North Vietnamese response. Moreover, the report of a second incident on August 4th apparently did not occur and may have been fabricated. See the declassified NSA article by Robert J. Hanyok, "Skunks, Bogies, Silent Hounds, and the Flying Fish: The Gulf of Tonkin Mystery, 2–4 August 1964," *Cryptologic Quarterly* 19, no. 4 and 20, no. 1 (Winter 2000/Spring 2001), 16. Robert S. McNamara (secretary of defense in 1964) later confirmed that the second incident on August 4 did not occur. See James G. Blight and Janet M. Lang, *The Fog of War* (Lanham, MD: Rowman & Littlefield, 2005).
6. Treaties and conventions on human rights do not provide a legal basis for armed intervention unless these abuses are threatening international peace and security, thus an Article 42 (chapter seven) basis under the

UN Charter. On the other hand, some argue that a right to intervene for humanitarian or human rights purposes is a construction that is emerging in customary international law. The more states intervene for such purposes, the stronger is the argument that a customary international law basis obtains.

7. The empowering UN Security Council resolution that remains in effect resulted from a vote taken after the Soviet representative stormed out of the Security Council meeting in protest. No permanent Security Council member has repeated this tactical error since.

8. The reality with which diplomats had to deal, of course, was that when World War II in Europe was in its last phases and finally ended in 1945, the Soviet Red Army was in occupation of most of the countries in Eastern Europe. The defeat of Germany at tremendous human cost to the Soviet Union—some 20 million or more dead the price for this victory— also left them in *de facto* control of the territories they had "liberated" from German hegemony.

9. Both claims of "selling Eastern Europe down the river" and "losing China" to the communists played heavily in the partisan politics of the day as Republicans, whether militant internationalists or not, blamed these losses on the Roosevelt and Truman Democratic administrations.

10. Freemason James Monroe in his doctrinal statement refers explicitly to fellow "brethren" to the South (though not by name), anticolonial, proliberal republican freemasonic "brothers" the likes of Simón Bolívar (Venezuela), Miguel Hidalgo (Mexico), José de San Martín (Argentina), Bernardo O'Higgins (Chile), and Francisco Miranda (Venezuela).

CHAPTER 4

INSURGENCY

The American Revolution was an insurgency; the British response an example of a failed counterinsurgency.[1] Given the early American experience as backdrop, we turn to twentieth-century examples of groups or movements challenging those in authority in particular states or regions and now, in the twenty-first century, arrayed against governments and populations worldwide.

First, to think strategically about these challenges requires a causal understanding of what is at issue. In this regard, grievances in a population—real or imagined, just or unjust—provide the fertile ground that insurgent leaders need to develop an organization, advance an ideology to galvanize opposition to authorities, seek external support, and take actions against those in power or close to them. Second, we place insurgency in the turbulent context that globalization has spawned. Third, we examine how "modern" challenges to the "traditional" societies insurgents wish to preserve lead them to formulate reactionary ideologies that legitimate terrorism and other forms of political violence adverse to liberal societies.

The American Revolution: An Insurgency

Benjamin Franklin, Thomas Jefferson, and John Adams were senior members of the insurgency's political wing. George Washington led its military wing. Their *grievances* were specified famously in the ideologically liberal Declaration of Independence, drafted in 1776 by Jefferson to legitimate their cause. In the struggle for popular support domestically, Britain had the edge among royalists and others still loyal to the British Crown.

Cross-cutting church and commercial ties among the colonists were links that helped them organize and coordinate insurgent efforts from New England across the Middle Atlantic colonies to those in the South. The insurgents were led by successful agricultural and business elites of the day, not all, but many of them, freemasons—"brothers" in a network of lodges spread across the colonies.[2] These connections facilitated coordination of revolutionary activities in a time when transportation and communications were so much more difficult than they are today.

Even as Britain maintained control of key cities, the insurgents depended on the domestic support they could muster from men and women in the countryside. As for external support, Franklin cultivated it in a diplomatic mission to Paris (1776–1785).[3] The connections among Parisian elites that Franklin established also had diplomatic purposes.

Aid secured by Franklin from the French monarchy—arrayed as it was against its British counterpart—later proved decisive in assuring insurgent victory in 1781 at Yorktown. Little did the Parisian authorities know at the time that their support for the American revolutionaries would blow back against them just eight years later. Indeed, in 1789 Thomas Jefferson, Minister to France and Franklin's successor, was in close contact with the Marquis de Condorcet and other French revolutionaries in their liberal quest to overthrow the monarchy.

Recruiting citizen soldiers committed to the fight and supported by the local population was the model George Washington followed in raising an army that could defeat the British professionals. In doing so, he was following a path blazed by Oliver Cromwell in the 1640s during the English civil war—a Puritan revolution or insurgency against the English Crown fought by commoners recruited into a citizen army.

Prominent among George Washington's generals were the fellow freemasons he relied upon in a network of mutual-trust, fraternal relationships. Joining them in this liberal, antiroyalist cause were "brothers" from France (the Marquis de Lafayette), Prussia (Baron von Steuben), and Poland (Thaddeus Kosciuszko and Casimir Pulaski; the latter was the "father" of the American cavalry). The political leadership also advanced its liberal ideology that saw British governance as the problem. Overthrowing royal authority and creating a limited, popularly supported government in its place were the ultimate objectives.

Figure 3. Insurgencies: A Causal Outline of Principal Factors.

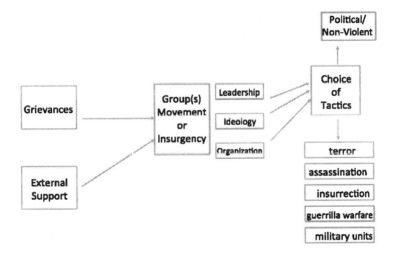

When we reflect on this American revolutionary experience, we find the essential elements of a successful insurgency present: (1) *grievances*

against governing authorities upon which *domestic support* was mustered; (2) *leadership* with its *organizational structure* in place, informed and motivated by a widely accepted *ideology*, and (3) *external support*, if needed, to tilt the balance against governing forces. Figure 3 depicts the causal relations among these factors.

Thinking Strategically About Countering Insurgencies

A causal understanding of the phenomenon—how the leaders organize their effort in response to grievances, cultivate internal and external bases of support, establish a common ideological identity, and make choices on tactics to use—also helps those whose task it is to think strategically about countering a particular insurgency.

We can learn from the British experience in America. Governing authorities lost touch with the common people, particularly in rural areas. Actions taken against opposition groups—as in the Boston massacre— only fanned the flames of the growing rebellion. Such actions undermined the colonial regime's legitimacy which, in turn, contributed to increasing popular support for the insurgents.

Doing something about grievances that underlie popular support for the insurgency is one obvious approach to countering an insurgency. Yet, there may be little one can do in present-day circumstances when grievances are broad based—as in objections by Muslims in many Islamic societies to the imposition of Western values that challenge more traditional, culturally, or religiously based understandings. Reversing globalization, even if that were desirable (and most of us would agree the benefits of globalization outweigh its very real costs), cannot be accomplished merely by waving a wand.

The best one likely can do is not only to try to mitigate adverse impacts in these societies, but also attend to lesser grievances, dealing with them as best one can. The purpose of such efforts is not to concede on issues just for the sake of making concessions in relation to grievances, but rather to remove a basis of popular support on which the insurgents depend. Whatever can be done about existing grievances, a priority is to avoid additions to the list that effectively strengthen the insurgent domestic support base. To use a current example, minimizing collateral death and destruction from hitting targets in Middle East countries or elsewhere by aircraft and unmanned vehicles has to remain a high priority, whatever else may be at stake.

Removing or lessening grievances and countering ideological appeals —ideally with wide distribution of well-thought-out, widely disseminated messages in diverse media and other targeted communications—chip away at the insurgent domestic support base. Drying up or intercepting external support of money and supplies to the insurgents is another task. Sometimes this can be done quietly by freezing accounts or otherwise blocking the flow of capital and material to the insurgents. Diplomacy and other communications with state and nonstate actors supporting the insurgents are also means to undermine the external support base.

Self-serving reasons on both sides open the door to meeting, discussing issues, negotiating and finding remedies or, conversely, delivering threats. The key criterion is whether there is a reasonable basis that communicating with insurgent leaders can be productive in terms of objectives sought. However despicable the conduct of these leaders may be to decision makers, direct communications with the leadership of insurgent groups or indirect exchanges conducted through intelligence services of one or another country or other third parties need not be rejected out of hand. Strategists and decision makers who think strategically are inherently pragmatic, always seeking the diverse ways and means of achieving the national purposes they have in mind.

Finally, following Clausewitz, the military option is to destroy the capabilities the insurgents need to carry out their attacks or defend the territory they occupy or in which they reside. Targeting the leaders, headquarters or operations centers, their command-and-control communications networks, and other means at their disposal may disrupt or slow down the insurgents—the success of this military option a function in part of the degree of resilience of which the insurgent organization and leaders are capable.

LEGITIMACY OF CAUSE AND POPULAR SUPPORT

The American Revolution as an insurgency against the British Crown and their royalist supporters was by no means new in the English experience that informed the American colonial insurgents. Though usually presented as separate, English history really is also part of an American history well known by eighteenth-century British subjects then in America who, along with royalists, constituted the leadership elites in the colonies. As with antiroyalist battles in Scotland and Ireland, the seventeenth-century English civil war helped legitimate in the minds of the eighteenth-century American colonial descendants of those engaged in these earlier struggles what they understood as their right to take up arms against the Crown once again.

Popular support in the English civil war had come predominantly from Presbyterians and other Calvinists—"puritans" led by Oliver Cromwell. Although a few aristocrats joined the cause, most of those who took up arms against the king's professional army were commoners. This "new model army," composed of citizen soldiers trained to fight by Cromwell and those who joined with him, finally prevailed against the king's professional army.

Paramount in thinking within the political wing of the American insurgency (and a view also shared by General Washington) was avoiding anything like the authoritarian excesses of the army-backed Cromwell regime that eventually assumed power in England after the 1649 trial and execution of King Charles I. Following the American insurgent victory in 1781, the post–George III period, by contrast, was to be one in which government was constrained—lacking centralized power and authority lest, in their minds, it become the enemy of the people. For his part, Washington decidedly did not want to become another Cromwell!

Those who settled in the American colonies and their descendants tended to engage in market-oriented, agricultural pursuits; the latter particularly in the south and other rural areas further west. In America those supporting the insurgency were no more royalist in orientation than they had been abroad. British authority and practices in the colonies that undermined their business interests or infringed on their liberties were among the grievances articulated in the Declaration of Independence. Their laissez-faire, classical liberalism was fully compatible with these views.

As noted earlier, leadership ranks in both political and military wings were filled heavily by freemasons—historically an under-reported network of commercially and politically influential persons who helped organize and conduct the insurgency against the British Crown. As previously noted, transportation by land was difficult and communications were slow. Notwithstanding these obstacles, politically motivated freemasons could come together as "brothers" across the thirteen colonies in a common cause. Some, of course, remained on the Tory or royalist side, but others coalesced outside of their lodges in what became a transcolony movement.

It was an insurgency committed to a liberal, pluralist ideology that put emphasis on individuals and their liberties. Put another way, in liberalism individuals (this includes groups of individuals) matter. What they do singly or collectively also matters. No religious test for public office, no establishment of a state church, and freedom to practice (or not to practice) a religion of personal choice were secular, liberal values incorporated later in the US Constitution and its Bill of Rights.

Among other things the new liberal order legitimated free markets, provided for a national currency, offered patent protection for inventions, and allowed federal regulation focused not on state and local business, but rather on interstate and international, commerce. The new government was far more constrained in relation to local market transactions, which accommodated the expectations of the commercially oriented citizenry who had broken with the Crown. They had been decidedly less inclined to accept the burdens of taxation and observe other restraints imposed by British authorities.

British counterinsurgency efforts relied on popular support from royalists and others not persuaded by the revolutionary cause. Its Tory base predominantly in the cities, the Royal Army—augmented by mercenaries—conducted raids in the countryside. For their part, the insurgents relied on the use of guerrilla, hit-and-run tactics against British forces as well as regular, anti-British colonial units they had organized and trained in Washington's Continental Army. On the political side, untoward incidents before and during the war—famously the Boston "massacre"—provided fodder for the insurgents in their effort to undermine widespread popular support for the British.

In the set of present-day options used by insurgents, the American revolutionaries engaged in political action to strengthen their popular and external bases of support, but restricted themselves in the use of violence to regular and guerrilla warfare. Unlike many twentieth- and twenty-first-century insurgencies, using such violent tactics as terrorism, torture, and assassination was decidedly not part of their game plan. Given their internalized understandings of what was proper, leaders in both the political and military wings of the insurgency would have been repulsed by such measures so commonplace today.

The Turbulence of Societal Change

One of the "predictable" effects of societal change within and across societies is turbulence—upsetting established political and economic patterns in relation to the social structure and culture in particular societies. Whatever else they may be about, insurgencies are contests over legitimate authority. Challenges to authority are plentiful.

This turbulence is one of the byproducts of increasing globalization in our time—not just within states and their societies, but also worldwide.[4] Turbulence, then, is the context within which present-day insurgencies occur. They are both a product as well as a contributing factor to the domestic, regional, and global turbulence or instabilities we observe.

The American insurgency that succeeded in separating the American colonies from Britain in the Revolutionary War resulted in political regime change. It did not alter to any significant degree the economy, social structure, or culture—societal elements that remained essentially the same as they had been before taking up arms against British colonial leaders. By contrast, the twentieth- and twenty-first-century insurgencies we focus on in chapter 5—Vietnam, Afghanistan, Iraq-Syria, and Yemen —are part of much larger (and more sweeping) changes marked by decolonialization in Vietnam and the impact colonialism and globalization in the postcolonial period have had on "traditional" societies in the Middle East.

Beyond the American first-hand experience in the American Revolution, other insurgencies that have informed American understandings of the phenomenon and counters to it include: (1) opposition to the US presence in Cuba and the Philippines in the Spanish-American War (1898); (2) the anti-Turkish campaign in World War I influenced by British Colonel T.E. Lawrence ("Lawrence of Arabia") and his Arab fighters;[5] (3) the anti-German Yugoslav coalition in World War II led by Tito; (4) Mao Tse-Tung's people's army before and after World War II that defeated the American-supported Nationalists in 1949; (5) the anti-French campaign in Algeria in the 1950s (until France under President Charles de Gaulle finally capitulated in 1962); (6) the British campaign in Malaya against communists in the 1950s; and (7) the insurgent victory led by Fidel Castro that overthrew the Battista regime in 1959. For his part, Che Guevara sought unsuccessfully to extend the Castro revolution to Bolivia and elsewhere in South America.[6]

To understand insurgencies, we take a step back first to understand what is going on in a particular *society*—a challenge to the political order with economic and social implications. Whether the United States stays outside of the conflict for power among the contenders or intervenes on one side or the other is a recurring challenge policy makers face, particularly when the insurgency itself is anti-American and supported by other states or nongovernmental actors like ISIL (Islamic State in Syria and the Levant, which includes Iraq, Syria, Jordan, Lebanon, Israel, and parts of the eastern Mediterranean), or one or another of the al Qaeda factions. Transsocietal insurgencies led by affiliates of al Qaeda or the Islamic State, for example, can be understood in this respect, at least in part, as reactions against globalization—the imposition of "Western" understandings of modernity on traditional societies by the forces of globalization identified primarily with the United States and European countries.

In stepping back for a societal overview, we identify four analytical elements that define any society: the political regime or *state*—its institutions and processes, the economy, social structure and culture in relation to the regional or global environment (see figure 4). Politics—the processes or the ways and means by which authoritative choices are made in a particular society—and governance are questions of power and authority in relation to social structure, culture, and economy that have engaged humankind over the millennia. How much order we seek (or how much disorder we are willing to accept) with respect to the degree we seek of liberty, equality, and community (and the balance among them) varies substantially from country to country.

Taking the long view, globalization is the latest chapter in a transformation that accelerated in the nineteenth century. Industrialization in Europe, North America, and elsewhere transformed some societies (redefining them as "modern"), thus leaving others intact (defining them as "traditional"). The historical sociology of a country or region matters.

Indeed, what has happened in and to a society in the past typically has significant effects on the present.

Colonization of the Western Hemisphere began to unravel with the American Revolution in the last quarter of the eighteenth century with the rest of Latin America following suit by the 1820s. The gradual demise of nineteenth-century imperialism from Africa to East Asia and the Pacific (and the British, French, Belgian, Dutch, Portuguese, Spanish, Italian, German, and American colonies or territories that accompanied this European and American outreach) occurred in the twentieth century after the two world wars.

The process of this decolonization and the creation of new states picked up speed after World War II and reached a high point in the 1960s, particularly on the African continent. Political independence from former colonial powers in Africa, Asia, and Latin America was accompanied as well by increasing industrialization, urbanization, and other changes in these societies.

Globalization and the global imposition of Western economic, social, and political values it constitutes are characteristic of this postcolonial period. Deep grievances in more traditional societies result in reactionary movements that dream of a presumed golden age of the past they wish to reincarnate. In the Middle East the idea of recreating a caliphate based on Islamic law has become a galvanizing purpose. Tradition is celebrated even as modern means of communication and war-related technologies are incorporated as means to accomplish what turn out to be reactionary or backward-looking goals.

THE TRADITION-MODERNITY DICHOTOMY

Although the tradition-modernity dichotomy was core to sociology and comparative politics in mid-twentieth century and for several decades afterward, it has been less prominent in the present-day, postcolonial discourse. Fads come and go in academic disciplines. One objection was that this literature treated traditional society pejoratively when, in fact, unlike the cold, barren, care-less aspects of the modern city, traditional societies provide a very rich, socially warm, committed space in which human beings thrive, finding the nurturing and caring they need so much. Related to this objection was the claim that writers often portrayed the shift from tradition to modernity as progressive, if not an inevitability, then at least a more desirable outcome.

We set these normative biases aside here, focusing only on the analytical utility that the tradition-modernity dichotomy provides for understanding resistance to globalization (particularly its liberal values that challenge traditional, often religiously based societies). If we abandon the understandings in this informative tradition-modernity literature altogether as biased or antiquated, we do so at our own peril.

The "traditional" society, still prevalent in rural areas that Islamist groups to a greater or lesser degree wish to preserve, has religiously grounded cultural rather than the secular values identified with "modern" or "Western" societies. As byproducts of postcolonial globalization (as in the earlier colonial and imperial imposition of "Western" values), the culture of "modern" society challenges traditional ways in these countries, particularly the deep religious underpinnings found particularly in rural areas.[7]

It would have been helpful if those making policy at the highest levels on whether and how to intervene in places like Iraq, Afghanistan, and nearby tribal areas of Pakistan (and those tasked with implementing these decisions) had had a clearer understanding of tribal or clan-based societies and the more traditional values associated with these social structures.[8] Invading Iraq in 2003, the under-resourced way in which the invasion was conducted, de-Baathification—removing followers of Saddam Hussein associated with his Baath Party who had held important posts in the governing structure, and demobilization of the Iraqi army during the occupation period destabilized not just Iraq, but also the entire region. De-Baathification, coupled with removing army leaders from their positions, effectively liquidated the civilian and military infrastructure upon which secular governance had depended. In Iraq, the Shia were the principal beneficiaries of these colossal errors while the Sunni, who had been in power, were effectively marginalized. It is not surprising that military members in the latter would become central players in a new, post–Saddam Hussein insurgency—the Islamic State.

Our return to this literature here, however, is not just about these events in the Middle East. It also stems from deep misunderstandings about "traditional" societies among many senior US officials that were most apparent in the lead up to wars in Vietnam in the 1960s and Iraq, Afghanistan, and Pakistan in the first decade of the twenty-first century. The mistake oftentimes was to see them as societies that were pluralist or individualist in character, much as Americans and Europeans understand themselves to be. The compelling role of tribe and extended family or clan had to be learned on the ground. To their credit, US Army officers often had a greater understanding of the complexity of social structure and cultures of these countries than many of the civilian officials senior to them who made the high-level decisions about strategy and policy.[9]

Insurgencies are contests over legitimate authority. *Legitimacy*—a right to rule—is probably the greatest prize any office holder, agency of government or the regime as a whole can have.[10] Multinational insurgencies like ISIL, al Qaeda, and such affiliates as al Qaeda in the Arabian Peninsula (AQAP) seek legitimacy that will allow them to displace existing governments. *Da'esh*, the Arabic-language version of the same ISIL acronym has a negative connotation in Arabic which, as noted in the preface, contributes to its common use by anti-ISIL Arabs and increasingly by Western governments. US and other news media also refer to it as ISIS (Islamic State of Iraq and Syria), but this understates the territorial ambitions of the insurgent leaders that go well beyond these two countries.

The Palestinian Hamas and Iranian-backed, Shia-oriented Hezbollah are examples of other important groups with differing agendas, particularly in relation to Israel. ISIL, AQAP, and al Qaeda as a whole pose a greater and more direct threat to US than the other groups thus far have done. For its part, ISIL considers itself as having established a state, albeit one not recognized by any sovereign states. This bow to the "modern" construct of state in fact is superseded in practice by claims to having established a postcolonial caliphate that draws on Islamic tradition and rejects existing state boundaries. After all, these boundaries were constructed particularly during the post–World War I, post-Ottoman colonial period in which the West so decisively altered the geopolitics of the entire region.[11]

It is a call for a return instead to the religious-political form established in the succession from Muhammad that preceded the post-Ottoman, Western colonial period when Britain and France carved up the region, creating divisions in Araby that they could manage more easily with a smaller number of colonial administrators reporting to European capitals. In the postcolonial period, successor regimes have conformed to the Western model of a world composed of sovereign states, thus perpetuating the divisions in Araby (and the Islamic world as a whole)—a construct that conveys advantages both to local elites and Westerners abroad.

Any legitimacy for ISIL's caliphate regime rests on a *traditional* basis —a reactionary interpretation (with which most Muslims disagree) of Islamic Shari'a law, the Koran, and the Sunnah (the sayings and teachings of the Prophet Muhammad). Nevertheless, the idea of restoring an Islamic caliphate does draw followers, such as men and women in their late teens, twenties, and thirties who have joined ISIL.[12] Boko Haram in Nigeria is among those that have linked themselves to ISIL. The caliphate idea has a widespread appeal that draws many followers wishing to reverse the postcolonial legacy of borders established by European countries to serve their own interests.

INSURGENT IDEOLOGIES

Zionism—a nationalist movement that began in the late nineteenth century—sought a homeland for Jews. The holocaust in Europe that caused the deaths of some six million Jews and displacement of countless others in the 1930s and during World War II led finally to the establishment of Israel as a state in 1948 under UN auspices. Opposition among Palestinians and other Arabs to the idea of an exclusive Jewish state took the form of an anti-Zionist ideology, held most intensely by displaced or otherwise adversely affected Palestinians .

Israel prevailed in the 1948 war and three subsequent wars with Arab states, but the anti-Zionist ideological die had been cast. It quickly became a basis used by such anti-Israel insurgent groups as the Palestine Liberation Organization (PLO)—a collection of anti-Israel factions—and later by Hamas, Hezbollah, and others. Anti-Zionism became a rallying cry for opposition to Israel not just by Palestinians, but also by many in the Arab world and other non-Arab Islamic countries to include Iran.

The ideologies embraced by the Islamic State, al Qaeda, and its affiliates are laced with anti-Zionism, but the malaise runs much more deeply. Instability in Islamic societies stems not just from domestic factors. Other factors seen as influencing the region adversely include tribal or clan conflicts; the millennium, long-standing, religious-cultural divide between Sunni and Shia Muslims; and other grievances directed toward external actors (states, corporations, international, or nongovernmental organizations).

Immersion in an increasingly globalized world to which they are intimately connected also imposes secular values and norms that challenge the traditional sociocultural bedrock. Thus al Qaeda, ISIL, and other insurgent groups emerge in reaction to (and against) "modern" or secular values (or the lack of them) they see as being imposed from the outside. For them, returning to their particular interpretations of Islamic norms and practice is imperative.

Fueling these grievances are deep-seated resentment and anger against the colonialism imposed by the West on the region upon the demise of the Ottoman Empire in the aftermath of World War I. As noted earlier, the territorial boundary lines of British and French colonial spheres effectively carved up Araby in the image and likeness (and to the advantage) of European states. The *idea* of Islamic *caliphate* that, at least in principle, had survived during the Ottoman Empire, was set aside during the colonial period and later was displaced by the more secular governments of new states. There never was, however, the degree of separation of church (or mosque) and state which one finds in Europe and the Americas.[13]

Insurgent leaders typically are motivated by particular ideologies that they also use to cultivate followers. The American insurgency against British rule was driven by a liberal ideology. We address two other ideologies next—the Marxist-Leninist ideology that drove the insurgency in Vietnam and an antiglobalization ideology (often anti-US or anti-West) that motivates insurgents in ISIL, al Qaeda, AQAP, their affiliates, and other insurgent groups across the Islamic world from Morocco in the West to the Philippines in the East. These ideologies are instrumental social constructions with substantial implications for societies in which insurgents operate, particularly now in low-income, capital-poor countries. They tend to "reject foreign values and institutions completely" but do want "the foreigner's most powerful techniques" to restore "the purity of an earlier golden age."[14]

By contrast, in the Vietnam case also discussed in chapter five, the Marxist-Leninist or communist brand advanced by Ho Chi Minh and his followers sought to rid the country of foreign influence and alter class relations in which some were dominant while others subordinated or disadvantaged. As with liberalism, it was a forward-looking revolutionary ideology, but one that sought major change in society—to make a future for the people that was better than it ever has been in the past. Ending foreign domination was the first step toward that end. Unlike liberalism, of course, it charted a very different course—not the liberal focus on secular society composed of individuals with liberties and rights vis-à-vis the state.

Ideologically speaking, followers of al Qa*eda*, AQAP, ISIL, and related groups are in a "restorative" or reactionary category. For them, the task at hand is resisting the forces of globalization that impose the Western, liberal understandings of modernity that challenge the cultural and religious foundations of the Islamic societies they are defending.

Quite apart from religio-cultural differences between Islam and Judeo-Christian understandings is imposition of the Western-oriented "modern" state of Israel that displaced Palestinians from their homes and homeland. Living in the present, they envision a future close to an idealized past. Hence reestablishing the Islamic caliphate and returning to what they see as a pure and good form of Islam and Islamic law are what they are about. It is this reactionary vision that challenges not just Israel, but also postcolonial Arab states constructed earlier primarily under British and French influence.

INSURGENCY IN SOCIETY

To be successful, those who organize and lead insurgencies or, by contrast, those who wish to defeat them, must understand the social context in which these movements take place. Insurgents challenge state authority and, if they succeed, change the regime to one of their liking. In the American case, the insurgents replaced British rule but did not seek to transform the society itself. The economy, social structure, and culture were left in place. Arrayed as a four-pointed diamond, the relations depicted in figure 4 capture analytically the essential elements of society those in power typically wish to maintain, but one that insurgents want to change to one degree or another.

Figure 4. The Elements of Society.

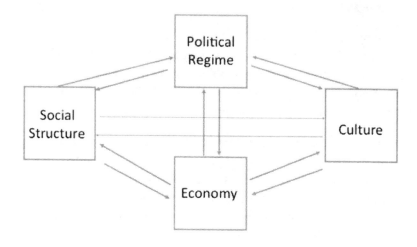

As such, forcible regime change in the American colonies was a more modest, liberal undertaking than liberal revolutionaries in France sought just eight years after the military defeat of the British by George Washington and his fellow insurgents. In 1789 Thomas Jefferson, Minister to France, had established links to freemasons[15] and other insurgents in Paris, some of whom had far more sweeping changes in mind, namely transformation of the society as a whole: (1) the political regime (replacing the monarchy with a republic), (2) the social structure (eliminating the aristocracy by seizing their lands and executing those seen as enemies of the republic), (3) the economy (redistributing land to peasants and facilitating commerce favored by market-oriented *bourgeois* interests), and (4) the culture (ending church dominance, even replacing the church-oriented calendar for a time with a secular one, and advancing the then radical, democratic agenda of *liberté, égalité, fraternité*). In contrast to the French Revolution, the American experience was modest—at most, revolution with a "small" (or lower-case) "r" that left intact the major elements of society.

Table 7. Society: Analytical Elements.

- **Political Regime or "State"**—government, bureaucracy, or administrative institution, rulers or other authorities, and associated groupings such as political parties one finds in most present-day societies;

- **Economy**—actors, institutions, and processes one associates with production and distribution of goods and services;

- **Social Structure**—social units and their relation to each other (classes, individuals and groups, elites and masses, patrons and clients, etc.); and

- **Culture**—historically grounded, socially constructed values or norms operative throughout or in parts of a particular society.

Although the four elements as factors or variables are empirically intertwined (and thus difficult in fact to distinguish one from another), we can separate them analytically. If we ignore one or more of these four variables, our understanding of the dynamics in any society, particularly one in which an insurgency is underway, will be incomplete at best, misleading at worst. Quite apart from us as observers, the effectiveness of insurgents (and those seeking to counter them) depends upon a deep understanding of the elements of society—the regime, social structure, economy, and culture.

Arraying the four elements as a diamond allows us to visualize more readily the relations that exist among them. The "diamond" in figure 4.2 explains or predicts nothing, but does give us points of focus that have substantial analytical utility. It is merely a device that helps us deal readily with the essential elements in a given society. It leads us to raise the right questions about the relations among the political, economic, social-structural, and cultural factors that are relevant to decisions made by both insurgents and counterinsurgents.

Reducing the primary focus to just four analytical factors or variables and relations among them is a parsimonious approach to understanding what is going on in a particular society. Lest we err, however, by oversimplifying the complex reality of politics, we take pains to explore each analytical factor to identify its underpinnings—the social units or individuals that make up these units or influence their operation in society.

Moreover, we effectively immerse the diamond in regional or global society with the understanding that just as external factors can influence what happens in a given society, so it is that what happens in a particular society can influence other societies as well. Notwithstanding our effort to simplify analytically the reality we observe, we are left with substantial complexity with which policy makers must still grapple.

This approach—viewing *politics in society* analytically in terms of the four factors we have identified and how they relate to the external, regional, or global context in which they are immersed—provides a comprehensive approach policy makers can put to good use. It helps focus attention both on what has been put in and what has been discounted or left out. The cases we take up in chapter 5—Vietnam, al Qaeda, AQAP, and the rise of ISIL from the failures in Iraq—focus on both the insurgencies and American efforts to counter them or the tactics they employ. Terrorism has moved from al Qaeda's high-explosive attacks on predominantly Western targets to ISIL's assassinations designed to terrorize or intimidate their opponents not just in Europe, the United States, and elsewhere outside of the region, but also in the Islamic world as a whole.

For its part, al Qaeda and ISIL have become insurgencies with many affiliates worldwide. Given the relative autonomy of its parts in places as diverse as Afghanistan and Yemen, al Qaeda is not, strictly speaking, an organization with licensed franchises. Rather, al Qaeda and its affiliates are bound together only loosely through reactionary Islamist-based, ideological threats posed against the United States and other Western-driven values. For its part, ISIL is more regionally focused in its caliphate-building exercise, notwithstanding the articulated dream that one day the caliphate could become worldwide in its scope. What brings al Qaeda and ISIL together conceptually is their ideological opposition to liberal, "modern" values advanced by globalization that adversely impact traditional, religiously grounded cultures in the Islamic world. This is the root or underlying basis of their particular grievances against the West.

INTERCOMMUNAL STRIFE

Unlike the Middle East insurgencies we are discussing that are multinational in scope, cases of intercommunal strife have tended to be contained within countries inhabited by particular ethnic groups at odds with each other. Because these conflicts are contained within a narrower territorial space, US decision-makers have tended not to see them as a direct threat to American national security interests. In the minds of US decision-makers, ISIL, al Qaeda and its affiliates do challenge American security interests more directly in the Middle East and beyond.

At the same time, ethnic conflicts exacerbated by insurgent actions or civil war displace persons from their homes in cities and villages who must then seek refuge in safer areas either locally or abroad. Certainly this has been the case for conflict areas like Syria where many Shia, Sunni, and Alawites and other groups have fled, seeking refuge primarily in European countries. Syrian refugees have posed extra-regional challenges in Europe, given its proximity, and to a lesser extent in the United States, Canada, and other countries receiving them.

In the 1950s, Britain still the colonial power in Malaya, countered a communist insurgency drawn predominantly from the Chinese population there. The British were able to capitalize on ethnic divisions, countering the insurgency by mobilizing ethnic Malays (the majority) and Indians against the Chinese insurgents. For its part, the Vietnamese insurgency in the late 1950s, 1960s, and early 1970s was contained within the boundaries of North and South Vietnam, except for transit of supplies (mainly across eastern Laos—the Ho Chi Minh trail) and sanctuary (mainly in eastern Cambodia for the North Vietnamese, and Viet Cong for southern insurgents).

The postcolonial period has been marked by intercommunal strife in places as diverse as west Africa: civil war among Ibo, Yoruba, and Hausa-Fulani in Nigeria (1967–1970); South Asia: religious-ethnic divides in Sri Lanka between Tamil-Indian insurgents of Hindu identity against Sinhalese government forces of Buddhist identity (1983–2009); and in central Africa: tribal divisions between Hutus and Tutsis leading to genocide in the mid-1990s in Rwanda, Burundi, and Congo.

The Middle East insurgencies are similarly marked by ethnic divides. There is competitive conflict between al Qaeda (of Saudi origin, but also with non-Arab fighters from tribes in Afghanistan, Pakistan, and other areas) and AQAP, its Yemeni-Arab affiliate that is decidedly different with its own set of tribal-ethnic identities. For its part, ISIL is also ethnically in a different place with fighters drawn from Iraq, Syria, and even European and North American locations. Al Qaeda, AQAP, and ISIL do have Sunni identity in common, but that puts them at odds with the Alawite regime in Syria as well as Hezbollah and other Shia in Lebanon, Syria, Iraq, and Iran. Separate from ISIL, the Sunni al-Nusra Front is al Qaeda's affiliate in Syria. For its part, Boko Haram—an ISIL affiliate—has a Sunni identity, but one composed of Nigerian tribes. It is indeed a complex set of diverse or competing identities.

Not just a Middle East, African, and South Asian phenomenon, national and ethnic conflicts emerged in the Balkans (1991–2001), which resulted in genocide and the breakup of Yugoslavia into separate nation-states. It remains an ongoing problem between Greeks and Turks on Cyprus. Put another way, national and ethnic strife is a human problem that becomes acute when identities become mutually exclusive. In the absence or breakdown of overlapping identities or underlying links, ethnic conflict easily becomes violent. Genocide and other human-rights violations may eventually bring the United States and other forces to intervene in an effort to stop the bloodshed, but such interventions are by no means assured. This is not just because American decision-makers may prefer to avoid the role of world's police, but also because they tend not to see interventions of this sort as driven by core US national security interests.

AFTERWORD

Insurgencies, the turbulence they cause (and from which they are spawned), and the political violence they employ within and outside their regions likely will remain a major challenge on the American national security agenda for decades to come. Intercommunal strife, by contrast, has tended to focus on particular (and neighboring) countries inhabited by the particular ethnic groups at odds with each other. Human-rights violations and the various forms of violence, including genocide, occur with devastating effects on the inhabitants, but these actions are still local and thus not normally exported beyond the borders of the countries or region directly involved. Nevertheless, the migration of persons in these conflict areas to safe havens elsewhere does pose challenges to countries receiving these refugees.

Notes

1. See Michael Rose, *Washington's War: The American War of Independence to the Iraqi Insurgency* (New York: Pegasus Books, 2008).
2. Franklin, Washington, and likely Jefferson were most prominent among them. Adams was not a freemason. See the scholarly research on identifying the network of freemasons active in this American insurgency conducted by Ronald E. Heaton, *Masonic Membership of the Founding Fathers* (Silver Spring, MD: The Masonic Service Association, 1965).
3. While in Paris, Franklin brought Voltaire into freemasonry in the Paris-based *Loge des Neuf Soeurs*.
4. See James N. Rosenau, *Turbulence in World Politics: A Theory of Change and Continuity* (Princeton, NJ: Princeton University Press, 1990).
5. T.E. Lawrence, *Seven Pillars of Wisdom* (New York: Anchor Books, 1991). See also Charles Edmonds, *T.E. Lawrence* (New York: D. Appleton-Century Co., 1936) and, more recently, Scott Anderson, *Lawrence in Arabia: War, Deceit, Imperial Folly and the Making of the Modern Middle East* (New York: Anchor Books, 2014) and Michael Korda, *Hero: The Life and Legend of Lawrence of Arabia* (New York: Harper Perennial, 2010).
6. See Ernesto Che Guevara. *Guerrilla Warfare* [*La Guerra de Guerrillas*] (New York: Barnes and Noble, 2008).
7. Sociologist Talcott Parsons (1902–1979) developed an analytical summation of this tradition-modernity dichotomy—a convenient, five-factor summary of nineteenth- and early twentieth-century literature that specifies the contrast between these two ideal types. These five-pattern variables listed with traditional first, modern second are affectivity vs. affect neutrality, collectivity orientation vs. self-orientation, particularism vs. universalism, ascriptive vs. achievement criteria, and functional diffuseness vs. functional specificity. Edward Shils and Talcott Parsons, eds., *Toward a General Theory of Action* (Cambridge, MA: Oxford University Press, 1952 and New York: Harper & Row, 1962): 48–49, 77–84, 91, 187–188, 203–204, and 207–208.
8. For a thorough treatment of US policy, see Dan Caldwell, *Vortex of Conflict: U.S. Policy Toward Afghanistan, Pakistan, and Iraq* (Stanford, CA: Stanford University Press, 2011).

9. Many were trained in US civilian graduate programs as Foreign Area Officers (FAOs), typically a two-year master's degree with one year living in a country of specialization.

10. In his now-classic statement, Weber identifies three grounds or pure types of authority that historically have been used to validate such claims to legitimacy—rational-legal, traditional, and charismatic. See Max Weber, *Economy and Society,* Guenther Roth and Claus Wittich, eds. (Berkeley: University of California Press, 1978: vol. I), 215–216.

11. On post–World War I decisions carving up the Ottoman Empire among victorious European allies, particularly the British and French, that put in place the boundaries defining states that in the postcolonial period would be the basis of present-day conflicts in the region, see David Fromkin, *A Peace to End All Peace: The Fall of the Ottoman Empire and the Creation of the Modern Middle East* (New York: Holt, 1989, 2009).

12. For more on the ISIL or ISIS insurgency, see William McCants, *The Isis Apocalypse: The History, Strategy, and Doomsday Vision of the Islamic State* (New York: St. Martin's Press, 2015).

13. The post-Ottoman Turkish construction of secularized state and society advanced by Kemal Ataturk, a freemason with European backing, became a model for more secular regimes elsewhere in the region.

14. For a useful taxonomy of ideologies, see Ernst B. Haas (1924–2003), *Nationalism, Liberalism, and Progress,* vol. 1, *The Rise and Decline of Nationalism* (Ithaca, N.Y.: Cornell University Press, 1997), vii and viii, and vol. 2, *The Dismal Fate of New Nations* (Ithaca, N.Y.: Cornell University Press, 2000), 1–4, 7–12, 14–16, 19–22, 25–32, 34–41, and 43–45. Revolutionary ideologies seeking to transform societies are either liberal of "Whig" (gradualist and incrementalist) or "Integralist" (forward-looking communist or backward-looking fascist) varieties. "Syncretist" ideologies, by contrast, seek to preserve religiously based traditions and broadly are of three kinds: "reformist" that advocate only moderate change, "traditionalist" that contain or keep agents of change within certain bounds, and "restorative"—the most radical of the three—that seek a return to an idealized past. The ideologies of the Islamic State, *al Qaeda,* and their affiliates fit into this last category.

15. On the role of freemasons in the French revolution, see Roger Chartier, *The Cultural Origins of the French Revolution,* trans. Lydia G. Cochrane (Durham, NC: Duke University Press, 1991), esp. 162–167.

CHAPTER 5

COUNTERING INSURGENCIES AND TERRORISM

Terrorism is only one of a number of tactics a movement, insurgency, or group can use to accomplish its objectives. Their leaders make choices. Countering them requires an understanding of what gives rise to (and sustains) these perpetrators of political violence.

The insurgencies that will be discussed were reactions against colonialism or the imposition of Western understandings of modernity and, later, the forces of globalization that insurgencies identified with the United States and other high-income or capital-rich countries. Thus, French colonialism in Vietnam, followed by Japanese occupation in World War II and, after that, the return of the French, galvanized the Vietnamese nationalist opposition to foreign influences—grievances upon which the insurgency built its domestic base of support. After the French defeat in 1954, the United States entered the fray, viewed by many as the "new" French—the new neocolonial power imposing Western values upon the Vietnamese people.

In succeeding decades, the clash between the forces of modernity confronting tradition was coined as the currency of *globalization*—the ongoing worldwide expansion of capital and all of the more liberal, "modern" values with which it is associated. In this sense, the reaction to this Western liberalism took form, most prominently in the 9/11 attacks on the World Trade Center in New York (symbol of global capitalism) and the Pentagon (symbol of the American military's worldwide influence). The failed attempt to attack either the White House or the US Capitol was focused even more broadly against the US government.

Terrorism is highly rational. Insurgent leaders choose among different forms of violence to attain their political goals: organized uprisings or insurrections that may become violent, terror, assassination, guerrilla warfare, and combat with regular units. In the Vietnam case—a nationalist effort to rid the country of foreign presence or influence—insurgents under Ho Chi Minh ultimately seized power, first from the French, later from the United States and its allies. By contrast to such insurgencies *within* particular countries are those that have regional (or even global) aims like the Islamic State in Iraq and the Levant (ISIL), al Qaeda, and their affiliates.

RATIONALITY OF TERRORISM

German sociologist Max Weber (1864–1920) identified *instrumental rationality* (*zweckrationalität*)—choosing options purposefully—the stuff of cost-benefit calculations (maximizing gains or minimizing losses). Instrumentally rational insurgent leaders have also capitalized on another form of rationality also identified by Weber—*value rationality* (*wertrationalität*) found, for example, in the suicide bomber.[1]

Going into a burning building as a first responder (as was the case for many firefighters in New York on 9/11) or diving into a river to save lives during a flood are examples of putting one's life in danger for a noble cause. An amphibious landing on a beach under enemy fire, parachuting behind enemy lines, and engaging in battle on land, in the air, or at sea are actions taken by military personnel in the line of duty. The suicide bomber takes his life for a cause in which typically a young male[2] in his late teens or early twenties strongly believes.

Why do they do such things? Israeli and Palestinian psychiatrists and psychologists who have studied the suicide-bomber phenomenon assure us that the perpetrators are not insane. Weber gives us a helpful insight when we reflect on his concept of value rationality. The ideals of duty, honor, service, patriotic commitment to country, loyalty, courage, or bravery (sometimes referred to as military or "martial values") are also the "value-rational" motivations of some decisions, behavior, or conduct that we might otherwise consider irrational.

To Weber, commitment to values is neither irrational nor a "non-rational" criterion for social action, but yet another dimension of human rationality that accounts for some decisions and other forms of social action. As Weber observes, social action thus finds its bases in affect (or emotion) or in the traditional (or religious) expectations ("ingrained habituation") of proper behavior.

For the most part, the leaders of an insurgency are instrumentally rational. They plan the actions they take and usually avoid putting their own lives in jeopardy. At the same time, however, they are only too willing to cultivate the value rationality of their followers. Putting the suicide bomber or others at risk—those who put their lives in jeopardy for the cause—nicely fits their instrumentally rational purposes. Destroying a target and creating fear and intimidation through terrorist acts thus are part a larger strategic plan for undermining a regime they are against.

We take up in the pages that follow two very different types of insurgencies: (1) the Vietnam war by Vietnamese nationals first against the French and later against the United States and its allies engaged in a counterinsurgency effort and (2) Middle East insurgencies in Afghanistan and tribal areas of northern Pakistan where al Qaeda has sought sanctuary as well as Al Qaeda in the Arabian Peninsula (AQAP) in Yemen, ISIL in Iraq and Syria, and affiliates of either or both in other countries to include al Shabaab in Somalia and Boko Haram in Nigeria.[3]

What differentiates the two categories of cases is that for Vietnamese nationalists it was about getting rid of the vestiges of colonialism and the United States and its allies that took France's place whereas in Afghanistan and the border areas of Pakistan, Iraq, and Syria, the struggle is against the forces of globalization, the postcolonial creation of states constructed in the Euro-American Westernized style that undercuts traditional patterns of life. In the minds of ISIL, and other insurgents, an Islamic caliphate would "restore" their particular forms of Islam and also eliminate Israel as a Jewish state.

The 9/11 attacks in 2001 on the World Trade Center and Pentagon were directed symbolically against globalized businesses and the American military role associated with them. Hijacked United Flight 93 that crashed in Pennsylvania was directed against the US government directly, targeting either the White House or, more likely, the Capitol.

Viewed more broadly, the al Qaeda and ISIL cases exhibit many of the same factors we find operative in Iraq, Syria, and elsewhere. Their agendas are informed by a reactionary ideology—a step backward in historical time with the attempt to establish a religiously based caliphate, not just another modern nation-state.

COUNTERING INSURGENCIES AND TERRORISM

Decisions to intervene and the conduct of wars in Vietnam and, in more recent decades, Iraq and Afghanistan, have been made without a full understanding of the complexity of the societies to which American forces have been sent. Ethnic divides, tribal and clan structures, and cultural differences sometimes have been minimized—"leaving such matters to anthropologists," as some would say—if not overlooked, in a strategic thinking dominated by firepower and other purely military considerations.

The German strategist Clausewitz understood "people's war" as a societal phenomenon, the social context that commanders must take into account.[4] Although he represents people's war as a method of a popular, national defense against invaders, his formulation has obvious applicability to insurgencies against an incumbent regime and its military or security forces that rely on popular support bases against those in power sustaining the existing order. He lays out rather specifically some of the principal attributes,[5] arguing that:

> the war is carried on in the interior of the country;
> it is not decided by a single catastrophe;
> the theater of war embraces a considerable extent of country;
> the national character supports the measures; and
> the country is of a broken and inaccessible nature, either from being mountainous, or by reason of woods and marshes, or from the peculiar mode of cultivation in use.

In such a war, "armed peasants . . . when scattered, disperse in all directions for which no elaborate plan is required." The locals know the ins and outs of their homeland and can engage regular forces at will in guerrilla, hit-and-run attacks. Thus, "the march of every small body of troops in a mountainous, thickly wooded or otherwise very difficult country becomes very dangerous, for at any moment the march may become an engagement."[6] He is extraordinarily skeptical about the efficacy of governmental response:

If it is a question of destroying roads and blocking narrow defiles, the means which outposts use or raiding parties of an army can apply to that purpose bear about the same relation to those furnished by a body of insurgent peasants as the movements of an automaton do to those of a human being.[7]

People's war to Clausewitz is a "kind of nebulous vapory essence"[8]—a substantial insurgent challenge to any commander of regular forces organized to combat it. When American forces are deployed to such diverse Islamic societies as Iraq and Afghanistan, they are effectively intruding in societies marked by distinct cultural and social-structural tradition. The "intruder" necessarily has impact on these social relationships and, in turn, suffers consequences.

For their part:

> Armed peasants cannot and should not be employed against the main body of the enemy's army, or even against any considerable forces; they must not attempt to crunch the core; they must only nibble at the surface and the edges.[9]

Persistence—solidifying their support in the countryside—works over time to the advantage of the insurgents:

> The fire spreads as it does in heather, and reaches at last that stretch of ground on which the aggressor is based; it seizes his lines of communication and preys upon the vital thread by which his existence is supported.[10]

Diverse writers, based on their own experiences, further developed these themes that Clausewitz took up well before them. Guerrilla hit-and-run tactics used in World War I against the Ottoman Turks by British Royal Army Colonel T.E. Lawrence (Lawrence of Arabia) and his Arab cohort are the stuff of legend—putting theory into practice.[11] It was Mao, of course, who gave "people's war" its prominence in the mid-twentieth century.[12] Others like Ho Chi Minh and his follower, Võ Nguyên Giáp,[13] also put these ideas to work in Vietnam against both the French and the Americans.

Grounded in these sources and the American experience with insurgencies in the twentieth and early twenty-first centuries, Bard O'Neill provides a definition of the phenomenon that captures its essentially political character. To O'Neill, an insurgency is "a struggle between a nonruling group and the ruling authorities in which the nonruling group consciously uses *political resources* (e.g., organizational expertise, propaganda, and demonstrations) and *violence* to destroy, reformulate, or sustain the basis of legitimacy of one or more aspects of politics."[14]

Insurgency thus is a highly rational, purposive political enterprise. Putting on our analytical (or intelligence) lenses, we focus here on three components of any insurgency—its leadership, ideology, and organization. Leaders first secure and try to grow their base, appeals typically grounded in grievances—real or imagined, just or unjust—that resonate with at least some segments in the society or societies with which they identify.

Because external support may prove to be decisive, securing these sources becomes a high priority. Thus, Benjamin Franklin became the American insurgency's diplomat seeking and ultimately gaining direct support from France against the British.[15] In Vietnam, Ho Chi Minh sought and received assistance from both the USSR and China in his insurgency, first against France and later against the United States and its South Vietnamese ally. So it is today with al Qaeda, its affiliates, and other insurgent groups like ISIL that seek and depend upon external support.

Both the US and Vietnamese insurgencies were motivated by progressive or forward-looking, transformative, left-of-center or left-wing ideologies. In the American case, the insurgents advanced a liberal ideology—left-oriented in its time, but more Whig (moderate, more gradual change) than the Jacobin variant that occurred in the French Revolution (radical and, as discussed in chapter 4, more prone to effect change through revolutionary violence). Contrary to either form of liberalism, in the Vietnam case we find a Marxist-Leninist ideology—a forward-looking vision, left-wing ideology that anticipated the coming of better societal conditions than had ever existed heretofore. The American insurgency against British rule was progressive—liberal and antimonarchical, radical for its time. The Marxist-Leninist dream of a future of widespread prosperity in a classless society defined in integralist terms—a radical agenda for Vietnam that focused on overthrowing the American-backed regime in Saigon.

By contrast, al Qaeda, ISILand other insurgencies adhere to one version or another of reactionary, right-wing Islamist ideologies that try to take societies back to what they see as a purer time. In fact, both progressive-left and reactionary-right ideologies are more about vision than reality, but that is beside the point. Indeed, a principal purpose or function of ideology is to solidify the insurgents in a common cause.[16]

Finally, when leaders put their organizations to work, their intent is to take effective action toward achieving particular objectives they have set. In this regard, the leaders have a multiple choice of both violent and nonviolent political actions as tactical *means* to achieve their goals.

THE POLITICAL, "NONVIOLENT" WING

Some insurgencies have political wings that conduct themselves (or masquerade) as nonviolent organizations, even though they have close links to those organizational elements conducting violent actions in support of the same cause. One example from the 1980s is the leadership of Gerry Adams of Sinn Féin that then served, in effect, as the nonviolent political arm of the Irish Republican Army (IRA), which was composed of a number of violent factions. Having a political wing—Adams's position in Sinn Féin and his connections with IRA factions—proved instrumental, later negotiating the peace settlement with the United Kingdom (and northern Irish parties) that came into force in 1999. The good offices of former US Senate Majority Leader George Mitchell contributed to reaching the settlement, aided by networks of contacts with the United Kingdom, Ireland, Sinn Fein, and other groups.

Another example from the 1970s and 1980s is the Palestine Liberation Organization (PLO) then under Yasser Arafat's leadership. Violent insurgent factions at the time engaged primarily in guerrilla, hit-and-run attacks against Israel. On the public stage these violent acts led the United States and other supporters of Israel to deny legitimacy to the PLO, labeling it as a "terrorist organization." At the same time, however, Arafat's PLO was its political arm that provided a peaceful venue for secretive contacts with the United States and other players with interests in peaceful resolution of the Palestine-Israel conflict. The group was headquartered in various Arab countries during this time after being forced from Jordon to Lebanon in 1971 and later moving to Tunisia.

Political wings thus develop what amount to diplomatic contacts with state officials. Thus, with the support of the Norwegian government, the PLO and Israel negotiated the 1993 Oslo Accords that legitimated a Palestinian authority to exert limited control over Israeli-occupied territories in the West Bank. Political wings typically are also an insurgency's propaganda or public-information arm that relies on media contacts in addition to its direct appeals—a capacity expanded substantially with the advent of the internet and social media.

Another option for political wings is to organize demonstrations and, in some cases, insurrections or popular uprisings that give violent factions a basis for action. In Arafat's time, the first intifada began in 1987; it diminished with the Madrid Conference (1991) and finally ended with the Oslo Accords two years later. Given the grievances about actions taken by the Israeli government against Palestinians and Palestinian interests, Arafat was instrumental in a second intifada (2000–2005). Contributing to the end of this second intifada was conflict among Palestinians, specifically between Arafat's Fatah and the rival Hamas faction, coupled with Arafat's death in 2004.[17]

The Arab Spring of street demonstrations that began in Tunisia and spread to other Arab locations as diverse as Egypt, Libya, and Bahrain became insurrections that toppled regimes in Egypt and Libya, but were thwarted by authorities in Bahrain and Syria. Gains in Egypt were also reversed. Nevertheless, whatever their actual involvement, political wings typically try to maintain a public face of at least arms-length distance from the perpetrators of political violence.

Neither al Qaeda nor ISIL have established open political wings which, to say the least, complicates any efforts by governments or other outsiders to communicate with their leaders. Conveying messages through third parties is extraordinarily difficult, although some channels do exist among the sources of external support for al Qaeda and ISIL within the Arab or, more broadly, Islamic world to include those residing in Europe or elsewhere outside of the Middle East. Instead, communications generally become a matter of public rhetoric as in making threats, countering threats, and expressing outrage. Supplying anti–al Qaeda or anti-ISIL forces and dropping of ordnance by aircraft or using unmanned vehicles against ISIL or al Qaeda targets are the nonverbal forms of "communication" that the United States and other counterinsurgent governments have adopted.

Advances in technology have also facilitated communications by instantaneously bringing together people around the world in ways that the political wings of the twentieth century could not do. ISIL has demonstrated that social media and the Internet can be useful ways for extremist movements to mobilize in the twenty-first century—attracting fighters and sympathizers from even advanced Western societies. Al Qaeda and its affiliates also have proved quite capable of promoting their ideological message and the call for violent jihad via the Internet and such outlets as AQAP's magazine *Inspire.*

Counterinsurgency efforts also have taken to the Internet to combat the recruitment methods and tactics of groups like al Qaeda and ISIL. Preventing organized terror groups from inspiring and mobilizing the disenfranchised and disillusioned likely will remain a key task for the United States and other governments in the years ahead. At the same time, however, any restrictions on the openness of the Internet are fraught with ethical and legal questions with global implications.

Terrorism as Political Violence

Since the September 11, 2001, attacks by al Qaeda, US officials have focused the bulk of their efforts on preventing (or at least minimizing the adverse effects of) terrorism. We avoid here governmental, journalistic, or other casual use of the term *terrorism* or *terrorist.* Not everyone using one form or another of violence is a terrorist. We also set aside narrow definitions tied bureaucratically to particular roles and missions of US government agencies. Terrorism certainly includes nongovernmental actors who direct political violence against civilians, but conceptually the purposeful use of fear goes much further both in terms of perpetrators and their intended targets.

Bard O'Neill defines the term *terrorism* as "the threat or use of physical coercion primarily against noncombatants, especially civilians, to create fear in order to achieve various political objectives."[18] The definition, though correctly emphasizing attacks or threat of attacks against civilian noncombatants, also includes intimidation of government and military personnel. What matters is the intent of the perpetrators. An attack on a target for strictly military purposes—to destroy or weaken a war-fighting capability, for example—may produce intimidating effects as a byproduct, but this effect in itself does not make it a terrorist event.[19] Only if producing fear is purposeful, does the same act rises to the level of terrorism.

Terrorists are not alone in using fear or intimidation in efforts to sway populations. Indeed, states can and have used terror for their own political and military purposes. Bombing targets in Iraq at the outset of war in 2003 was aimed not just at destroying air defenses and other targets of military value, but also to cause "shock and awe"—intimidating the Iraqi population and its leadership in an effort to undermine morale and weaken the will to resist the armed intervention by American and British forces then underway.

The definition we adopt here, then, follows O'Neill's lead, but formulates it somewhat more broadly in scope: terrorism is purposive—the rational or purposeful use of the irrational—intimidating effects intended to achieve some purpose, usually political. This definition does not limit the kinds of perpetrators or, for that matter, their targets. Anyone and everyone falls within the scope of this definition, then, who has the capacity and seeks to use the intimidating effects (or the threat of) violence in an effort to influence civilian noncombatants, other governmental personnel, or both.

Finally, terrorism is only one form of political violence insurgents may use. Assassination, insurrection, guerrilla fighting, and combat with regular units are other means that insurgents may employ. Of course, these tactics often have intimidating or terrorizing effects, even if these were not their primary purpose. It is useful, however, to acknowledge that insurgents have a multiple choice of different forms of violence that may serve their purposes.

Aided by information from the FBI, CIA, and other intelligence agencies, the "home game" against terrorist acts in the United States falls under the federal Department of Homeland Security (DHS) and its Federal Emergency Management Agency (FEMA) that act in relation to state and local police, fire, emergency management, health care, and other first-responder organizations. Intelligence that provides early warning is a high priority to prevent the attack from occurring in the first place. When attacks do occur, the effort shifts to managing consequences. Planning beforehand to reduce vulnerability and accessibility by terrorists to known or anticipated targets can reduce or mitigate damages. By contrast, the "away" game abroad falls primarily on the shoulders of the Defense, State, Treasury and other departments, intelligence agencies, and the FBI working at home and abroad with counterparts among allies and coalition partners.[20]

The insurgency in Vietnam did not threaten the US homeland directly in the way al Qaeda did on September 11, 2001. Thus, strategy for dealing with the former was primarily an "away game." Since 9/11, the "home game" is also an integral part of any strategy for dealing with insurgents operating abroad.

THE VIETNAM CASE: THE BACK STORY IN BRIEF

As with other European powers, the French imperial reach extended south to Africa, west to the Americas, and east to Asia and the Pacific. In many respects Vietnam was a prized possession for the rich culture of its peoples, its verdant seacoasts, lush rice-growing deltas, and mountain splendors—Saigon then referred to as the French pearl of the Orient. Much as local persons in business or government elite circles elsewhere in the French colonies selectively could become French citizens, many Vietnamese did so as well. Indeed, these francophone Vietnamese adopted the French language in daily use, identifying with the French language and Roman Catholicism as well as French cuisine and culture (music, literature, and the arts).

Under Nazi influence and confronted in Southeast Asia by Japanese military force, in 1940 the Vichy government in France succumbed to Japanese military presence in Indochina, albeit with the French administration to remain in place. This effectively set the stage for the nationalist, anticolonial insurgency organized by Ho Chi Minh (1890–1969) and initially directed against the Japanese and their Vichy French collaborators. The nationalist Chinese released Ho from prison, which allowed him and his cohort to organize the Viet Minh. Ho's efforts thus received Chinese and other Western allied support to include the US Office of Strategic Services (OSS)—the World War II predecessor of the CIA.

Given the Japanese defeat and withdrawal from Vietnam in 1945 and his Viet Minh organization now in place, Ho turned his attention entirely to the French who were bent on reestablishing their control. For Ho and others in his cohort, the Japanese occupation in World War II presented an opportunity to take a strong position against all outside powers who would exercise hegemony over the Vietnamese. Anti-Japanese sentiments were generalized against all foreigners to include the French and, later, the Americans. After the defeat of Japan, the French effort to return to the *status quo ante* thus was fraught with difficulty. Though their stay was short, the Japanese had indeed challenged whatever legitimacy French colonialism had in Vietnamese society. At the end of the day, neither the Japanese nor the French were welcome.

Ho's declaration of Vietnamese independence marking the birth of the Democratic Republic of Vietnam in 1945 drew from the Franco-American legacy—that "all men are created equal" and that the Vietnamese people have "the right to life, the right to be free, and the right to achieve happiness." Having lived, traveled, and worked in France, the United Kingdom, and the United States as a young man, the declaration also reflected Ho's intimate familiarity with the West. Identifying with the left in France, he also traveled to the Soviet Union, China, and elsewhere pursuing political activities that defined his communist commitments.

In 1945, reflecting their weakened position at the time, the French initially agreed as a tactical move to an autonomous Vietnamese state within the French Union. They subsequently reversed this position, which led the Viet Minh finally to declare war on the French Union in 1946. Following Mao's victory over the Chinese nationalists in 1949, Ho successfully garnered support from Beijing—actions that also received Soviet blessings.

As in the American case almost two centuries before, the essential elements of a successful insurgency were present: (1) *grievances* against governing authorities upon which *domestic support* was mustered; (2) *leadership* with its *organizational structure* in place, informed and motivated by a widely accepted *ideology*, and (3) *external support*, if needed, to tilt the balance against governing forces. With external support in place, the Viet Minh expanded their numbers, attacked French forces, and ultimately brought them to a disastrous defeat in 1954 at Dien Bien Phu in the northern part of Vietnam.

Key to achieving this and subsequent victories was the thinking of Ho's principal military strategist, Võ Nguyên Giáp. Quite simply, the American understanding was that Ho was a communist, not a national leader upon whom the United States could rely. Some in the State Department may have seen Ho as "the Thomas Jefferson of southeast Asia," but this was by no means the consensus view in Washington. True, the United States had accommodated Josip Broz Tito in Yugoslavia as a communist leader independent of Joseph Stalin and thus operating outside of the Soviet orbit. But that was in Europe beginning in the late 1940s. In the American mind of the 1950s and 1960s, by contrast, Southeast Asia lay in China's shadow and thus was decidedly different.

Besides, reflecting US history, the American self-image was as an anticolonial power that had established its independence from Britain in the late eighteenth century, tested briefly in the War of 1812. From the American perspective, this was reason enough not to aid the French substantially in their recolonization effort any more than it actively had supported British efforts to sustain its empire following World War II— India an early and significant loss to the British raj.

For their part, Britain, France, and other imperial powers allied with the United States in the North Atlantic Treaty Organization (NATO) saw the American position through decidedly similar lenses. For them, it was not so much an anticolonial sentiment in America as it was a US effort to displace them to the American advantage—or so many thought. To many French and British observers, American anticolonialism was merely an American cloak to cover the assertion of American power and position in their place. In this regard, Article 6 of the North Atlantic Charter (1949) was a formal denial of any American commitment to imperial restoration or maintenance of European hegemony, the geographic scope of collective defense explicitly excluding areas outside of the North Atlantic area. The only exception was Algeria, then considered by Paris not a colony but an integral part of France.

France's military defeat at Dien Bien Phu in 1954 resulted in the French ouster from the colony as a whole. Ho's communists now controlled the north, the fate of the whole of Vietnam not yet decided. In Geneva talks, the United States assumed a prominent role in guaranteeing nation-wide elections to be held in 1956 to decide the political outcome for a unified country. As it became clear in the United States that Ho Chi Minh and his fellow communists would prevail, however, the elections never occurred.

Instead, the United States effectively replaced the French as guarantors of a noncommunist south. Ho and his followers remained committed to their vision. As Ho put it in 1956: "The reunification of the whole nation is the lifeline of all our people. Great unity is the force that's bound to win."[21] By the 1960s, Ho and his followers remained in both the north and the south—the latter the Viet Cong—had extended their organizational efforts throughout the country, the strongest bases of support found among peasants in the countryside. As was the case in places as diverse as China and Yugoslavia, Vietnamese nationalism was strengthened by the mere presence of foreigners seen by them as occupying the country through links with a puppet regime in the south that depended upon American support.[22]

From the US perspective, what many saw as a civil war had become a matter of North Vietnam invading the South. This certainly was the argument set forth again and again by then secretary of state Dean Rusk. That the American-supported regime in South Vietnam requested US military assistance gave the legal basis for American military intervention. To say it was a civil war would have removed this legal fig leaf used by Washington to justify the US intervention.

Quite apart from legal niceties, however, American decision makers at the time were driven by their anticommunist understandings. Failing to contain the Soviets and, in Southeast Asia, the Chinese, was adverse to US national security interests as they understood them. Defending a "democratic" regime in the Republic of Vietnam (RVN) against invasion by the communist Democratic Republic of Vietnam (DRV) became the expressed purpose of the American intervention.

From 35,000 troops (mainly advisors and Special Forces) present in 1965, numbers quickly rose by 1968 to some 550,000.[23] The conscription that facilitated this surge in numbers gradually eroded the American domestic support base for the US effort, particularly when casualties mounted. Evening news programs that reported killed-in-action (KIA) levels above 300 per week and even larger wounded-in-action (WIA) statistics galvanized opposition to the war.

The course of the war had shifted from just antiguerrilla actions to use of American main force units to drive the North Vietnamese Army (NVA) and Viet Cong from any territorial positions they held. Air force and navy aviation units undertook a substantial effort to bomb and thus interdict the daily flow of supplies under jungle cover from North to South along the so-called Ho Chi Minh trail that connected North Vietnam to the South via Laos.

In any insurgency, the "outsider"—whether the British in the American case or the French (succeeded by the Americans) in the Vietnamese case—is at a severe disadvantage. Insurgents cultivate domestic sources, articulating their grievances and committing the movement to changing the status quo. Ideologies (liberal in the anti-British American case, socialist or communist in the anti-French and anti-American Vietnamese case) frame the issues insurgent leaders and their organizations take on. Depicting those they are against as "outsiders" or "enemies" of the people focuses the energies of the insurgents and their domestic supporters.

Organized, well-led, and focused insurgencies tend to attract external support from those seeing gains to be had from insurgent victories over incumbent authorities in a particular society. In his mission to Paris (1776–1785), Benjamin Franklin successfully cultivated these external contacts and realized the needed support from doing so. His diplomacy proved decisive in the insurgent victory at Yorktown during the revolution against Britain. So it was in Vietnam where Ho and his cohort secured Chinese and Soviet assistance.

The US defeat in Vietnam was due to a number of factors. As with the French, the insurgents successfully painted the United States as an outsider meddling in Vietnamese domestic matters, wreaking great destruction of life and property. Collateral death and destruction from bombing campaigns against targets on the Ho Chi Minh trail and in both

North and South Vietnam—whatever their military value—strengthened popular support in the countryside for the insurgents.[24]

Reflections in Washington on insurgency in the early 1960s had produced a persuasive, but false analogy to British success against communist insurgents in Malaya (1948–1954). As noted in chapter 4, the British had successfully separated the insurgents from the population as a whole—effectively denying them the popular support base they needed. The same, it was thought, could be done in Vietnam. What was overlooked in this narrative was that in the Vietnamese case, notwithstanding regional and demographic differences, all major players were ethnically Vietnamese.[25]

By contrast, in multiethnic Malaya (with Malay, Chinese, and Indian populations) the communist insurgents were predominantly Chinese operating with support from China. Not all Chinese in Malaya were communists or communist sympathizers, of course, but most of the insurgents were of Chinese identity. The majority population was Malay, while the Chinese as well as north and south Indian populations were distinct minorities. British success, then, was achieved by isolating the insurgents—turning the non-Chinese majority of the country against them.[26] The situation in Vietnam, on the other hand, was decidedly different. Although non-Vietnamese minorities were present, it was a country in which armed forces in both the North and South and the Viet Cong insurgents shared in common a Vietnamese identity not as easily split ethnically into contending camps.

From a military perspective, destroying war-making capability and unseating the regime in Hanoi required a ground invasion of North Vietnam supported by air force, marine, and navy aviation units. Both the Johnson and Nixon administrations ruled out this option, however, concerned as they were that doing so might prompt intervention by China or the Soviet Union, thus dramatically expanding the military and political stakes.[27]

Restricting military options in the north to airstrikes and limiting those to targets away from the port of Haiphong or elsewhere one might find Soviet ships or other Soviet or Chinese presence, the war became one of attrition. Casualty counts mounted on both sides. Matters came to a head during the dry season in the February 1968 Lunar New Year or "Tet" offensive launched by the North Vietnamese and Viet Cong against American positions in South Vietnam. North Vietnam and the Viet Cong attacked again in May at the end of the winter dry season, but before the monsoon rains, mud, and flooding made any follow-on offensive more difficult.

Casualties on both sides were high. When the dry season returned in late fall and the winter and early spring months, the Americans expected follow-on offensives.[28] In fact, North Vietnamese and Viet Cong losses in the two offensives were far greater than the Americans and their South Vietnamese ally realized. The expected follow-on offensives did not occur after all, but the damage to the American position had already occurred, albeit on a very different, domestic front.

Support for the war had begun to wane even before the Tet offensive. Tired of the war and the several hundred American soldiers, sailors, and airmen killed or wounded every week,[29] the US antiwar movement grew even stronger. Drafting young men at eighteen and older picked up speed. Vulnerable to the draft, both undergraduate and graduate students —the men, usually supported by their significant others—tended to see themselves potentially as cannon fodder on Vietnamese battlefields. They took action both on and off campus.

Protests grew in intensity. Indicative of this malaise and the damage done to his administration, President Johnson announced in March 1968 he would not seek reelection. The Democratic Party being in disarray effectively divided into three campaigns—Vice President Hubert Humphrey the Democratic centrist candidate formally supportive of Johnson administration policies, the antiwar left headed by Senator Eugene McCarthy, and the right wing American Independent Party that enjoyed strong southern Democratic support led by Alabama governor George Wallace and his running mate, retired Air Force General Curtis E. Lemay. With effectively three Democrats running (thereby dividing their share of votes significantly), Republican former Vice President Richard Nixon won the election with a plurality—just 42% of the popular vote!

Indeed, candidate Nixon had claimed to have a secret plan for ending the war but, in fact, continued the struggle and, in 1970, extended the war to Cambodia. The army finally got its way, clearing sanctuaries in the "Parrot's Beak"—the Cambodian salient extending into Vietnam like an arrow pointing at Saigon (or so it was portrayed)—and elsewhere in the Cambodia-Vietnam border area. The action provoked a domestic response well beyond what had occurred previously. In one tragic incident that occurred on May 4, 1970, Ohio National Guardsmen fired upon students at Kent State University who were protesting the US invasion of Cambodia. Four students were killed and nine wounded.

In a division of labor, the air force and navy depicted the Ho Chi Minh trail as a series of segments or "route packages"—each service responsible for destroying trucks carrying supplies or making different parts of the trail impassable. The burden was entirely upon airpower (US Air Force and US Navy) during the winter dry season, monsoon rains in the summer months substantially slowing the north-to-south movement of supplies.

Interservice rivalry took a new form with the competition between the air force and navy, each claiming an edge over the other. One air force general, the director of intelligence at the US Air Force headquarters in Saigon, became famous among visiting policy elites at the time for his briefings, each some two hours that combined post-strike, damage-assessment photos taken over a period of several years. The impression left with sympathetic visitors from Washington was one of an extraordinarily successful bombing campaign. Hyperbole reigned. Air force intelligence (the general) claimed that operations had interdicted 85% of supplies on the trail going to the northern part of South Vietnam (a tactical zone referred to as I Corps),[30] 100% going to points further south (tactical zones referred to as II, III, and IV Corps)!

For its part, the army wanted to deny sanctuary in Cambodia to the North Vietnamese and Viet Cong. During the last days of the Johnson administration, a senior official from the CIA[31] was dispatched to Saigon for consultations with military officers only to learn that reports of supplies coming from Cambodia into Vietnam were scarce and of questionable reliability. Quite apart from intelligence reports to sustain the case, the military reasoning was that air force interdiction had been so successful that supplies going to insurgents operating in South Vietnam had to be coming from somewhere. Hence, in briefings Cambodia became the "back door" to Vietnam. The Johnson team was not persuaded, but the Nixon administration that assumed office early in 1969 ultimately made the decision to extend the war to Cambodia in what became the war's major turning point.

Misjudgments based on faulty intelligence (or particular interpretations intended to influence policy makers) were only too commonplace. Enemy casualties were routinely overstated—several times US losses—as many as 2000 or more enemy allegedly killed each week, which suggested that the United States and its Vietnamese and other allies were winning (or at least holding their own in) the war. Misrepresentation or omissions occurred not just at the strategic but also at the tactical level.[32] Perhaps varying in degree, overstating enemy losses has also more recently occurred in the Iraq and Afghanistan campaigns discussed later in this chapter.[33]

Contributing to domestic malaise in the United States were two incidents in 1968 and 1969: My Lai (some 100 miles south of Da Nang) and "Hamburger Hill" (in the A Shau Valley near the Laos border). The former was the site of the March 16, 1968, mass murder of some 300–500 villagers by American soldiers. On May 10–20, 1969, frontal assaults against North Vietnamese positions with no particular military or other strategic value on a location labeled Hill No. 937 caused massive casualties on both sides, earning it the tragic name "Hamburger" Hill. The conflict in Vietnam had become a war of attrition in which numbers killed mattered to officials more than destroying or weakening the enemy's warmaking capability.

Particularly troubling to the American public and the Congress were such decisions to commit troops in this war of attrition—taking enemy positions at great human cost and then abandoning them. Infamous among these ventures, Hamburger Hill was by no means unique. US losses were 72 killed and 372 wounded, the North Vietnamese reportedly losing more than 600. Killed-in-action counts for the United States at the time were some 250 to 300 or more per week. As noted above, weekly enemy counts were reported on the order of 2,000 or more.

Adding fuel to the domestic protest movement, the My Lai event was finally disclosed to the press ten months into the Nixon administration (November 1969). To say the least, the just-war concept of sparing noncombatants seemed an abstraction, except for the few soldiers who tried to shield these civilians. Somehow the Clausewitzian understanding of war had been lost—that the way to win any battle (or an entire war for that matter) was to destroy or substantially weaken the enemy's war-making capability. By this, Clausewitz did not mean body counts (as if the contest could be settled quantitatively by counting which side had lost more soldiers either absolutely or proportionally).

Invading the north, thus disrupting military command-and-control and destroying war-making capability on the ground, was understand-ably precluded by fear of Chinese or Soviet intervention that would have expanded the war substantially. The invasion option was just too dangerous. On the other hand, right-wing advocates were likely correct that taking invasion off the table and limiting attacks to air strikes made the war unwinnable. If so, to fight unwinnable wars is a strategic mistake. It also contradicts a basic just-war tenet that going to war must have some chance of success.

Many contended then (as they do now) that such a war should never have been undertaken in the first place. Even if invasion of the north been pursued, there was no assurance that popular support for the

American-backed regime in Saigon could have trumped that enjoyed by the North Vietnamese and their Viet Cong cohorts in the south in what was a nationalist struggle in which the "outsider" is inherently in a deficit position. Failure by senior policy makers to understand this was catastrophic for the soldiers, sailors, airmen, marines and others who lost their lives in the conflict as well as the national treasure misallocated to an unwinnable war.[34]

The Nixon administration would eventually adopt a "Vietnamization" policy—reducing the American ground combat presence and relying on the South Vietnamese Army to assume the lead role. Ultimately, this failed with the fall of Saigon to North Vietnamese forces on April 30, 1975. Just as the shift to local (South Vietnamese) forces failed, this localizing of the conflict again would fail in Iraq three and a half decades later....

US INTERVENTIONS IN AFGHANISTAN AND IRAQ AND THE RISE OF THE ISLAMIC STATE

Al-Qaeda, using its safe haven in Afghanistan under the Taliban regime, attacked the United States on September 11, 2001. NATO members invoked Article 5 of the North Atlantic Treaty (an attack on one is an attack on all) and came to America's aid. Allied and other coalition forces invaded Afghanistan and, with support of some anti-Taliban tribes, quickly effected regime change in Kabul. Much was left to be done, but priority later given to Iraq by the Bush administration diverted resources that might have been expended in Afghanistan for follow-on stabilization of the regime and fighting insurgents in the countryside.

Even though Saddam Hussein in Iraq had no real connection to al Qaeda and its leader, Osama bin Laden, it suited members of the administration to cast this as a broad war on terror that included an "axis of evil"— including parties as different as Iraq, Iran, and North Korea. According to the administration, all three were becoming nuclear powers. Indeed, the lens through which decision makers see circumstances profoundly impacts their interpretations of what is at issue and the actions, if any, to be taken.

Motives for invading Iraq thus included the claim of Saddam Hussein being bent on Iraq becoming a nuclear power. After all, he already had chemical weapons of mass destruction that had been used not only against Iranians (1983–1988) during the Iran-Iraq war but also against Kurdish tribes (1988) and Shia in the southern part of Iraq (1991).[35] If that were not enough, Iraq's alleged link to al Qaeda made it part of the administration's new Global War on Terror (GWOT). Neither of these principal premises—Iraq's nuclear weapons capability and Iraq's link to al Qaeda—proved in fact to be the case.[36]

We probe more deeply for the understandings that underlay the decisions taken. Vice President Richard (Dick) Cheney had been secretary of defense during the George H.W. Bush administration when the United States and its coalition partners forced Iraq to withdraw its forces from Kuwait in 1991. Both he and the vice president's long-time friend and political ally, secretary of defense Donald Rumsfeld,[37] were supported by neoconservatives who wanted to complete what they considered the job left unfinished by the George H. W. Bush administration. To them it was not enough to have liberated Kuwait in 1991. In their view, pushing on to Baghdad and ousting Saddam Hussein from power would have removed a major threat to the region in general and Israel in particular. Instead, the United States and its coalition partners had left the Saddam Hussein regime intact, particularly because, in the George H.W. Bush administration's view at the time, doing so maintained Iraq as a key regional balancer against Iran.

The al Qaeda attack on the United States provided an opportunity not just to remove the Taliban from power in Kabul, but also finally to effect regime change in Baghdad. The United States committed 150,000 troops. The British joined the United States in the campaign with 46,000 and the Australians 2,000 troops as part of a multinational force of some twenty-four countries. Most of these committed token-only forces numbering in the hundreds, some less than a hundred troops on the ground. The parties subsequently shared the burden of occupation and postinvasion stabilization.

The invasion, though initially successful, was decidedly under-resourced. Secretary of Defense Rumsfeld had tangled with both his army secretary, whom he replaced, and the army chief of staff, who subsequently retired. Both had sought but were denied a much larger invasion force. Rumsfeld successfully kept the lid on the size of the invading US forces but, as a consequence, there were insufficient numbers of troops to help restore order and even secure weapons and ammunition depots.

US officials in Baghdad, carrying out the neoconservative agenda set in Washington, oversaw the removal of Baathists that had been so central to civilian government administration and military command under the old regime. Reconstituting both meant bringing more Shia into government and military service in an attempt to establish a more balanced governing structure with greater sectarian representation of Shia and Sunni Arabs and Kurds (the latter also Sunni). In time, however, the new Iraqi army would in fact become more of a Shia army, marginalizing Sunni representation.

Taken together, de-Baathification and dismantling the Iraqi army contributed substantially to the long-term destabilization of the country.[38] When the United States withdrew its mainline units[39] in 2011, Prime Minister Nouri al-Maliki's regime remained in place. With the Americans gone and no longer under the same real-and-present pressure to be more inclusive of Sunni Arabs and Kurds, the Maliki government tightened its grip, marginalized Sunni participation, and arrested Sunni seen as adversaries. Imprisonment and torture were back in vogue, this time not under American but rather Iraqi Shia auspices. The predominantly Shia army was also directed to take violent actions against Sunni civilian groups challenging the regime.

We return to where we started in the previous chapter. Grievances held by the Sunni against the Shia, who were newly in power, were what Sunni leaders needed to transform al Qaeda *in Iraq* into a new organization, ISIL. Indeed many of the dispossessed Sunni Baathists and military officers, many previously loyal to Saddam Hussein, brought important administrative and military skills to what became the Islamic State. The ironic outcome of the American-led campaign to rid Iraq of Saddam Hussein was that by subsequently stripping Iraq's Sunnis of power and facilitating a Shia government that would thrive on Sunni exclusion, the seeds were sown for insurgents to rise to power a decade later on the shoulders of the country's disenfranchised Sunnis.

The ideological component draws heavily from the thinking of ISIL's leader, Abu Bakr al-Baghdadi (born c. 1971 in Samara, Iraq), who earned a doctorate in Islamic Studies at the University of Baghdad. He was imprisoned by the United States in February 2004 but was eventually released in December. The ideology he advances is of the most reactionary, restorative form. On June 29, 2014, al-Baghdadi publicly announced restoration of a borderless caliphate with Islamic law at its core, thus formally reconstituting an idealized past dating to the time of Muhammad. As head of the new caliphate, he has assumed the title Caliph Ibrahim with all the historically grounded deference owed to the leader.

That neither the Islamic state nor the caliphate has recognition by Arab states, much less outside of the region, is beside the point. To ISIL's leaders, the Islamic State (or caliphate) is an important work in progress. The purity to be reestablished by incorporating their interpretation of the Koran, Shari'a law, and Sunna within the caliphate drives the leadership, followers, and new recruits. Leadership, ideology, and organization are all in place as ISIL's leaders pursue their restorative agenda.

By contrast to al Qaeda, which has used terror mainly through high-explosive attacks, ISIL leaders have added assassination by beheading or immolation to the list, claiming a right under Shari'a law to do so. Many in the Islamic world have objected strenuously to this radical interpretation. To them, justifying such tactics by reference to scripture is heretical.

AFTERWORD

Counterinsurgencies fail when the insurgents have substantial support from the local population, particularly if they also are the recipient of external aid. Rather than try to deal with insurgencies by securing an entire country, more limited commitments directed against those using terror and other forms of political violence have a greater chance of success. In practice, the line between a counterinsurgent and counterterror strategy is thin, but it is a useful analytical distinction that helps focus limited resources on the sources of threat. Success in a counterinsurgency that attempts to transform a society abroad is usually beyond available means—much less knowhow, as indeed the empirical record amply substantiates.

Notes

1. On instrumental and value rationality as they relate to social action, see Weber's *Economy and Society,* ed. Guenther Roth and Claus Wittich, vol. I (Berkeley: University of California Press, 1978), 24–26 and 29.
2. Although a few women or girls have been suicide bombers, they are exceptions that make it a male-dominant enterprise.
3. See Michael Morrell, *The Great War of Our Time* (New York: Twelve/ Hachette, 2015).
4. Karl von Clausewitz, *On War* in Caleb Carr (ed.), *The Book of War* (New York: The Modern Library, 1999), 776–782. See also Michael I. Handel, *Sun Tzu and Clausewitz Compared* (Carlisle Barracks, PA: U.S. Army War College, 1991).
5. Carr, *The Book of War,* 777–778.
6. Ibid., 779.
7. Ibid.
8. Ibid., 778-779.
9. Ibid., 778.
10. Ibid. 778.
11. T.E. Lawrence, *Seven Pillars of Wisdom* (New York: Random House/ Anchor Books, 1926, 1991).
12. See Mao Tsetung, *Six Essays on Military Affairs* (Peking: Foreign Languages Press, 1972) and *Selected Military Writings of Mao Tsetung*(Peking: Foreign Languages Press, 1972).
13. See Võ Nguyên Giáp, *Poeple's War, People's Army.* (New York: Bantam Books and Frederick A. Praeger, 1962).
14. Bard E. O'Neill, *Insurgency & Terrorism* (Washington, DC: Potomac Books, 2005), 15.
15. During his time in Paris, Franklin cultivated, among others, his relationship with Voltaire, in the freemasonic *Loge des Neuf Soeurs.*
16. As Frank Talbert, a US Army officer drawing from the American experience in Afghanistan and Iraq, told me in 2014: "The leadership [of these insurgencies] does not want the foot soldiers truly educated in the cause. They just want to stoke the fire within them and impart their ideology so they [the "soldiers"] will unquestioningly do their bidding and [even] die for the cause."

17. An exhumation in 2012 with data examined by Swiss scientists indicated radioactive poisoning (polonium) may have been the cause of death. Fatah, Arafat's organization, put the blame on Mossad, Israel's intelligence agency. Not surprisingly, the Israeli government denied the allegation as unfounded.

18. O'Neill, 33.

19. I recall the deep, rumbling sound and rattling of windows we heard and felt in Saigon (1968–1969) due to B-52 ("arc light") bombing of targets some 10–12 kilometers away. To be so close to the "enemy" was an intimidating effect on American forces, but this was hardly the purpose of the strikes.

20. On strategy for homeland security, see Paul R. Viotti, Michael A. Opheim, and Nicholas Bowen, Editors. *Terrorism and Homeland Security.* Boca Raton, FL: CRC Press/Taylor & Francis, 2008. My contribution to that effort is an article "Toward a Comprehensive Strategy for Terrorism and Homeland Security," 3–31.

21. Ho Chi Minh Museum, Ho Chi Minh City (Saigon), April 4, 2015.

22. Chalmers Johnson found that nationalism was central to communist insurgencies in both China and Yugoslavia. See his classic *Peasant Nationalism and Communist Power* (Stanford, CA: Stanford University Press, 1962).

23. Under Eisenhower there were some 600 advisers, and 16,000 under Kennedy.

24. This has also been the case in Afghanistan, Iraq, and Syria, of course, as collateral death and destruction by aircraft and drone attacks or ground operations strengthen insurgent appeals to the domestic support base.

25. Differences among Vietnamese relate to their historical and geopolitical experiences—the north more influenced culturally by China; the south by India; and between the south and Huế yet another Vietnamese identity.

26. See Robert Komer, *The Malayan Emergency in Retrospect: Organization of a Successful Counterinsurgency Effort*, RAND Report R-957-ARPA (Santa Monica, CA: RAND Corporation, 1972).

27. On the embedded thinking of policy elites about the strategic importance of Vietnam and how that led to problematic policy choices, see Leslie H. Gelb and Richard K. Betts, *The Irony of Vietnam: The System Worked* (Washington, DC: Brookings, 1979).

28. The army provided defense of its own installations with combat troops and military police. The air force relied on its security police as the first

line of defense of air bases, calling on *ad hoc* units of personnel assigned
to these bases as reinforcements lest the bases be overrun. The author,
then an Air Force lieutenant, was Deputy Flight Commander of one such
unit. See Roger P. Fox, *Air Base Defense in the Republic of Vietnam, 1961–
1973* (Washington, DC: Office of Air Force History, United States Air
Force, 1979).

29. Average US killed in action (KIA) in 1968 was 278. The average number
of draft notices was 30,000 per month. Source: Dan Caldwell, Pepperdine
University.

30. Pronounced "eye" corps.

31. A CIA member of the agency's Estimates Office, a GS-18, then the highest civil service grade, was sent by the Johnson administration to examine intelligence claims that Cambodia was the logistical "back door" to
Vietnam used by the Viet Cong. His conclusion was that the claim was
not supported by the evidence. Invasion of Vietnam, favored by the army
and air force, would have to await the Nixon administration that took
office in January 1969.

32. For example, notwithstanding interest expressed by the Director of
Operations in receiving tactical reports, the Director of Intelligence
pulled one such report the author made of a Viet Cong threat specifically
directed against C-130s flying into or out of Pleiku in central Vietnam,
which he argued was unduly upsetting to the operations people who
might overreact. In fact, a C-130 was shot down within the week; a C-130
pilot, a friend of mine, was killed on June 23, 1969. Had the report been
received, another C-130 pilot commented that Operations likely would
have altered take-offs and landings with steep ascents and descents—the
modified flight paths reducing vulnerability to ground fire. My friend's
and other deaths might have been avoided had analysts not been so constrained in the rendering of such threat reports.

33. Private conversation with a U.S. Army officer.

34. See Secretary of Defense McNamara's later apologia in James G. Blight
and Janet M. Lang, *The Fog of War: Lessons from the Life of Robert S.
McNamara* (Lanham, MD: Rowman & Littlefield, 2005).

35. American service members suffered casualties from exposure to chemical agents found in Iraq. See C. J. Chivers, "The Secret Casualties of Iraq's
Abandoned Chemical Weapons," *New York Times*, October 14, 2014.

36. Other possible motives difficult to substantiate, but offered by observers,
included the United States seeing Iraq as a strategic base for US operations, securing oil not just in Iraq but also in the Persian Gulf region

as a whole, and settling scores with Saddam who allegedly sought the assassination of President George H. W. Bush.

37. Rumsfeld also had held that position in the Ford administration when Cheney was Ford's Chief of Staff.

38. For a critical view of US policy in Iraq, see Emma Sky, *The Unraveling: High Hopes and Missed Opportunities in Iraq.* (New York: PublicAffairs/Perseus Group, 2015).

39. Among the few mainline units still remaining were various special operations and explosive ordnance destruction units and trainers.

CHAPTER 6

INTELLIGENCE

Logistics, technology, popular support, leadership, and operational capabilities are essential to success in wars, armed interventions, and countering insurgencies and the political violence they use. So is intelligence that assesses enemy capabilities accurately, gives early warning of attack, anticipates enemy actions, and assesses the situation as combat operations proceed. Making longer-term national estimates is also an important part of the intelligence enterprise.

Spying on adversaries (and being spied on by them) is the stuff of espionage. Whom can you trust with secrets? Even those loyal to the American cause may make honest mistakes that reveal classified information. Others may have a political or personal axe to grind as they disclose state secrets. Still others may do it just for money. As the Soviets discovered during the Cold War, relatively few Americans are likely to turn coat for purely ideological reasons. The alleged appeals of Marxism or Marxism-Leninism were a relatively hard sell to Americans in the post–World War II period.

The more recent Bradley Manning and Edward Snowden cases discussed later in the chapter, though massive in the scale of classified information revealed, are by no means new to the American experience. Espionage, counterespionage or counterintelligence, and questions of loyalty date from the American Revolutionary period nicely captured by the intrigue between Major General Benedict Arnold, considered a "traitor" to the American cause (and to his commander, Major General Washington) and a thirty-year-old British major, John André, dubbed a British spy. We begin this chapter with this story, reflecting on these ever-present intelligence challenges.

André's Loyalty to King and Arnold's Betrayal of Washington's Trust

Major John André, under arrest and on trial for his life, looked out the window across the creek from the house in which he was held. André was quartered in a private residence about a hundred yards or so from the makeshift court in the Dutch church in the center of the town. In and around the town were ancient trees that marked the hilly, beautifully wooded area—a piedmont leading to the Catskill Mountains further to the north.

Tappan really was not a town—more a hamlet, a small community settled mostly by Dutch men and women when, before the British takeover, the colony was New Amsterdam. Not surprisingly, many of these Dutch settlers held anti-British sentiments and thus were sympathetic to the revolutionary cause—a sentiment much appreciated by George Washington and his fellow generals who depended upon these and other domestic bases of support.

Indeed, General Washington resided as guest in the de Wint house down the road along the creek about a quarter of a mile just past the "old tar tree"[1] used by the revolutionaries as a lookout—a warning post lest British soldiers catch them off guard. Given its location on the New Jersey border, the town had always been an area transited by both English and Dutch settlers. Though now formally British subjects, Dutch liberals like the de Wint–Blauvelt family[2] were reliable supporters of the revolutionaries.

At the same time, of course, British forces also had their supporters. A few miles east of Tappan on the west bank of the Hudson River lived Mollie Sneden (1709–1810), a pro-monarchy "Tory" who ran a cross-river ferry from Sneden's landing that, until she was shut down, accommodated pro-British elements.

Frederick Blauvelt and his wife, Maria de Wint, welcomed the distinguished general, accompanied by his aide de campe, Colonel Alexander Hamilton, as Washington awaited the outcome of the court martial he had ordered. Their daughter Elizabeth and her husband lived in the nearby house[3] where André was kept under guard awaiting trial.

It was not an ordinary proceeding. The custom in courts martial is to assemble a board of officers who are the same rank or higher than the accused (subordinates not allowed to sit in judgment of their seniors). In this case, however, General Washington upped the ante significantly. Rather than assemble fellow majors and lieutenant colonels with, perhaps, a colonel or brigadier general presiding, Washington directed 14 one- and two-star generals to consider the case. Eight brigadiers (Parsons, Clinton, Knox, Glover, Patterson, Hand, Huntington, and Starke)—and six major generals—then the highest rank in the Continental Army (Greene —President of the Board, Stirling, St. Clair, Howe, the French Marquis de la Fayette, and the Prussian Baron von Steuben) came to Tappan to sit on the court martial. All were freemasons, as were Andre and Arnold. Washington sought consensus among his senior "brothers" if he were going to preside over the execution of another mason.

Although not much was said publicly about it at the time, the generals certainly knew why they had assembled. Major General Benedict Arnold, one of their own and Washington's commander at West Point, had betrayed both the revolutionary cause and Washington's trust. Secretly passing to André papers with details on the layout and defenses of the very strategic Hudson River post he commanded at West Point,

General Arnold gave aid and comfort to the enemy—high treason as the revolutionaries saw it. With these plans in hand, British General Sir Henry Clinton, Lt. General James Robertson (his deputy), and their commanders were in a position to take the post, thus severing lines of communication in the Continental Army between forces in New York and New England with those in New Jersey, Pennsylvania, and locations further south of the Hudson River.

Clinton and his generals controlled Manhattan, the surrounding New York area, and for some distance up river. As noted earlier, had West Point fallen into British hands, Clinton would have had operational control of the river, thereby denying Washington's movement to the east bank of the river to points further north and effectively splitting revolutionaries in the middle-Atlantic states and further south from those in New England —an extraordinarily important strategic victory for the British.[4]

Arnold found refuge behind the British lines, but the revolutionaries captured André. Fresh in Washington's mind was the British execution on September 22, 1776, of Nathan Hale, the twenty-one-year-old patriot spy who, upon his hanging, famously proclaimed his regret for having only one life to give for his country. Was André to be treated any differently? Why should he be spared? If the British command had used Hale's execution to send a message to the insurgents, hanging André would return the message in kind.

The question before the court was whether André was, in fact, a spy who had engaged in espionage. His defense rested upon the fact that his military position was Adjutant in the British Army under General Clinton's command—he was not a spy at all. It was Arnold who had sought him out, passing him the documents.

The claim was not persuasive to the court martial. That André had removed his uniform, changing into civilian clothes in order to conceal his identity, convinced the court that he, in fact, had acted as a spy. Finding him guilty of espionage, capital punishment was the verdict the generals recommended. Given this unanimous concurrence by the fourteen, General Washington issued the death warrant.

André pleaded eloquently to Washington to respect his standing as an officer and afford him the gentleman's privilege of execution by rifle shot rather than by hanging. In an October 1, 1780, letter to the general, André stated:

> Buoyed above the terror of death by the consciousness of a life devoted to honourable pursuits, and stained with no action that can give me remorse, I trust that the request I make to your Excellency at this serious period, and which is to soften my last moments, will not be rejected.

> Sympathy towards a soldier will surely induce your Excellency and a military tribunal to adopt the mode of my death to the feelings of a man of honour.

> Let me hope, Sir, that if ought in my character impresses you with esteem towards me, if ought in my misfortunes marks me as the victim of policy and not of resentment, I shall experience the operation of these feelings in your breast, by being informed that I am not to die on a gibbet.

André's request came upon the heels of pleas in his behalf by British Generals Clinton and Robertson. Even Benedict Arnold had asked Washington to spare André. It was not particularly helpful to André that Arnold wrote to Washington in a very threatening tone. After his summary of the facts as he saw them, Arnold asserted:

> If, after this just and candid representation of Andre's case, the Board of General Officers adhere to their former opinion, I shall suppose it dictated by passion and resentment; and if that Gentleman [John André] should suffer the severity of their sentence, I shall think unhappy myself bound by every tie of duty and honour, to retaliate on such unhappy persons of your army,

as any fall within my power, that the respect due to flags, and to the law of nations, may be better understood and observed.

I have further to observe, that forty of the principal inhabitants of South Carolina have justly forfeited their lives, which have hitherto been spared by the clemency of His Excellency Sir Henry Clinton, who cannot in justice extend his mercy to them any longer, if Major Andre suffers; which in all probability will open a scene of blood at which humanity will revolt.

Suffer me to intreat [sic] your Excellency, for your own and the honour of humanity, and in the love you have of justice, that you suffer not an unjust sentence to touch the life of Major Andre.

But if this warning be disregarded, and he suffer, I call heaven and earth to witness, that your Excellency will be justly answerable for the torrent of blood that may be spilt in consequence.

All of this was to no avail. Washington would have none of it. Why should André be treated differently than Hale some four years earlier? André's request for an officer's execution by rifle shot was met by silence. On the morning of October 3, 1780, André was instead taken to a nearby hill about a half mile to the west and hanged. The place still bears the name André Hill, and a monument honoring André remains there to the present day.

Those witnessing the hanging were effusive in praise for the young officer, commending him for his bravery and even his gallantry. Washington joined in this chorus, acknowledging that the cruel code of war had forced the execution of an otherwise honorable man. Buried after the hanging at the top of the hill, in 1821 the British Consul General at New York oversaw the exhumation of André's remains, returning them to a final resting place of honor at Westminster Abbey in London. It was a time of Anglo-American *rapprochement* in the decade after the War of 1812.

So why was a convicted spy honored but his coconspirator condemned? The intended effect, of course, was to draw a sharp distinction between

André and Arnold—between the spy and the traitor. André had been loyal to his sovereign, engaging in the collection of strategic intelligence. By contrast, Arnold not only had betrayed the cause but also his fellow generals. He was a turncoat.

The reality, of course, was far more complicated than that. Those defending Arnold's action saw him as having initially gone astray when joining the revolutionary cause, but ultimately returning to the fold in loyalty to his sovereign. From this Tory perspective, Washington, his generals, and those of lesser rank who fought with him as well as the political wing, made up of Franklin, Adams, Jefferson, and others, were the disloyal ones who deserved to be hanged. It was hardly a temperate period in the American experience.

For our purposes here, however, we underscore the distinction between the spy as patriot who gathers intelligence for his country and the agent or double agent who sells his or her country short. It is a perspective deeply set in the American historical understanding as illustrated by this story of Major André and Major General Arnold. Indeed, the intelligence world today remains a mix of intelligence collection by both technical means and human source or espionage in which both agents and double agents and their multiple contacts traffic. Then, as now, networks of human beings matter.

INTELLIGENCE COLLECTION, COVERT ACTIONS, AND SPECIAL OPERATIONS

Intelligence collection, espionage (the use of spies to collect information), covert actions, and special operations by US government agencies have played a prominent role in US foreign and national security policy, particularly since the end of World War II.[5] The principal mission of intelligence is the collection and analysis of information about adversaries, but clandestine operations have also been employed as the conduct of policy by extraordinary means—coups, organizing insurrections, assassinations, and other activities that raise important moral and legal questions addressed later in the chapter (see table 8 for a partial list of clandestine activities).

THE INTELLIGENCE "COMMUNITY"

Intelligence, as we use the term here, refers to the information that governments seek as they monitor and anticipate the actions of both state and nonstate actors. Engaged in this task are sixteen government agencies—referred to as "elements"—that constitute a "community" overseen by the Director of National Intelligence (DNI) who works directly for the president. It is the stuff of spying or *espionage*—using all sources, human and technical, to paint for policy makers as accurate a picture as possible of what others, particularly adversaries, are doing or likely will do. Aware that others—including adversaries as well as allies, coalition partners, and the nonaligned—are doing the same, the community also engages in counterintelligence to deny information or block its collection by adversaries.[6]

As becomes clear when one reads the following paragraphs, the "community" is an alphabet soup of agencies and offices. Prior to the DNI's creation by legislation (2004)[7] in response to the 9/11 attacks in 2001, the president's "overseer" of the intelligence-community was the Director of Central Intelligence (DCI), who also was director of the CIA.

Table 8a. Clandestine or Secret Activities: Covert Actions and Special Operations.

Angola	1976–1992: CIA and military support South African-backed groups
Bolivia	1986: Special Forces support counter-insurgency
Brazil	1964: CIA-backed *coup* against President João Goulart that brings General Castello Branco to power
Cambodia	1969–1975: CIA-backed *coup* against Prince Norodom Sihanouk that brings Lon Nol to power
Chile	1973: CIA-backed *coup* against President Salvador Allende
Congo	1960: CIA-backed *coup* and assassination of Prime Minister Patrice Lumumba; 1965: CIA-backed *coup* against President Joseph Kasavubu that brings Joseph Mobutu to power
Cuba	1960–1965: Failed CIA attempts to Assassinate Fidel Castro; 1961: CIA-backed invasion by anti-Castro Cubans that failed at Bay of Pigs
Ecuador	1963: CIA-backed *coup* against President Velasco Ibarra
El Salvador	1981–1992: CIA and Special Forces support counter-insurgency
Ghana	1966: CIA-backed *coup* against President Kwame Nkrumah
Greece	1947–1949: counterinsurgency
Guatemala	1954: CIA-backed *coup* against President Jacobo Árbenz 1966–1967: counterinsurgency
Haiti	1991 and 2004: CIA-backed *coups* against President Jean-Bertrand Aristide

Source. Adapted from Global Policy Forum data.

Table 8b. Clandestine or Secret Activities: Covert Actions and Special Operations (*Cont'd*).

Indonesia	1965: CIA-backed *coup* against President Sukarno that brings General Suharto to power
Iran	1953: CIA-backed *coup* against Prime Minister Mohammad Mossadegh 1980: Special Forces mission to rescue American hostages fails
Iraq	1992–1996: CIA-backed efforts against regime of President Saddam Hussein
Italy	1948: CIA influences elections in favor of the center-right, especially Christian Democrats (DC)
Laos	1962: CIA-backed military *coup*
Nicaragua	1981–1990: CIA organizes and directs "Contra" campaign against Sandinistas
Oman	1970: counterinsurgency operation
Philippines	1948–1954: CIA-backed "secret 'commando'" war; 1989: CIA and Special Forces support counter-insurgency
Vietnam	1960–1964: military advisors and special forces begin activities prior to escalation with regular forces in 1965

These terms *overseen by* (rather than *directed by*) and *overseer* capture the relative lack of authority in relation to budgets and personnel that are, for the most part, still under the control of the elements listed in table 9, which also details the alphabet soup of agency names. If one is to "control" any large organization administratively, the essential levers are those dealing with budget and personnel or human resources—their hiring (or firing), compensation, training, and promotion. In fact, the DNI does not control the intelligence community because it remains decentralized with most budgetary and personnel authority still held by the component elements.

Nevertheless, the DNI's voice is heard on program, budget, intelligence, and other matters directly by the president and within the Executive Office of the President (EOP), particularly by the Office of Management and Budget (OMB) and, on intelligence matters, within the National Security Council (NSC). Creating the DNI effectively reduced the CIA's formal position within the intelligence community by displacing the CIA Director's primacy within the NSC. Interagency national intelligence estimates, previously coordinated across the intelligence community by the Director of Central Intelligence, now come under the DNI's National Intelligence Council (NIC). As a practical matter, even with the loss of the DCI function, the CIA voice is still heard as the lead intelligence agency outside of the DoD orbit.

For its part, the Office of the Director of National Intelligence (ODNI) monitors an annual budget of more than $50 billion with some $4 billion allocated to "overseas contingency operations" engaged in by the intelligence agencies.[8] In addition to this National Intelligence Program (NIP) figure is more than $20 billion in the Military Intelligence Program (MIP) budget under the Defense Department. Thus, when the NIP and MIP are added together, overall annual US spending on intelligence tops $70 billion, which does not include funding by allies or partners in joint ventures.

The high cost of the National Security Agency (NSA), National Geospatial Agency (NGA), and the National Reconnaissance Office (NRO) in northern Virginia—not to mention DIA, the DoD's own intelligence agency in Washington, DC,—accounts for the disproportionately large share of the intelligence budget in DoD's hands. Signals intelligence (SIGINT), which includes communications (COMINT) and electronic (ELINT) intercepts, falls under the NSA at Fort Meade in Maryland just outside of Washington, DC, as well as the military intelligence units that also collect such data—a task they have performed since before World War II.

The NGA is at the top of collection and interpretation efforts directed toward imagery of all kinds—principally photographic, but also infrared or other energy-based images. Imagery intelligence (IMINT) in general, photographic intelligence (PHOTINT) in particular, and other information related to Earth-based, natural and man-made objects of national security interest—so-called geospatial intelligence (GEOINT)—are the NGA's domain. The NGA thus performs functions performed by earlier organizational entities—the National Imagery and Mapping Agency (NIMA) and, still earlier, the National Photographic Interpretation Center (NPIC).

The CIA's organizational structure follows the agency's principal tasks. Under the director and deputy director come three principal units —the directorate of intelligence responsible for analysis, the "directorate of operations" responsible for clandestine activity, and the directorate of science and technology. Similarly, the Defense Intelligence Agency (DIA)—the senior military-intelligence agency—has a parallel structure: a directorate of analysis, a clandestine service, and a science-and-technology directorate. For its part, the CIA has added a new directorate of digital innovation and has created "mission centers" to bring together individuals across the directorates.

CIA remains the principal agency involved in covert actions, but DIA has expanded its role substantially in both espionage and covert actions. In addition to a worldwide network of military attachés engaged in overt intelligence collection, DIA now has covert operatives of its own. The armed services use the term *special operations* to capture their own military-related covert activities. Their effectiveness, of course, has not been limited to the battlefield or military-support operations. In one of the most celebrated cases, the Navy Seals stormed al Qaeda leader Osama bin Laden's compound in Pakistan, which resulted in his death on May 2, 2011.

Table 9. The US Intelligence "Community."

Director of National Intelligence (DNI)

1. Central Intelligence Agency (CIA)

Department of Defense (DoD)
    2. Defense Intelligence Agency (DIA)
    3. National Security Agency (NSA)
    4. National Geospatial-Intelligence Agency (NGA)
    5. National Reconnaissance Office (NRO)
    6. Air Force Intelligence, Surveillance and Reconnaissance
      Agency(AFISRA)
    7. Army Intelligence and Security Command (INSCOM)
    8. Marine Corps Intelligence Activity (MCIA)
    9. Office of Naval Intelligence (ONI)

United States Department of Energy
    10. Office of Intelligence and Counterintelligence (OICI)

United States Department of Homeland Security
    11. Office of Intelligence and Analysis (I&A)
    12. Coast Guard Intelligence (CGI)

United States Department of Justice
    13. Federal Bureau of Investigation, National Security
      Branch (FBI/NSB)
    14. Drug Enforcement Administration, Office of National Security
      Intelligence (DEA/ONSI)

United States Department of State
    15. Bureau of Intelligence and Research (INR)

United States Department of the Treasury
    16. Office of Terrorism and Financial Intelligence (TFI)

INTELLIGENCE AGENCY COMPETITION

It would not be correct to characterize these government agencies as constituting a "community." In fact, it is more accurate to describe them as an often-competing set of intelligence units—each having its own agenda, organizational culture, and purposes (see table 9, which identifies the principal components of the intelligence community).

Dysfunction associated with the stovepipe metaphor was most apparent in the September 11, 2001, surprise attack by al Qaeda on the World Trade Center in New York and the Pentagon in Washington, DC. Intelligence was not so easily shared across government agencies, even if they had wanted to do so.

In addition to bureaucratic competition between them, a barrier stood between the CIA and the FBI. By statute, a division of labor between the two put the FBI in charge of information related to domestic law enforcement while the CIA focused on intelligence abroad and was thus kept from domestic spying. As a practical matter, the FBI routinely interacted with its law-enforcement counterparts in other countries, while the CIA pursued foreign intelligence connections in the United States. Both agencies also shared common interest in espionage by foreign operatives within the United States.

Although their work at home and abroad thus overlapped to some degree, the functional distinction between law enforcement and intelligence gathering was a criterion explicitly designed to keep the CIA from spying on American citizens. It also gave bureaucratic ground for not sharing information with other agencies related to advising policy makers of threats and providing them with early warning of attacks, which would allow them to make decisions and take actions to prevent them or, at least, mitigate the consequential damages.

Failure to "connect the dots" and provide actionable intelligence was obviously problematic. Bits of important information tended not to be readily shared not just between the CIA and FBI but also among the fourteen other intelligence agencies. Part of the problem was managing the sheer volume of information collected by agencies like the NSA. But even when the needles in haystacks—important bits of information— were found, it remained more a "community" of stovepipe organizations possessing information that was not so easily shared.

Given the 9/11 experience, an immediate need was to aggregate intelligence collected on terrorist threats into a single place. Creating a Terrorist Threat Integration Center (TTIC) in 2003 was an early response to this challenge which, with the creation of the DNI, has become the National Counterterrorism Center (NCTC). Separate intelligence agencies now channel their bits of information to a single, bureaucratically independent place within the ODNI where, in principle, analysts can connect the dots in timely fashion, providing decision makers with the best available, actionable intelligence.

The remedy to the larger problem of coordination among intelligence agencies on any number of issues was the creation of a Directorate of National Intelligence (DNI). Since 1947, the Director of CIA had also been the Director of Central Intelligence (DCI). In principle, the DCI as senior intelligence officer in the US government would bring all of the components together into one intelligence community. In fact, the DCI had no such authority. Although the DCI occupied the senior intelligence position on the National Security Council (NSC), he was not really coequal with the two principal cabinet officers dealing with foreign policy and national security—the secretary of state and secretary of defense.

Moreover, as noted earlier, the largest part of the intelligence budget is spent by the Department of Defense. Without any direct control over the DoD intelligence budget—much less DoD personnel assigned to intelligence—the DCI was not really in a position to challenge the authority of the secretary of defense in intelligence matters. The NSA, NGA, and NRO report to the secretary of defense, as does DIA. Indeed, DIA was created during the Kennedy administration to give the secretary of defense and chairman of the Joint Chiefs of Staff a consolidated military-intelligence source apart from the intelligence units that remained within the separate military service departments.

The State Department performs a relatively small intelligence function centered in its Intelligence and Research (INR) bureau. At the same time, however, the State Department oversees a global network of embassies and consulates that routinely gather and report information—both classified and open-source or unclassified—that often has intelligence value. Embassy "cables" and "telegrams"—terms reflecting earlier telecommunications technologies—have long been distributed not just within the State Department but also across the government, including military headquarters both at home and abroad.

In addition to confidential, secret, and top-secret classifications and No Foreign Dissemination (NOFORN) labels[9] that apply across the US government, the State Department developed its own set of labels limiting dissemination: Limited Official Use Only (LOUO), Executive Dissemination (EXDIS), and No Dissemination (NODIS)—the last kept within the State Department or shared, perhaps, with the White House or very selectively with other agencies.

The large volume of messages prepared by staffs in diplomatic missions are sent under the last names of the ambassador, consul general, or chargé d'affaires to the secretary of state are, in fact, typically passed to the appropriate bureaus and desks for action or information. Although only a few actually reach the secretary's desk, ambassadors dealing with issues of great concern to the secretary also may have a direct message or voice channel open to them. For the secretary's part, although only a relatively few messages actually emerge from the secretary's office, by tradition all messages dispatched from the State Department bear the secretary's last name as, symbolically at least, the last word in the bottom line.

Finally, CIA depends upon the State Department, which provides the CIA station chief and staff a venue within any US embassy or diplomatic mission. The station chief is a member of the "country team," as are other CIA principals within a particular embassy, and thus enjoy the privilege of diplomatic cover and the immunity from arrest that goes with it. The ambassador heads the country team, although the station chief reports directly to the CIA headquarters in northern Virginia. Similarly, the Defense Attaché reports directly to DIA, and military attachés in the defense attaché's office also reporting to their respective army, navy, or air force intelligence offices in the Pentagon.

UNPACKING THREATS, CONSTRAINTS, AND OPPORTUNITIES

Intelligence depends upon a continual awareness of what is happening or might occur; this pertains not only to the threats and constraints imposed from the world around us but also the opportunities to be found there. Identifying threats, constraints, and opportunities—distinguishing among and making sense of them, separating wheat from chaff—is the stuff of intelligence analysis. We deal with either a deluge of information or, alternatively, the lack of needed facts to make what are essentially subjective judgments.

Analysts review both classified and open-source intelligence (OSINT) available to the public from diverse communications media, including the Internet. Whether from open or intelligence sources, massive data can be sorted and searched, documents translated, and indicators constructed to give warning of what may happen, but none of these displaces the role of the analyst who must make sense of what is before her or him. As always, raw data or "facts" do not speak for themselves. They must be interpreted to assess their implications for national security or other purposes. Intelligence remains at its core a highly subjective enterprise demanding human judgments.

The seasoned analyst does this routinely without taking too much time to reach a reasoned judgment. As with most skills, however, it takes years—perhaps a decade or more—to perfect and, finally, to master these analytical capabilities. Although the cognitive or analytical part of the brain receives data and calculates, it is the subconscious brain that bears the bulk of the burden. The expertise required to sift rapidly through data and reflect accurately on the meaning of what the analyst observes depends upon the training and direct experience achieved over thousands of hours. *Knowing* comes at a very high price in time.

Connecting the dots is a metaphor for causal analysis—conceptual understandings of cause and effect to be found in the wealth (or dearth) of data before the intelligence analyst. It is a puzzle-solving process. Using multiple sources of information collected for their use, the analyst and colleagues try to assemble the main outlines of a puzzle in which some important pieces may be missing. Moreover, their efforts may be confounded by a veritable avalanche of data—the problem not a lack of "dots," but rather too many to make sense of their meaning or assess their implications.

Moreover, in some cases the analyst is dealing with a mystery, not a puzzle. The "puzzle metaphor" assumes that if we simply collect enough dots, the intelligence "picture" will eventually emerge. As a practical matter, however, some things (like what a foreign leader may be thinking) are inherently unknowable. On such questions, the analyst may engage in informed speculation, but the conclusion drawn may be tenuous at best.

Perception and misperception are opposite sides of the same cognitive coin.[10] Prior understandings may keep the analyst from making correct inferences from the data observed. The commonly held thought in December 1941 that the Japanese navy did not intend (or was not in a position) to attack American ships, aircraft, and military installations in Hawaii led those receiving radar-based and other indicators to overlook or not interpret them as evidence of a forthcoming, massive attack by carrier-based aircraft.

Another example of prior understandings leading to misinterpretation was the mindset prior to the October 1973 Egyptian attack across the Suez Canal on Israeli positions in the Sinai desert. Intelligence analysts in the United States relied heavily on what their Israeli counterparts also thought —that Egypt did not have the military capabilities to pull off a cross-canal operation and thus would not dare try to do so. Analysts tended to rationalize assembly of bridging equipment and other military activities that they observed on the east side of the canal as mere posturing by the Egyptian army. When the Egyptian army nevertheless established itself in positions west of the canal, Israel counterattacked.[11] The United States assisted militarily in a massive resupply effort and, after Israel made major gains on the ground against both Egypt and Syria, diplomatically helped broker an end to the fighting.

Instructive in these and other examples of prior understandings leading to misinterpretations is Leon Festinger's suggestion that we have a human tendency to avoid cognitive dissonance.[12] Unwittingly, we may blind ourselves to seeing what runs counter to our preestablished take on reality. Worse, our prior (and possibly incorrect) understandings may be reinforced when these are also commonly held by others whose judgment we trust. We become in these circumstances, as Irving Janis put it, victims of "groupthink."[13]

One remedy to avoid (or, at least reduce the likelihood of) intelligence "failures" due to cognitive dissonance and groupthink is to designate a naysayer (or a team of analysts) as having the responsibility for making cases contrary to the widely held conventional wisdom or the findings in a particular analysis or estimate. By institutionalizing and thus legitimating the naysayer's task, we seek to remove the stigma associated with challenging the view held by one's colleagues or supervisors. The hope in this process is to increase the likelihood that analysts and estimators will not miss in advance what in the aftermath becomes obvious.[14]

Notwithstanding best efforts, intelligence failures still occur. "Post-mortem," after-action assessments of what, if anything, went wrong, have the obvious benefit of 20-20 hindsight. It may be that the necessary information was just not there—more an intelligence "surprise" than a failure. Or it may have been bottled up in one agency at one level or another, thus effectively denied to the analysts or policy makers in positions of authority who need it to make decisions. Put another way, it is clearly dysfunctional when intelligence organizations become like "stove pipes," keeping information within rather than sharing it with others, particularly policy makers with a need to know.

SECURITY FUNCTIONS AND DYSFUNCTIONS

The best way to keep a secret is not to tell anyone. Short of that, keeping secrets depends on telling as few people as necessary—those who have a "need to know" and, for very sensitive information, telling only those who "*must* know." The downside of limiting dissemination of information, of course, is that policy makers not in the know may be blindsided. Even other intelligence analysts without requisite special or "compartmented" clearances may not receive intelligence reports produced by their colleagues and are thus denied information that may be relevant to their work.

Policy makers and the intelligence analysts who support them may also be blindsided by too much information. The sheer volume of data collected and the time it takes to separate wheat from the chaff limit timely access to important intelligence. Put another way, how long does it take to find the needle in the haystack? Worse, there may be several "haystacks" at issue—data collected from diverse sources that are not directly connected. Data search engine technologies applied to classified documents—looking for names or key words in masses of intercepted communications—may help navigate the flow of data, but the human task remains formidable. Again, intelligence involves highly subjective judgments. "Facts" do not speak for themselves. What we take (or refer to) as facts are more often than not really interpretations made individually by the analyst or collectively in collaborative efforts.

Indeed, intelligence is classified confidential, secret, and top secret for understandable security reasons, such as the sensitivity of the information itself or merely to protect the source. This concern to hide from an adversary the ways and means by which intelligence is collected leads to further compartmentalization that restricts access to those who *must* know particular information or the source from which it was collected.

Some intelligence is shared with allies or coalition partners, often as part of an agreed intelligence exchange. Thus, as noted above, some documents may be classified NATO Secret or NATO Confidential. Others may bear the label "No Foreign Dissemination Except for...." Exceptions include allies like the United Kingdom, Canada, Australia, and New Zealand.

Thus, limits are imposed on the distribution of information collected from human or other sources lest their identities be disclosed. The analyst who receives the information may be told about the reliability of the source and the likely validity of the information, but little else. This can be very frustrating to the analyst whose interpretations and judgments would benefit from greater access to (or information about) the source.

Communications and electronic intercepts and various forms of reconnaissance are the stuff of technical intelligence. Agencies tasked with collecting information from these technical sources create compartments within secret and top-secret classifications, limiting access to those who must know—a highly subjective judgment in itself. Thus, secret or top-secret information may be assigned a code word that designates to those in the know the technical source from which it was collected— satellites, aircraft, and unmanned and ground or sea-based collection platforms. For example, SIGINT sources—COMINT and ELINT—have their own sets of classified labels and code word designators, as does GEOINT imagery (as noted, frequently referred to as IMINT or PHOTINT) gathered from satellite or airborne platforms.[15]

These compartments are inherently exclusionary, providing information to a select few who "must" know, but denying it to others. Worse, as observed in the previous section, intelligence may become bottled up in a particular agency tasked with collecting or analyzing it. The intelligence community is replete with these metaphorical stovepipes that obstruct the dissemination of intelligence even to those who "must" know as in the LIMDIS, EXDIS, and NODIS limits imposed by the State Department.

Sometimes dissemination limits imposed by one agency are ignored by another. For example, military or civilian Defense Department employees with security clearances and access to State Department documents may decide to pass some of them to others within DoD, who are not the intended recipients. This collection of intelligence held by one agency by another is one way of overcoming the stovepiping dysfunction. This informal sharing of intelligence, however functionally justified, may not be known by the agency originally classifying the report. Put another way, "leaks" occur within the executive branch, sometimes extending to Congress, committees, and staffs. In the politics of the Potomac where information is a key asset, leaks by officials are also made to the press and other communications media—the motive typically being to garner public support or understanding for their positions on some issue.

Quite apart from leaks across government agencies or to the media, some individuals with security clearances—either government employees or contractors—have taken it upon themselves to disclose classified information, thus breaking the law and violating their contract to keep state secrets. During the Cold War, such disclosures by Americans tended to be for private gain rather than for ideological motivations. KGB or other foreign agents generally found monetary payments more effective as a recruitment tool than anticapitalistic, other ideological, or cause-based appeals.

Matters of conscience and policy disagreement also led some individuals and organizations to reveal state secrets. The Pentagon Papers—a collection of policy and intelligence assessments related to the Vietnam War—were leaked by Daniel Ellsberg and subsequently published in 1971 by the *New York Times* and *Washington Post*. The ensuing political firestorm eventually reached the Supreme Court, which upheld the right of journalists to publish such documents under the Constitution's freedom-of-the press guarantee.

In the mid-1970s, CIA agent Philip Agee became disaffected by what he considered moral abuses by CIA operations in Latin America. In his *Inside the Company: CIA Diary* (1975), he revealed the activities and identities of some 250 CIA officers and others engaged in assassinations and other covert actions. Ultimately finding protection in Havana, Agee died there in 2007 at the age of seventy-two, apparently of natural causes.

More recently, in 2010 Private First Class Bradley Manning exposed US policies and actions with which he personally disagreed. Given the access he had as a technician, Manning transferred a massive number of classified embassy and State Department cables to the WikiLeaks organization, which made them public. Upset by US policies in Iraq and Afghanistan, his motivation was to disclose what he found offensive about the conduct of American foreign policy. Manning was convicted in 2013 by a military court martial and sent to prison on a 35-year sentence for violations of the Espionage Act—disseminating classified information.

Of even greater impact on disclosing sources and methods was thirty-year-old civilian contractor Edward Snowden's leaking of selections from a cache of as many as 200,000 documents, which he passed to the *Guardian* (UK) and the *Washington Post*.[16] A libertarian who saw himself as a whistle blower, Snowden exposed NSA monitoring of domestic communications as well as those of allies (including cell phone conversations of political leaders such as German chancellor Angela Merkel). Underscoring the commitment among journalists to freedom of the press and the public's right to know, the Pulitzer Prize was awarded in 2014 to both newspapers. Not surprisingly, most government officials—especially those in intelligence committed to safeguarding sources and methods—take a decidedly different view.

The issue is by no means new. In 1929, President Herbert Hoover's secretary of state, Henry L. Stimson, closed down his department's SIGINT effort, famously remarking that "gentlemen do not read other gentlemen's mail." But those were simpler times. Or were they? Snowden's revelations produced a firestorm of commentary at home and abroad about the extent of the NSA's spying. His supporters consider Snowden a hero for exposing this government intrusion into the communications of private citizens. Others—not surprised by the revelations and somewhat more sympathetic to the government position—saw the problem not so much in the intelligence collected, but in getting caught doing it.

It is an old story. Aware that he was being spied upon, liberal English political philosopher and activist, John Locke (1632–1704), used coded language to mask the intent of written communications that could be intercepted by intelligence agents loyal to the English monarchy. Locke's apparent involvement in the Rye House plot against the Crown (1683) finally led him to self-generated exile to the Netherlands.

To government officials, of course, the damage done by Snowden was very real. Intelligence classification into confidential, secret, and top-secret categories and special, restricted compartments is not just to safeguard intelligence information, but also to protect sources and methods used. Once those countries, groups, and persons know the means by which intelligence is collected on them, they not unexpectedly take steps to close off further intrusion. Foiling terrorist plots thus becomes more difficult as perpetrators find other ways to communicate or find ways to disguise the content of communications by cell phone. Angry that Snowden had violated his trust, US officials sought his extradition. Rather than face prosecution in the United States, Snowden made his way to Russia where he was granted temporary asylum.

Newspapers—sensitive to national security concerns—reviewed the documents and assessed government arguments before publishing them. Claiming a right to do so under *New York Times v. United States* (1971), the American press concurred with the US government in some but not all instances. In the domestic political arena, then, Snowden was reviled in intelligence, policy-making, and politically more conservative circles, but in other, more libertarian (and civil-libertarian) corners he has been celebrated as a hero for exposing the extent of NSA and other US government collection of private communications.

The Obama administration's response, while condemning Snowden, was to seek an agreed balance between intelligence collected for counterterrorism and other national security purposes and the privacy rights of citizens as well as German and other allies, their political leaders and populations. Striking such a balance is, of course, more easily stated than achieved. Not purely a matter of executive branch decision, most reforms require amending the Foreign Intelligence Surveillance Act (FISA), thus assuring a Congressional role.

After studying the options, the president proposed, among other safeguards, that Congress "authorize the establishment of a panel of advocates from outside government to provide an independent voice in significant cases before the Foreign Intelligence Surveillance [FISA] Court." He also proposed curbing NSA's holding indefinitely its own archive of telephone calls made by citizens, the government instead relying on regulated government access to records held by the telephone companies through the FISA court process.

The related dispute between Apple and the FBI underscores the conflict between government's need to know for law-enforcement or other intelligence purposes and, at the same time, securing private communications and other data contained on personal cell phones from government or other unwarranted intrusions. Demands that Apple provide government with the electronic "key" to "unlock" cell phones was met by substantial resistance not just by Apple, but also by other telecommunications firms. Perhaps because they have (or more easily can develop) technologies to break into or intercept communications from these devices, there has been decidedly less concern by NSA or other intelligence agencies that Apple or other corporations be forced to provide keys to unlock secure devices. From the perspective of many in the US intelligence community, routinizing such access by other governments (or private-sector units) may be contrary to the US government's interest.

INTELLIGENCE AND POLITICS ON THE POTOMAC

Quite apart from individuals who, for whatever motivation, take it upon themselves to disclose classified information, are those who do so for political gain. As observed in the previous section, competing agendas among administration officials, members of Congress, staffs, and lobbyists linked to them lead many to leak information helpful to a particular (often politically motivated) cause.

Plugging leaks is more easily said than done. For their part, highly placed administration officials, sometimes the president himself, release information previously kept from the public eye. Because members of the executive branch are responsible for classifying intelligence and other information in the first place, they not infrequently see themselves as authorized to declassify and thus selectively release information.

Members of congress or their staffs sometimes do the same. A classic case was Alaska Senator Maurice "Mike" Gravel who read the Pentagon Papers into the Congressional record of the subcommittee he chaired in June 1971. After all, the US Constitution in Article I, Section 6, protects senators and representatives from being prosecuted for what they say in the Senate or House of Representatives.

Beyond their own commitment to security, however, a strong motivation for senators or representatives not disclosing intelligence classified by the executive branch, of course, is losing future access to this information. Accordingly, intelligence oversight committee members in both houses avoid such disclosures. Other members of Congress and their staffs understandably may be less committed to following rules put in place by the executive branch to protect the sanctity of intelligence information, as well as the sources and methods of collection.

In the intelligence community (as elsewhere in Washington), information is core to the power bases of particular agencies and the individuals within them. Motives for withholding intelligence—benign or otherwise—vary substantially. In some instances, not disseminating information may be due to uncertainty about either its validity or importance. In other cases, however, disclosing the information may adversely affect understandings of a particular agency's interest or position in the bureaucratic competition that defines politics on the Potomac. The idiosyncrasies and particular interests of bureaucrats may also obstruct access to intelligence kept bottled up.

Protecting executive branch policy or other prerogatives is a strong motive for reluctance to disclose some intelligence or intelligence methods to members of Congress. Aside from concerns lest some senators or representatives not keep executive branch secrets, disseminating information may result in unwanted challenges oftentimes cast in partisan terms. Competing bases of authority between the branches spawned by separation of powers, along with extremely polarized partisan politics, contribute substantially to the intelligence dysfunctions that complicate the making and implementation of US foreign and national security policy.

Congressional prerogatives are also at stake. Presidents had authorized covert actions undertaken by the CIA during the first three decades of the Cold War with little, if any, disclosure or involvement by the Congress. Revelations in the 1970s about operations conducted by the CIA (referred to as the "family jewels"), the FBI, and other government agencies resulted in demand for Congressional oversight of executive branch intelligence activities.

Among the "family jewels" described in Senate hearings before the Church Committee (1975) were coups (e.g., in 1953 against the Mohammad Mossadegh regime in Iran, reinstating the Shah; in the following year against the Jacobo Árbenz regime in Guatemala; in 1963 against South Vietnamese President Ngo Dinh Diem; and in 1973 against the Salvador Allende government in Chile), assassination attempts, surveillance to include spying on journalists and other American citizens, secretly opening private mail, human-subject drug experiments, and illegal wiretapping.

The obvious remedy was to expand oversight of intelligence operations, particularly covert actions. The Hughes-Ryan Intelligence Oversight Act (1974) thus gives oversight authority to intelligence committees in both houses and requires the president to report all CIA covert actions to these two committees.

Although presidents might still try to distance themselves from controversial covert actions, the legislation effectively ended the doctrine of "plausible deniability"—that the president (or his staffers) could claim he knew nothing about any particular operation. This fig leaf which presidents had stood behind since World War II positioned the CIA to take the hit should there be any unauthorized disclosure of controversial covert actions. In the new order of the day, given that the president is the one who authorizes covert actions, it is the chief executive's desk where the buck is supposed to stop.

INTELLIGENCE COLLECTION AND COVERT ACTIONS: MORAL, LEGAL, AND PRAGMATIC CONSIDERATIONS

Intelligence collection includes exploiting human sources for national security purposes. In a ritualized acceptance of this reality, officials routinely use the term *exploitation*, referring explicitly to these human sources. To them, the compelling rationale for doing so is national security. It is an honest statement of what they do. But does this end justify any means? Where are the moral limits? Where are lines to be drawn?

Enhanced interrogation—a euphemism for torture of prisoners in Iraq, Afghanistan, and Guantánamo in Cuba, and in secret prisons elsewhere— was US policy during the Bush administration. The administration also authorized extraordinary rendition—arresting or kidnapping persons of interest located in other countries and subjecting them to enhanced interrogation—which became established practice. To them, avoiding new (even more catastrophic) attacks on the homeland than 9/11 meant national security stakes that were high enough to warrant using these extraordinary measures. Not everyone agreed.

Both treaty and domestic law prohibit use of torture. US law against torture dates from the earliest days of the republic. Eighteenth-century liberal understandings clearly prohibited such measures. For the United States or anyone else to do so was unconscionable. Like piracy, anyone committing such acts anywhere were subject to trial in US courts. For the most part, the official American view on such actions was sustained throughout the country's history to include the US-Soviet Cold War. It was also a basis for American advocacy of the antitorture treaty.

Exceptional times do produce exceptional circumstances, at least in the minds of those less persuaded by absolutes. Use of torture by US interrogators in Iraq, Afghanistan, Guantánamo in Cuba, and elsewhere was not without its historical precedent. In 1899, after victory in the Spanish-American War, the US military in Philippines used water and other forms of torture to gain intelligence from revolutionaries opposed to the American occupation. Not alone in using such measures, atrocities abounded on all sides.

Defining torture narrowly became the George W. Bush administration's work around. Under the new dispensation, one could conduct interrogations using methods that fell short of the line between life and death. For example, to get information through interrogation one could subject an individual to waterboarding (i.e., pouring a large volume of water over his mouth until, gasping for breath, he began to ingest water into his lungs. In between bouts the hope was that the prisoner would give up secret information to his interrogators.

Waterboarding was a euphemism for what previously (and historically) was referred to simply (and more honestly) as the water torture. Officials also called it *simulated* drowning when, in fact, the victim was actually beginning to drown. So long as the person administering the torture could avoid causing death, he was said to be free of legal liability for such actions.

Waterboarding was just one tactic among several designed to make prisoners break. Depriving prisoners of sleep, bombarding an individual with loud music played continuously, forcing individuals to remain standing for many hours, humiliating them with forced nudity and other sexually oriented actions, hanging them by their wrists (sometimes dislocating their shoulders), threatening to do harm to their family members, and intimidating them with the presence of ferocious dogs were among the tactics military and civilian interrogators used.

These measures failed on three grounds. First, they were morally repugnant. Second, they were illegal. Finally, from a pragmatic perspective, they did not work as intended. Information drawn from individuals subject to such torture was inherently unreliable. With ample motive to deceive their torturers, many of the victims did just that. Telling minor truths mixed up with lies became the modus operandi among them. How one could unpack them, differentiating truths from lies, was by no means an easy process.

Rather than interrogation (much less accompanied by torture), after-action review conducted by DIA confirmed what had been known by intelligence and law-enforcement professionals—that the more effective way to get reliable information was to use "interviews" in which the questioner first gained the confidence of the interviewee. Reliable information is decidedly more likely to be forthcoming when one interviews and painstakingly gains the confidence of the source.

Reflecting on his own security-related experience earlier in his career, even Iraqi-deposed president Saddam Hussein was more willing to disclose information when he identified with the man asking him questions. It takes particular skill, of course, to establish this bond—a curious empathy between captor and captive, questioner and respondent, interviewer and interviewee. Although some may object ethically to the duplicity involved, this approach is far more effective for intelligence purposes and decidedly less morally damaging than the use of torture euphemized as "enhanced" interrogation techniques.

Quite apart from torture as an enhanced interrogation technique are covert actions that date from the earliest days of the CIA and its World War II predecessor, the Office of Strategic Services (OSS). Before revelations to the US Senate's Church Committee (1975), the agency had few external controls. As noted earlier, the record of assassinations and assassination attempts, coups d'état, and other paramilitary operations produced a firestorm of moral outrage at the time that resulted in strengthening oversight by Senate and House committees.

As with torture, assassination-as-policy fails on the same three grounds —morally, legally, and pragmatically. Such tactics are morally repugnant methods, however worthy the end or objective may seem. From a legal perspective, assassination-as-policy amounts to combining the roles of judge, jury, and executioner into one agent—hardly the process anyone is due, whatever the alleged offense.

As a matter of law in civil society, governments or their agents: (1) arrest or put a suspect in custody (or try to do so), (2) afford that person a fair trial for alleged offenses in a properly constituted court (or, perhaps, if the accused refuses to appear, trying the person in absentia in the same court), and (3) if guilty, apply the appropriate penalty that fits the crime committed. Prohibitions on assassination were put in place in the mid-1970s by the Ford and Carter administrations, solidified as Executive Order 12333 issued by the Reagan Administration (1981): "No person employed by or acting on behalf of the United States Government shall engage in, or conspire to engage in, assassination."

With the creation by Congress of the Director of National Intelligence (DNI) position, the George W. Bush administration formalized approval of covert actions at the presidential level. In this regard, Executive Order 13470 (2008) states:

> The NSC shall consider and submit to the President a policy recom-
> mendation, including all dissents, on each proposed covert action
> and conduct a periodic review of ongoing covert action activities,
> including an evaluation of the effectiveness and consistency with

current national policy of such activities and consistency with applicable legal requirements. The NSC shall perform such other functions related to covert action as the President may direct, but shall not undertake the conduct of covert actions.

The NSC, DNI, and CIA (or any other department or agency) thus do not have authority to undertake covert actions without presidential approval. This stipulation was not entirely new, of course. In fact, most such decisions previously had reached presidential level but, as noted earlier, presidents had enjoyed the privilege of plausible deniability, thus washing their hands of public accountability for covert actions gone wrong or leaked to the press and no longer under wraps.

In the American experience, the government is not above the law it formulates; government agents are proscribed from taking the law into their own hands. Nevertheless, sometimes they do and usually for pragmatic purposes. Policy makers like Dean Rusk, secretary of state in the Kennedy-Johnson administrations, saw assassination-as-policy through pragmatic lenses, referring to it in matter-of-fact terms merely as what goes on in the "back alleys of the world."[17] Blowback from Rusk's "back alleys of the world" is a reality difficult to grasp, much less control.

Indeed, as disclosed on Capitol Hill and in the "family jewels" document, in the 1960s CIA made more than forty failed assassination attempts against Fidel Castro in Cuba. In Vietnam, the Phoenix Program targeted the insurgent Viet Cong Infrastructure (VCI)—an effort to "neutralize" North Vietnamese influence in the south. The word *neutralize* is a euphemism for infiltrating, capturing, interrogating, and assassinating. The operations were conducted by South Vietnamese military and security services in coordination with CIA and American special operations units.

The agency was also directly or indirectly involved in a supporting role in a number of other covert actions. Military leaders and other Chileans hostile to the left-wing rule of Salvador Allende overthrew his regime in September 1972—the coup later referred to in Santiago as Chile's 9/11.

His followers alleged that Allende had been assassinated by the plotters, his opponents at the time claiming Allende had committed suicide.

In a larger frame, however, the incident fit into a broader Cold War, anticommunist scheme against the left perpetrated by right-wing regimes then in power in Argentina, Bolivia, Brazil, Paraguay, and Uruguay. Under General Augusto Pinochet, successor to Allende, Chile was added to the list.

With military aid and technical support from the United States, Operation Condor targeted left-wing elements in an effort to eradicate their influence. Tragically (and counter to most American expectations), the campaign took tens of thousands of lives. It was a time remembered infamously as one dominated by death squads run by the security or intelligence services in these countries.

For its part, the US Army School of the Americas, founded in 1946 and located in Panama, became a cornerstone of the US anticommunist, counterinsurgency effort in Latin America when the Kennedy administration gave it this task in 1961. Interrogation, torture, sniper training, and other "dark alley" methods apparently were part of the curriculum, thus legitimating in some minds the use of such techniques.

Dubbed by some as the School of Assassins, critics also observed that rather than successfully advancing democratic values, the school reinforced of military-authoritarian modes of governance. Indeed, a number of the school's graduates later became dictators displacing civil authorities. Expelled by the Panamanian government in 1981, the school then took up residence in Fort Benning, Georgia. Given its controversial track record, in 2000 the school was renamed the Western Hemisphere Institute for Security Cooperation (WHINSEC).

Not all US-supported clandestine ventures were as morally and legally problematic as these. Success in covert actions—part of the overall US and allied effort—contributed to neutralizing Soviet dominance of Eastern Europe. Another Cold War example was arming Afghans in their resistance to the 1979 Soviet intervention and occupation, which did directly contribute to the Soviet defeat and withdrawal a decade later. On the other hand, the United States had backed the Mujahideen resistance, which was also supported by Osama bin Laden, Pakistan's ISI, and others hostile to the Soviet takeover. Under bin Laden, al Qaeda later would establish its base in Afghanistan where it planned and executed the 9/11 attacks against the United States in 2001.

AFTERWORD

The post–Cold War period, now in its third decade, poses decidedly new challenges alongside the old ones. For example, the cyber sphere, discussed in chapter 1, has enormous implications for US national security, intelligence an important asset policy makers need as they grapple with new threats to telecommunications, transportation, energy, financial, and other infrastructure. Space is also a place in which both state and nonstate actors now traffic. Satellites and other assets there are subject to attack. It is another domain in which the intelligence community likely will play an increasing role in the decades to come.

At the same time, old problems remain. Terrorism is still a threat requiring worldwide surveillance to provide warning and, if possible, the means to thwart such attacks. Moreover, states still use force, sometimes invading other states. The idea that Russia would continue to accept the post-Cold War status quo proved unfounded with efforts to redraw boundaries in Ukraine in 2014, much as it had used force in Georgia six years earlier. China's military modernization and naval buildup puts it in a stronger position to pursue its interests in the East Asian region. It may be the twenty-first century, but we are not beyond states continuing to use force when their leaders see it as in their interest to do so.

Put another way, decision makers will continue to rely heavily on what they learn from the intelligence community. The national security and intelligence agenda contains a very substantial list of challenges.

Notes

1. A remnant of the "old tar tree"—long since dead, bare of bark and its upper branches cut—remained standing until the 1950s when it finally was cut down, much to the dismay of historically minded residents.
2. Frederick Blauvelt married Anna de Wint; her father, Johannes (a West Indies planter), purchased the house in 1746. The house was built in 1700 by Daniel de Clark, another Dutch settler who had come to New Amsterdam in 1676.
3. The place subsequently acquired the name "76 House" with exhibits commemorating André, his court martial, and subsequent execution while, at the same time, condemning Benedict Arnold (his portrait hung upside down above the fireplace).
4. Arnold's treason was an even deeper personal betrayal to Washington and Arnold's fellow generals. Washington, the generals he assembled to fight the war, including Arnold, were all "brothers" in freemasonry. This freemasonic link was an important component of the military wing of the revolutionary movement upon which Washington relied; the integrity and trust within the leadership of the Continental Army were an explicit extension of these brotherly loyalties. Adding further complication, André was also a freemason. Not about to single-handedly order the execution of a British "brother" on a charge of espionage, Washington assembled an all-Masonic court martial that gave collective cover for any decision they would reach. For an annotated list of freemasons engaged in the revolutionary war that documents evidence of their Masonic affiliations, see Ronald E. Heaton, *Masonic Membership of the Founding Fathers* (Silver Spring, MD: The Masonic Service Association of the U.S., 1965).
5. On the work of the intelligence "community," see Jeffrey T. Richelson, *The US Intelligence Community*, 7th ed. (Boulder CO: Westview Press, 2016); Paul R. Pillar, *Intelligence and U.S. Foreign Policy* (New York: Columbia University Press, 2011); and Mark M. Lowenthal, *Intelligence*, 6th ed. (Washington, DC: CQ Press, 2014).
6. See Hank Prunckun, *Counterintelligence Theory and Practice* (Lanham, MD: Rowman and Littlefield, 2012).
7. The Intelligence Reform and Terrorism Reform Act.

8. For FY2014 the total appropriations figure the Obama administration requested was $52.2 billion of which some $4 billion was for "overseas contingency operations." (ODNI News Release No. 13-13; June 27, 2013).

9. The label sometimes comes with exceptions, for example, No Foreign Dissemination Except UK (or other allies specified in the label).. Sometimes the classification is preceded by reference to shared information in an alliance as in NATO Confidential or NATO Secret.

10. See Robert Jervis, *Perception and Misperception in International Politics* (Princeton, NJ: Princeton University Press, 1976).

11. Walls of sand (the Bar-Lev line), thought to be an effective obstacle to tanks crossing, were demolished by a rather primitive but highly effective technology—high-pressure hoses drawing water from the canal.

12. Leon Festinger, *A Theory of Cognitive Dissonance* (Palo Alto, CA: Stanford University Press, 1957).

13. Irving Janis, *Victims of Groupthink* (Boston: Houghton Mifflin, 1972).

14. For more on this problem, see the now-classic argument by Richard K. Betts, "Analysis, War, and Decision: Why Intelligence Failures Are Inevitable," *World Politics* XXXI, no. 1 (October 1978): 61–89.

15. William M. Arkin catalogs these codewords in his *Code Names: Deciphering U.S. Military Plans, Programs, and Operations in the 9/11 World* (Hanover, NH: Steerforth Press, 2005).

16. See Luke Harding, The *Snowden Files* (New York: Vintage, 2014).

17. In 1975, Rusk met with some twenty graduate students (I was one) in a seminar on foreign policy held at the University of California, Berkeley. When I asked him his opinion on the legitimacy of assassination as US government policy, he answered metaphorically (as if he were a father educating a son) to what goes on routinely in the "back alleys of the world"—a realist acceptance of what later Vice President Cheney would refer to as the "dark side" of international politics. Rusk's understandings of "back alleys" likely stem from his professional experience in World War II as part of the Office of Strategic Services (OSS), predecessor of the CIA.

CHAPTER 7

CIVIL-MILITARY RELATIONS

A citizen-soldier is first and foremost a citizen. As general, and later president, George Washington put it:

> As to the fatal, but necessary operations of war, *when we assumed the soldier, we did not lay aside the citizen* [emphasis added]; and we shall most sincerely rejoice ... when the establishment of American liberty, on the most firm and solid foundations, shall enable us to return to our private stations....[1]

This was the model George Washington conveyed, both as army general and in his presidential role as commander-in-chief.[2] To him, it is the citizen who responds to military necessity, but later returns to civil pursuits.

As a personal matter, Washington anticipated the end of the Revolutionary War when he would be "translated into a private citizen"—able "to sink into sweet retirement, and the full enjoyment of that peace and happiness, which will accompany a domestic life."[3] This was the spirit in which he finally bade farewell to his officers and resigned his commission in December, 1783, thus taking "leave of all the employments of public life."[4] Quite simply, Washington saw himself merely as a *citizen* who *happened to be in uniform.*

We begin with discussion of the type and size of the armed forces, including Alexander Hamilton's opposition to large standing armies and the ongoing challenge he saw of maintaining civilian supremacy and control of the military. Should the military, given its combat mission, focus exclusively on war fighting and military preparedness, thus separating itself from the concerns of other societal components? Or should the military expand its horizon beyond merely this focus on warfare, thus integrating itself and its professional agenda more fully with the rest of society?

The Type and Size of the Armed Forces

Standing armies or armed forces in peacetime were so feared by most of the eighteenth-century Constitutional framers that they put explicit provisions in the US Constitution against (or at least to constrain) them.[5] The framers were reacting to the role the British army had played in abusing citizen rights in the colonial period—offenses listed in the Declaration of Independence (July 4, 1776).[6] The experience of the seventeenth-century English civil war also influenced their thinking. Whether soldiers were subject to king or Cromwell,[7] they could be used to threaten citizen rights and liberties.

General Washington reaffirmed military subordination to civil authority immediately after the Revolutionary War. He was no Cromwell willing to use the army as a power base. The general certainly had an opportunity to do so when disaffected soldiers, frustrated in their efforts to secure due compensation from Congress for their contributions to the war effort, wanted him to use the army to seize public lands in the west for redistribution to the troops in lieu of back pay, some even advocating he subsequently become king! Washington completely rejected any such idea. He told the soldiers: "If you have any regard for yourself or posterity, or respect for me, to banish these thoughts from your mind, and never communicate, as from yourself or anyone else, a sentiment of the like nature."[8]

To guard against any military abuse of private property rights, the third amendment to the Constitution stipulates that "no soldier shall, in time of peace be quartered in any house, without the consent of the owner, nor in time of war, but in a manner to be prescribed by law." Beyond that protection, the second amendment also upholds "the right of the people to keep and bear arms" as essential to "a well-regulated militia" tasked with maintaining "the security of a free State." For Constitutional provisions on the military in American society, see table 10.

Indeed, primary reliance was to be on the organized militia within the states or what is now the National Guard (army and air), in large part because of their proximity to the people and their peacetime control by the states. Standing forces were to be avoided or minimized. Article I, Section 8.12, empowers Congress "to raise and support armies" but provides that "no appropriation of money to that use shall be for a longer term than two years."[9] In other words, not only is Congress the authority that funds the armed forces, but also each new Congress is in a constitutional position to reverse prior decisions on the existence and size of any standing army.

When standing armies are necessary, the framers separate authority over them lest either executive or legislative branch use the military as an exclusive power base. The logic is explained in *Federalist Paper* No. 51: setting branch against branch to check or balance each other. Similarly, the federalism explained in *Federalist Paper* No. 10 gives states and localities the independence or autonomy they seek from central direction or control.

Table 10a. Civil-Military Relations and the US Constitution.

We the People of the United States, in Order to form a more perfect Union, establish Justice, insure domestic Tranquility, *provide for the common defence*, promote the general Welfare, and secure the Blessings of Liberty to ourselves and our Posterity, do ordain and establish this Constitution for the United States of America.

Article. I. Section. 8. The Congress shall have Power

To ... *provide for the common Defence* and general Welfare of the United States....

To borrow Money on the credit of the United States....

To *declare War*, grant Letters of Marque and Reprisal, and *make Rules concerning Captures on Land and Water* ...

To *raise and support Armies*, but no Appropriation of Money to that Use shall be for a longer Term than two Years

To *provide and maintain a Navy*

To *make Rules for the Government and Regulation of the land and naval Forces*

To *provide for calling forth the Militia* to execute the Laws of the Union, suppress Insurrections and repel Invasions

To provide for organizing, arming, and disciplining, the Militia, and for governing such Part of them as may be employed in the Service of the United States, reserving to the States respectively, the Appointment of the Officers, and the Authority of training the Militia according to the discipline prescribed by Congress;

To exercise exclusive Legislation in all Cases whatsoever, over such District .. as may... become the Seat of the Government of the United States, and to exercise like Authority over all Places purchased by the Consent of the Legislature of the State in which the Same shall be, for the Erection of Forts, Magazines, Arsenals, dock-Yards, and other needful Buildings....

Note. Italics have been added to emphasize particular clauses or phrases.

Table 10b. Civil-Military Relations and the US Constitution.

Section. 9. ...The Privilege of the Writ of Habeas Corpus shall not be suspended, unless when in Cases of Rebellion or Invasion the public Safety may require it....

Section. 10. ...No State shall, without the Consent of Congress ... keep Troops, or Ships of War in time of Peace ... or engage in War, unless actually invaded, or in such imminent Danger as will not admit of delay.

Article II. Section. 1. The executive Power shall be vested in a President of the United States of America.... **Section. 2.** *The President shall be Commander in Chief* of the Army and Navy of the United States, and of the Militia of the several States, when called into the actual Service of the United States.... *He shall have Power, to* ... nominate, and by and with the Advice and Consent of the Senate, shall *appoint ... all ... Officers of the United States* ... but the Congress may by Law vest the Appointment of such inferior Officers, as they think proper, in the President alone, in the Courts of Law, or in the Heads of Departments.... **Section. 3.** *He* shall from time to time give to the Congress Information of the State of the Union ... and *shall Commission all the Officers of the United States.*

Article. IV. Section. 3. *...The Congress shall have Power to dispose of and make all needful Rules and Regulations* respecting the Territory or other Property belonging to the United States.... **Section. 4.** The United States shall guarantee to every State in this Union a Republican Form of Government, and shall protect each of them against Invasion; and on Application of the Legislature, or of the Executive (when the Legislature cannot be convened), against domestic Violence.

Article. VI. ...All executive ... Officers, both of the United States and of the several States, shall be bound by Oath or Affirmation, to support this Constitution....

Amendment II. A well regulated Militia, being necessary to the security of a free State, the right of the people to keep and bear Arms, shall not be infringed.

Amendment III. No Soldier shall, in time of peace be quartered in any house, without the consent of the Owner, nor in time of war, but in a manner to be prescribed by law.

Table 10c. Civil-Military Relations and the US Constitution.

Amendment V. No person shall be held to answer for a capital, or otherwise infamous crime, unless on a presentment or indictment of a Grand Jury, *except in cases arising in the land or naval forces, or in the Militia, when in actual service in time of War or public danger....*

Amendment XIV. *(Passed by Congress June 13, 1866. Ratified July 9, 1868.)*

Section 3. No person shall be a Senator or Representative in Congress, or elector of President and Vice-President, or *hold any office, civil or military,* under the United States, or under any State, *who,* having previously taken an oath ... as an executive ... officer of any State, to support the Constitution of the United States, *shall have engaged in insurrection or rebellion against the same, or given aid or comfort to the enemies thereof.* But Congress may by a vote of two-thirds of each House, remove such disability.

Section 4. The validity of the public debt of the United States, authorized by law, including debts incurred for payment of pensions and bounties for services in suppressing insurrection or rebellion, shall not be questioned. But neither the United States nor any State shall assume or pay any debt or obligation incurred in aid of insurrection or rebellion against the United States..., but all such debts, obligations and claims shall be held illegal and void.

In Article II, Section 2, the framers vest the president as chief executive with the foreign policy power "to make treaties" and to "be commander in chief of the army and navy of the United States, and of the militia of the several States, when called into the actual service of the United States." Concerning treaties, presidential power is limited by the requirement that the president act "by and with the advice and consent of the Senate," securing concurrence by at least "two thirds of the senators present."

After all, each state has equal representation in the Senate and the states were not about to relinquish complete authority over foreign policy or security matters that had previously been their responsibility. Moreover, the states, acting through the Senate, retain by majority vote a check on executive appointments of all "ambassadors, other public ministers and consuls ... and all other officers of the United States."

The historical and continuing experience with the dispute between the executive and the legislature over war powers was, perhaps, an intended consequence of the framers' decision to separate powers over the armed forces. Supporters of executive authority have argued that even though only Congress may *declare* war, the president as commander-in-chief of the armed forces has the Constitutional authority to *make* war. Presidents since Franklin Roosevelt have tended to have a more expansive interpretation of executive authority conveyed by this "commander-in-chief" function, particularly concerning war-*making* powers, than historically has been the case.

Congressional claims to the war-*declaring* power under Article I, Section 8.11, challenge these executive claims to authority. Moreover, it is Congress that has the authority under the same article to appropriate money "to raise and support armies" and "to provide and maintain a navy." In this split between executive and legislative authority over the armed forces, the framers tipped the balance in favor of the latter by a broad grant of authority "to make rules for the government and regulation of the land and naval forces"—functions normally one might expect to be performed by an executive authority.

The framers in effect conceded that to be effective the armed forces need the unity of command provided by the executive. At the same time, however, their fear of standing armies led them to establish checks by the states (acting through the Senate) and by the people (acting through the Congress as a whole), but particularly the House of Representatives—the more democratic chamber elected directly *by* the people.

It is Congress that has this authority "to make rules for the government and regulation of the land and naval forces." Of the two branches, then, it is Congress that thus has the larger claim to formal, legal authority. In a narrow construction that may well have been intended by the Constitutional framers, executive power is formally limited to command

—preserving the military's functional necessity of unity of command, while reserving other prerogatives to Congress.

Even command of the militia by the president is subject to congressional authority. It is the legislature under Article I, Section 8, that has authority "for calling forth the militia to execute the laws of the Union, suppress insurrections and repel invasions." Congress also retains the authority "to provide for organizing, arming, and disciplining the militia, and for governing such part of them as may be employed in the service of the United States, reserving to the States respectively, the appointment of the officers, and the authority of training the militia according to the discipline prescribed by Congress."

The unresolved historic quarrel between an executive with constitutional authority as commander-in-chief to make war and a legislature with authority under the same Constitution to declare and pay for wars came to a head in 1974 at a time of executive weakness.[10] The outcome was the War Powers Resolution, passed in 1973 over President Nixon's veto. With some exceptions, the document limits to a 60-day window presidential authority as commander-in-chief to engage in warfare, pending approval for continuance by the Congress. In more than four decades since its passage, both Democratic and Republican presidents have objected to the War Powers Resolution on constitutional grounds because it infringes on executive authority. Nevertheless, all have tended to comply with its terms. None have wanted to submit the matter for resolution by the Supreme Court lest the latter make binding an interpretation adverse to the presidency.

Congress seeking to curb executive power is by no means new in the American experience. In this regard, there is a decided preference in the Anglo-American democratic tradition for smaller militaries— particularly smaller numbers of standing forces.[11] Alexander Hamilton —one of Washington's officers in the Continental Army—felt strongly that unity of the states and avoidance of European political entanglements made feasible a small army less injurious to civil liberties. The eighteenth-century framers of the US Constitution certainly thought so (see Hamilton's argument discussed in the next section) and Alexis de Tocqueville later allocated several chapters in his *Democracy in America* to this topic, noting that "a large army amidst a democratic people will always be a source of great danger." Consistent with these worries, standing forces in peacetime were kept small throughout the century and a half prior to World War II. By contrast, the large peacetime standing forces maintained by the United States during the Cold War (and to the present day) represent an historical aberration made necessary by understandings of national security concerns related to the US role as a global power.

Although a small military may be desirable in a democratic society, an isolated one decidedly is not. The ideal for the military member in a democratic society, then, is to be seen (and to be) a citizen like any other, but one who happens to be in uniform in direct service to the country. It was de Tocqueville who saw the importance in a "democratic army" of "the love of freedom and the respect of rights" as being "in common with their fellow-citizens."

ALEXANDER HAMILTON'S OPPOSITION TO LARGE STANDING ARMIES

Drawing on his own Revolutionary War experience in the Continental Army, New Yorker Alexander Hamilton addressed his concerns about challenges to civil liberties posed by the military in society.[12] He observes how security and order on the one hand can be at odds with civil liberties on the other:

> The violent destruction of life and property incident to war, the continual effort and alarm attendant on a state of continual danger, will compel nations the most attached to liberty to resort for repose and security to institutions which have a tendency to destroy their

civil and political rights. *To be more safe*, they at length become willing to run *the risk of being less free.*

In this regard, Hamilton warns against having large standing armies. They not only challenge the citizenry but also tend to increase the power of the executive, typically at the expense of the legislature that represents the people:

> The institutions chiefly alluded to are STANDING ARMIES and the correspondent appendages of military establishments. Standing armies ... are not provided against in the new Constitution; and it is therefore inferred that they may exist under it. Their existence ... is, at most, problematical and uncertain.

> But standing armies, it may be replied, must inevitably result from a dissolution of the Confederacy. Frequent war and constant apprehension, which require a state of as constant preparation, will infallibly produce them. The weaker States ... would first have recourse to them, to put themselves upon an equality with their more potent neighbors. They would endeavor to supply the inferiority of population and resources by a more regular and effective system of defense, by disciplined troops, and by fortifications.

> They would, at the same time, be necessitated to strengthen the executive arm of government, in doing which their constitutions would acquire a progressive direction toward monarchy. *It is of the nature of war to increase the executive at the expense of the legislative authority....*

Given these circumstances, Hamilton's remedy is to opt for a small army. In the absence of war, there is no need for large standing armies. Units in a small army called upon to deal with a small faction or other disruption in society will not threaten the population as a whole so long as the latter's numbers render them more than a match for military might.

> The smallness of the army renders the natural strength of the community an over-match for it; and the citizens, not habituated

to look up to the military power for protection, or to submit to its oppressions, neither love nor fear the soldiery; they view them with a spirit of jealous acquiescence in a necessary evil, and stand ready to resist a power which they suppose may be exerted to the prejudice of their rights. The army under such circumstances may usefully aid the magistrate to suppress a small faction, or an occasional mob, or insurrection; but it will be unable to enforce encroachments against the united efforts of the great body of the people.

Having been a soldier himself, Hamilton is well positioned to make an argument that, if made by another, might be dismissed as a prejudicial, antimilitary rant. No, Hamilton recognizes the importance of the military to defend the country and provide security to the citizenry. At the same time, however, he argues that small armies can accomplish this mission; small thus being not as threatening to civil liberties. He warns, however, how security challenges may lead to an expansion of the army:

> The perpetual menacings of danger oblige the government to be always prepared to repel it; its armies must be numerous enough for instant defense. *The continual necessity for their services enhances the importance of the soldier, and proportionably* [sic] *degrades the condition of the citizen.* The military state becomes elevated above the civil. The inhabitants of territories, often the theatre of war, are unavoidably subjected to frequent infringements on their rights, which serve to weaken their sense of those rights; and by degrees the people are brought to consider the soldiery not only as their protectors, but as their superiors. The transition from this disposition to that of considering them masters, is neither remote nor difficult; but it is very difficult to prevail upon a people under such impressions, to make a bold or effectual resistance to usurpations supported by the military power....

Finally, Hamilton notes how being across the Atlantic from European conflicts made large standing armies unnecessary for the new republic. At the same time, he notes the importance of maintaining security among the states through unity. Should the states divide—as they, in fact, would do in the Civil War, then large armies necessarily would form at the expense of civil liberties:

> If we are wise enough to preserve the Union we may for ages enjoy an advantage similar to that of an insulated situation. Europe is at a great distance from us. Her colonies in our vicinity will be likely to continue too much disproportioned in strength to be able to give us any dangerous annoyance. Extensive military establishments cannot, in this position, be necessary to our security.
>
> But if we should be disunited, and the integral parts should either remain separated, or, which is most probable, should be thrown together into two or three confederacies, we should be, in a short course of time, in the predicament of the continental powers of Europe—our liberties would be a prey to the means of defending ourselves against the ambition and jealousy of each other....

Hamilton's predictions were prescient. Indeed, civil liberties suffered infringement during and after the Civil War, particularly during the reconstruction period in the defeated South.

For most of the American experience, large armies were dismantled when the wars for which they were assembled had ended. The same historical pattern of demobilizing the army took place in the late 1940s after World War II had ended in the middle of the decade.[13] On the other hand, understandings of national security in the minds of decision makers had shifted dramatically from the Hamiltonian view that we could benefit from the insularity of the American geopolitical position. Decision makers in Washington now saw the United States as a global power, its national security integrally linked to events beyond American shores.

To them, the new reality that had emerged was the conflict between the United States and its allies on one side, and the Soviet Union and countries in its sphere of influence on the other. Crisis in a divided Berlin in 1948—with the Soviet Union denying access to American, British, and French forces the much-needed transit of supplies to the city—was a rude awakening for many who had not yet gotten the message that the Cold War had begun.

Consistent with the new grand strategy of containing the Soviet Union, formation of the North Atlantic Treaty Organization (NATO) in 1949 was the initial post-crisis response. Attack by communist North Korea against South Korea in 1950 sealed the argument in the minds of most American policy elites in both political parties. The United States was now a global power; its security was no longer afforded by a fortress America, stay-at-home foreign and national security policy. A large standing conscript army, navy, marines, and air force—augmented when needed by reserve and National Guard units—became the new order of the day.

CIVILIAN SUPREMACY AND CONTROL OF THE MILITARY

What, then, of Alexander Hamilton's concerns? With a large military establishment, the only remaining remedy lay in the long-standing American tradition of maintaining civilian supremacy and control over the armed forces. The new organization of the Defense Department in 1947 (see chapter 9) certainly reflected that concern. In the initial structure and subsequent reorganizations, the secretary of defense and secretaries of the three service departments (army, navy, and air force) remain positions held by civilians to whom the military chiefs of staff and commanders report. Accompanying this formal structure is the ongoing cultivation of the norm that, while inputs to decisions are routinely made by military officers, the ultimate decision-making authority lies in civilian hands. Indeed, the president to whom the civilians and their military commanders report is constitutionally the commander-in-chief of the armed forces—the entire military establishment.

Military challenges to civil authority have surfaced from time to time, but in each case the principle of civilian supremacy was not only sustained, but also strengthened. The most famous challenge in the post–World War II period was the clash over policy between President Harry Truman and five-star General Douglas MacArthur. Whereas the president wanted to take a more limited approach toward North Korea and China during the Korean War, the general favored a more assertive one. For his part, the general used the press and direct links to members of Congress to advance his case. When Truman subsequently relieved MacArthur in April 1951, the president underscored his rationale for doing so: "Military commanders must be governed by the policies and directives issued to them in the manner provided by our laws and Constitution."[14]

To buttress the public case for civilian supremacy over the military, the Kennedy White House supported the film production of the book *Seven Days in May*, a controversial Hollywood film with an all-star cast released in 1964.[15] The scenario addressed fears of a military coup by officers led by a General James Mattoon Scott—a combined caricature of two US generals famous for their right-wing views—Edwin A. "Ted" Walker (army) and Curtis E. LeMay (air force). In the film, General Scott develops a coterie of followers among generals and admirals, garners public support from speeches, and cultivates congressmen on Capitol Hill who share his right-wing, anti-administration views. In a similar vein, Peter Sellers and George C. Scott costarred in the 1964 celebrated cinema satire, *Dr. Strangelove*, which portrays a commander who—on his own volition—launches a B-52 bomber attack on targets in the Soviet Union.

These period pieces—reactions to military assertiveness by more outspoken generals—also tapped concerns about civilian control, norms more deeply held within American society. The issue was not new. Long-standing limits on the length of military service not only keep the forces younger than they otherwise might be, but also provide a hedge against politicization of the senior military leadership. Thus, mandatory retirement for all generals completing forty years of service (thirty-five years before a change in the law in 2007) is a legislative requirement intended both to keep the officer corps from aging and to provide upward mobility for more junior officers into positions vacated by officers joining the retired list.[16] At the same time, however, the requirement also keeps senior officers from having too much political power. Generals who reach four-star rank typically do not do so until their 30th or 31st years of service. Even then, as four-star generals or admirals, they may be moved about from place to place, one command to another.[17]

Were they inclined to do so, those stationed in Washington have too short a period of time to build a political base that in any way could challenge civil authorities. Exceptions to the thirty-five-year (now forty-year) mandatory retirement rule are rare, typically only afforded to the chairman of the Joint Chiefs of Staff (JCS) or other selected generals or admirals who serve at the pleasure of the president and secretary of defense. Not surprisingly, the only generals who achieve the status needed to become political are field commanders in wartime, like MacArthur, or those who have served as JCS Chairman for an extended period of time. For his part, Admiral Hyman G. Rickover—dubbed "Father of the Nuclear Navy" and who also cultivated personal allies on Capitol Hill —was finally forced by the Nixon administration to retire in 1982; he was then about to turn eighty-two years old, after some sixty years of commissioned service.

The longer that generals or admirals stay on active duty in Washington, DC, the more politically connected they tend to become. More important than any forty-year rule, rotations in command, or other administrative action, however, is the well-established, deeply embedded military norm of civilian supremacy that keeps military leaders in check, committed as they are to the missions that define their profession.

Machiavelli observed that "good laws and good armies" are "the principal foundations of all states." In this regard, he advocated reliance on "citizen armies" as the most effective form of defense for state and society. Those who share this view seek to approximate as many of the tenets of democratic civil-military society as are socially and politically feasible. Whether threats come from state or nonstate actors, *citizens who happen to be in uniform* have proven to be the most reliable contributors to national security.

The Role of Armed Forces in Democratic Civil-Military Society

Notwithstanding the eighteenth-century tradition of a military integrated with society, the American military in the nineteenth, twentieth, and twenty-first centuries has, in fact, followed more of a separatist path during the longer periods of peace between major wars. Reliance has been on smaller, professional standing armies backed up by the National Guard and reservists, except in major wars when military ranks swell with both conscripts and volunteers. Only since World War II, spurred by national security concerns during the Cold War and post–Cold War periods, have large standing armies, navies, and air forces been maintained in peacetime.

Large forces that draw heavily from society, particularly in the enlisted and noncommissioned officer ranks, tend by their nature to become somewhat more integrated than smaller professional militaries that run the risk of becoming isolated from the societal mainstream. Be that as it may, whether large or small, the degree of integration of standing professional forces that can or should be sought has remained a difficult and often contentious issue for the society and its policymakers.

As shown in table 11, personnel numbers in the US armed forces on active duty and in the reserves have declined since the All-Volunteer Force was established, particularly after the Cold War ended. Reduced numbers of ground forces have constrained US military options. The United States is no longer able to deploy troops at the 1991 Gulf War level of approximately 500,000 troops, much less at Vietnam-War level (some 550,000 in that country as well as others then deployed elsewhere in the region—Thailand, the Philippines, Taiwan, Japan, and South Korea), Europe and elsewhere. Commitments to Iraq and Afghanistan were relatively small compared to the Vietnam and Korean contingencies, which required many repeat tours of duty that degraded residual capabilities even further.[18] Even "surges" number only on the order of 30,000 when troops sought by commanders clearly exceeded these practical limits.

Table 11. Armed Forces: A Focus on the Army

	Armed Forces (All Services)	Active Duty Army	Army National Guard	Army Reserves
1973–1974 (Beginning of AVF)	2,391,000	801,500	402,300	261,300
1981–1982 (Beginning Reagan Era)	2,049,100	775,000	385,800	219,600
1989–1990 (End of Cold War)	2,124,900	766,500	587,000	610,800
2002–2003 (Post 9/11)	1,414,000	485,500	355,900	358,100
2013	1,520,100	600,450	358,200	205,000
2014	1,492,200	552,100	358,200	205,000
2015	1,433,150	520,000	354,200	205,000
2016	1,381,250	509,450	327,750	205,000
2019 (projected)		440,000–450,000		

Source. International Institute of Strategic Studies (London), *The Military Balance*, various annual issues, and DoD press release, February 24, 2014, for projected Active Duty Army strength in 2019.

MacArthur vs. Kennedy:
Separatist vs. Integrationist Arguments

What role should the military play in a society that puts civilians in operational control of the armed forces? What should be done by the military and what should be left for civilians—or should they be interchangeable? Speeches at the US Military Academy (West Point) by General Douglas MacArthur in May 1962 and a response by President John F. Kennedy at graduation ceremonies there in June outlined two very different views of the military and society—the role of the citizen as soldier.

For General MacArthur, as later with Samuel Huntington, the army (and implicitly the other services) should focus primarily on its military roles and missions, leaving other matters to civilian authorities. By contrast, as with Morris Janowitz,[19] President Kennedy urged the newly commissioned officers at West Point to think outside of the narrow military box and prepare themselves to take on a wide spectrum of policy-related tasks that are not solely confined to the military agenda.

In the absence of a draft that can draw from all segments of society, the American military does not reflect the demography, cultural values, and politics of the country as a whole, but rather these aspects of the parts of society from which its volunteers come. The historical, cultural, and legal traditions that underlie the concept of democratic civil-military society in the United States are also more along the lines of a more separatist military that both General MacArthur and Samuel Huntington advocated, as opposed to the more integrated one in the understandings of President Kennedy and Morris Janowitz, however more desirable the latter might be. We develop below these separatist and integrationist arguments, as framed respectively by General MacArthur and President Kennedy.

General MacArthur's professional life as a commander brought him into policy debates with civilian authorities. As noted earlier, differences with President Harry Truman over military strategy vis-à-vis North Korea and China during the Korean War resulted in MacArthur losing his command. The president (and many others among policy elites) believed that MacArthur had become too political. As President Truman (who as an army captain had served under General MacArthur's command in World War I) saw it, the general had exceeded his authority, the basis for relieving him of his command.[20] Hotly debated at the time—and accompanied by a ticker-tape parade in New York and a speech to a joint session of congress in Washington by MacArthur (the returning war hero to many)—this action nevertheless made crystal clear that civilian supremacy over the military was real.[21]

This episode aside, the general finally delivered his farewell address to West Pointers (and the army) in May 1962 at the age of eighty-two —from memory, without text or notes—more than a decade after being relieved of his command.

Framed succinctly, the question we pose here to both General MacArthur and President Kennedy is *Should the US military focus on combat alone—training and fighting wars in which they are called to serve (the "separatist" argument)—or is the mission broader, one that incorporates understandings of the armed forces in society both at home and abroad (the "integrationist" argument)?*

Notwithstanding his own practice and experience (or perhaps because of it), General MacArthur's rhetorical answer to this question is clear. In his May 1962 farewell speech delivered to the corps of cadets on the plain (parade ground) of the US Military Academy at West Point, New York, he stated: "Yours is the profession of arms, the will to win, the sure knowledge that in war there is no substitute for victory; that if you lose, the nation will be destroyed; that the very obsession of your public service must be: *Duty, Honor, Country.*"

He added:

> Others will debate the controversial issues, national and interna-
> tional, which divide men's minds; but serene, calm, aloof, you stand
> as the Nation's war-guardian, as its lifeguard from the raging tides

of international conflict, as its gladiator in the arena of battle. For a century and a half you have defended, guarded, and protected its hallowed traditions of liberty and freedom, of right and justice.

Let civilian voices argue the merits or demerits of our processes of government; whether our strength is being sapped by deficit financing, indulged in too long, by federal paternalism grown too mighty, by power groups grown too arrogant, by politics grown too corrupt, by crime grown too rampant, by morals grown too low, by taxes grown too high, by extremists grown too violent; whether our personal liberties are as thorough and complete as they should be. These great national problems are not for your professional participation or military solution. Your guidepost stands out like a ten-fold beacon in the night: *Duty, Honor, Country*.

Focusing on the youth before him, he honed in on what he thought should be their principal concern as future military officers—to fight and win the wars that the civilian leadership will put before them in their service to the nation:

You are the leaven which binds together the entire fabric of our national system of defense. From your ranks come the great captains who hold the nation's destiny in their hands the moment the war tocsin sounds. The Long Gray Line [of West Point alumni] has never failed us. Were you to do so, a million ghosts in olive drab, in brown khaki, in blue and gray, would rise from their white crosses thundering those magic words: *Duty, Honor, Country*.

This does not mean that you are war mongers. On the contrary, the soldier, above all other people, prays for peace, for he must suffer and bear the deepest wounds and scars of war. But always in our ears ring the ominous words of Plato, that wisest of all philosophers: "Only the dead have seen the end of war."

He poignantly concluded with personal reflections that brought him back to the separatist interpretation of "duty, honor, country" he so passionately advocated:

The shadows are lengthening for me. The twilight is here. My days of old have vanished, tone and tint. They have gone glimmering through the dreams of things that were. Their memory is one of wondrous beauty, watered by tears, and coaxed and caressed by the smiles of yesterday. I listen vainly, but with thirsty ears, for the witching melody of faint bugles blowing reveille, of far drums beating the long roll. In my dreams I hear again the crash of guns, the rattle of musketry, the strange, mournful mutter of the battlefield.

But in the evening of my memory, always I come back to West Point. Always there echoes and re-echoes: *Duty, Honor, Country.* Today marks my final roll call with you, but I want you to know that when I cross the river my last conscious thoughts will be of The Corps, and The Corps, and The Corps. I bid you farewell.

By sharp contrast, during the June graduation ceremonies the next month, President John F. Kennedy effectively responded to the general's thesis,[22] countering the separatist idea with an "integrationist" answer. First, Kennedy acknowledged increasingly complex, defense- and war-related responsibilities military officers assume:

I hope that you realize—and I hope every American realizes—how much we depend upon you. Your strictly military responsibilities, therefore, will require a versatility and an adaptability never before required in either war or in peace. They may involve the command and control of modern nuclear weapons and modern delivery systems, so complex that only a few scientists can understand their operation, so devastating that their inadvertent use would be of worldwide concern, but so new that their employment and their effects have never been tested in combat conditions.

On the other hand, your responsibilities may involve the command of more traditional forces, but in less traditional roles. Men risking their lives, not as combatants, but as instructors or advisers, or as symbols of our Nation's commitments. The fact that the United States is not directly at war in these areas in no way diminishes the skill and the courage that will be required, the service to our country which is rendered, or the pain of the casualties which are suffered.

Foreshadowing the large-scale US involvement in Southeast Asia during the Kennedy-Johnson years, Kennedy underscored the needed skills in unconventional warfare. It is not just a matter of confronting an enemy— infantry against infantry, armor against armor, artillery against artillery. To engage in such unconventional combat operations requires greater knowledge of the societies in which they conduct combat operations:

> To cite one final example of the range of responsibilities that will fall upon you: you may hold a position of command with our special forces, forces which are too unconventional to be called conventional, forces which are growing in number and importance and significance.... This is another type of war, new in its intensity, ancient in its origin—war by guerrillas, subversives, insurgents, assassins, war by ambush instead of by combat; by infiltration, instead of aggression, seeking victory by eroding and exhausting the enemy instead of engaging him. It is a form of warfare uniquely adapted to what has been strangely called "wars of liberation," to undermine the efforts of new and poor countries to maintain the freedom that they have finally achieved. It preys on economic unrest and ethnic conflicts. It requires in those situations where we must counter it, and these are the kinds of challenges that will be before us in the next decade if freedom is to be saved, a whole new kind of strategy, a wholly different kind of force, and therefore a new and wholly different kind of military training.

Having reinforced MacArthur's case that theirs *is* the profession of arms, Kennedy does not see it as their *only* task. In saying so, Kennedy challenges the narrower separatist argument offered by MacArthur. Adopting an "integrationist" perspective that includes, but goes well beyond merely the combat arms, Kennedy elaborated:

> But I have spoken thus far only of the military challenges which your education must prepare you for. The nonmilitary problems

which you will face will also be most demanding, diplomatic, political, and economic. In the years ahead, some of you will serve as advisers to foreign aid missions or even to foreign governments. Some will negotiate terms of a cease-fire with broad political as well as military ramifications. Some of you will go to the far corners of the earth, and to the far reaches of space. Some of you will sit in the highest councils of the Pentagon. Others will hold delicate command posts which are international in character. Still others will advise on plans to abolish arms instead of using them to abolish others.

Whatever your position, the scope of your decisions will not be confined to the traditional tenets of military competence and training. You will need to know and understand not only the foreign policy of the United States but [also] the foreign policy of all countries scattered around the world who 20 years ago were the most distant names to us. You will need to give orders in different tongues and read maps by different systems. You will be involved in economic judgments which most economists would hesitate to make. At what point, for example, does military aid become burdensome to a country and make its freedom endangered rather than helping to secure it? To what extent can the gold and dollar cost of our overseas deployments be offset by foreign procurement? Or at what stage can a new weapons system be considered sufficiently advanced to justify large dollar appropriations?

As future officers, they would be involved in major policy decisions including, but not just confined to, military matters narrowly construed:

You will need to understand the importance of military power and also the limits of military power, to decide what arms should be used to fight and when they should be used to prevent a fight, to determine what represents our vital interests and what interests are only marginal. Above all, you will have a responsibility to deter war as well as to fight it.... Our forces, therefore, must fulfill a broader role as a complement to our diplomacy, as an arm of our diplomacy, as a deterrent to our adversaries, and as a symbol to our allies of our determination to support them.

In a concluding thought, Kennedy brings the concept of duty—so central to MacArthur's speech—back into focus as encompassing combat, but so much more:

> West Point was not built to produce technical experts alone. It was built to produce men committed to the defense of their country, leaders of men who understand the great stakes which are involved, leaders who can be entrusted with the heavy responsibility which modern weapons and the fight for freedom entail, leaders who can inspire in their men the same sense of obligation to duty which you bring to it....
>
> The times, the weapons, and the issues are now more complicated than ever.... You and I leave here today to meet our separate responsibilities, to protect our Nation's vital interests by peaceful means if possible, by resolute action if necessary. And we go forth confident of support and success because we know that we are working and fighting for each other and for all those men and women all over the globe who are determined to be free.

Afterword

George Washington's assertion that "when we assumed the soldier, we did not lay aside the citizen" captures the ideal in US civil-military relations. Much later in time, another general—Douglas MacArthur—reminded us that the military purpose remains to fight and win America's wars. President Kennedy countered that performing the core combat mission, extraordinarily important as it is, was not enough. Much more will be expected of military officers in the decades to come, he said—total immersion in the national challenges of the day. Military members fully integrated with—not apart from—American society not only aid national purposes, but also provide a check, buttressed by strongly held military norms, against any military intervention in domestic politics.

Notes

1. B. Schwartz, *George Washington: The Making of an American Symbol,* (Ithaca, NY: Cornell University Press, 1987), 132. Early discussions with Norman Provizer, Metropolitan State University in Denver, underscored the importance of Washington's views on the "citizen soldier."

2. In *Soldier and the State,* Samuel P. Huntington observes: "Washington obeyed the Continental Congress not as a soldier but as a citizen." He also notes that "Washington and Hamilton were indeed the antitheses of the professional type, moving with ease from military to political office and back again."

3. Paul Leicester Ford, *The True George Washington* (Philadelphia, PA: J. B. Lippincott, 1902), 291.

4. Schwartz, *op. cit.*

5. In *Federalist Paper No. 8,* Alexander Hamilton argued that "the continual necessity for their services enhances the importance for the soldier, and proportionately degrades the condition of the citizen. The military state becomes elevated above the civil." Hamilton saw a remedy in the proposed union of states that would strengthen their security and reduce the need for large armies among them.

6. Referring to the British sovereign, the document asserts: "He has kept among us, in times of peace, Standing Armies without the Consent of our legislature; he has affected to render the Military independent of and superior to the Civil Power...; For quartering large bodies of armed troops among us: For protecting them, by a mock Trial, from Punishment; For any Murders which they should commit on the Inhabitants of these States."

7. The reference is to royalists to the Crown (the king and aristocracy) or to Cromwell (the popular forces—the nonaristocratic common people).

8. W. MacDonald, *George Washington: A Brief Biography* (Mt. Vernon, VA: 1973), 24 and 27 (originally published in *Encyclopedia Britannica,* 11th ed. 1910–1911).

9. In *Federalist Paper No. 41,* James Madison observes that "the best possible precaution against danger from standing armies is a limitation of the term for which revenue may be appropriated to their support."

10. The Watergate scandal led to the resignation of President Nixon.

11. In *Federalist Paper* No. 8, Alexander Hamilton states: "The smallness of the army renders the natural strength of the community an overmatch for it.... The army ... will be unable to enforce encroachments against the united efforts of the great body of the people."

12. See *Federalist Paper* No. 8 from which his words in this section are drawn. Italics have been added to emphasize key points in Hamilton's commentary.

13. In June 1945 there were 12 million Americans under arms. A year later, the number had dropped to three million and by June 1947 just 1.5 million. Figures on his rapid demobilization come from Dan Caldwell, Pepperdine University.

14. Truman's orders in annotated draft of message to Frank Pace, Douglas MacArthur, and Matthew Ridgway (c. April 1951): http://www.trumanlibrary.org/hst/l.htm (accessed November 29, 2013).

15. Based on a 1962 novel with the same title written by Fletcher Knebel and Charles W. Bailey II, the movie starred Burt Lancaster, Kirk Douglas, Richard March, and Ava Gardner. Press Secretary Pierre Salinger arranged White House availability for filming crews.

16. The Defense Authorization Act of 2007. On a case-by-case basis the president may also extend the mandatory retirement age from sixty-two to sixty-eight. See 10 USC 1253.

17. For more on civilian controls over the uniformed military, Peter D. Feaver, *Armed Servants: Agency, Oversight, and Civil-Military Relations* (Cambridge, MA: Harvard University Press, 2005).

18. See former secretary of defense Robert M. Gates's lecture at Duke University (September 29, 2010): "As a result of the multiple deployments and hardships associated with Afghanistan and Iraq, large swaths of the military—especially our ground combat forces and their families—are under extraordinary stress.... Consequences include more anxiety and disruption inflicted on children, increased domestic strife and a corresponding rising divorce rate ... and, most tragically, a growing number of suicides." On the secretary's perspectives of his time in office, see Robert M. Gates, *Duty: Memoirs of a Secretary of War* (New York: Vintage Books, 2014).

19. Morris Janowitz, *The Professional Soldier, A Social and Political Portrait* (Glencoe, IL: Free Press, 1960).

20. In a private meeting in December 1961 with President Truman in his Independence, Missouri library, historian Thomas Menza, then 17, recalls vividly how, when asked by him the rationale for relieving

MacArthur, Truman explained how he had been taught in the army under MacArthur's leadership in World War I to obey the chain of command. Had he not followed the chain of command, he (Truman) would have been held accountable by Macarthur or others under his command. MacArthur had deviated from that norm, so the president fired him. Per the author's conversations on several occasions with Thomas Menza, President Truman invited him into his office at his library in Independence, Missouri. Having just seen the library exhibit on President Truman relieving General MacArthur of his command in Korea, Menza innocently asked him why he had done that.

21. Some wondered why President Truman had taken so long to remove MacArthur from command. Truman's service under MacArthur in World War I and respect for his accomplishments as commander in the Pacific likely gave him pause. That both were "brothers" in freemasonry may have been another factor leading Truman to delay taking such an action. After all, Truman had been Grand Mason at the state level in Missouri, well acquainted with the freemasonic norms to which he subscribed.

22. At a West Point–sponsored student conference on U.S. affairs (SCUSA, c. 1990), I learned from faculty of the Social Sciences Department that their predecessors (who had been in communication with the President Kennedy's staff) had provided inputs to the speech writers. The integrationist theme in Kennedy's speech is consistent with the department's then-more expansive, progressive understanding of the military's role in society.

Chapter 8

A Diverse Military of Citizen Volunteers

Realizing the goal of the military member as the citizen who merely happens to be in uniform requires the armed forces to integrate successfully minorities, women, and persons of diverse sexual orientation or identity. An ideal or pure type provides a basis for assessing how near or far the American civil-military case is to each of the criteria identified with a democratic society. The end of the draft and formation of a new all-volunteer force in the early 1970s returned the country to its historical moorings that relegated the draft only to major wars, followed by dismantling the conscripted armed forces afterward. A Selective Service system remains in place should it be necessary to draft individuals over eighteen years old to their early-to-mid twenties, but expectations of a return to conscription are low in the absence of a major contingency. Finally, we take up the integration of minorities, women, and military members of diverse sexual orientation or identity in what remains an all-volunteer force.

AN IDEAL TYPE OF DEMOCRATIC CIVIL-MILITARY SOCIETY

Consistent with Max Weber's understanding, construction of an ideal or pure type gives us a benchmark or standard against which real-world cases can be compared. As such, a pure type of democratic civil-military society cannot, in fact, exist anywhere. The empirical can only approximate the ideal—this ideal or pure type a limiting case. Using pure types also gives us a degree of definitional precision in the use of concepts. Constructing an ideal or pure type of democratic civil-military society forces us to specify the attributes of such a society:

1. Military members are citizens in uniform. Members of the armed forces in a democratic society are full citizens completely integrated with other citizens in the society—*the military member is thus merely a citizen who happens to be in uniform.* Thus, these citizens in uniform have neither more nor fewer rights than those not in uniform. They **not only** have equal protection of the laws and other benefits **of citizenship, but also** the same obligations or duties **as civilians.** Military service is merely an activity the citizen may volunteer (or be called upon) to perform. It does not change his or her status as citizen.

2. The armed forces are representative of the people as a whole. The armed forces in a democratic society are representative of the people as a whole, *not drawn exclusively or disproportionately from particular segments:* socioeconomic classes; racial, ethnic, tribal, or other cultural identities; men or women regardless of sexual orientation or identity; or other categories that differentiate people in society. Thus, the armed forces are as diverse—as heterogeneous (or homogeneous)—as society is as a whole. Values held by military members also reflect the same degree of diversity found in society.

3. The military is separate from society only for military tasks. The military as corporate group is separated from others in society only to the extent that is functionally necessary to perform military tasks. Thus, combat effectiveness does require unit training and *esprit* *de corps* established within military units separated from those who are not part of these units. Military necessity, however, is narrowly construed as *the effort is not to separate but to integrate the military fully within society*. Separation from the rest of society is limited as much as possible by this narrow construction of military necessity. Some degree of separateness, of course, is true of any group; even nonmilitary citizens form to perform tasks in civil society. Pluralist, democratic societies are composed of groups, but these separate identities do not challenge democratic society so long as members of these groups remain integrated within society as a whole.

4. The military is politically subordinated to civil authorities. In democratic societies the military is politically subordinated to civil authorities who represent the people in society as a whole. Thus, society is inclusive of its military, which is not isolated from political or bureaucratic processes, but integrated within society as a whole and subordinated to civil authorities. Authority is delegated to military commanders who must carry out their assigned tasks, but military personnel are always accountable to civil authorities who retain ultimate responsibility and authority for the armed forces. The Clausewitzian view of the military as a means or instrumentality to policy ends, not as an end in itself, applies as much to democratic societies as it does to nondemocratic ones. Military inputs are part of the political or policy process; they are inputs similar to ones made by other citizens with expertise on issues facing policy makers.

In constructing this pure type, the focus is more on Morris Janowitz' s understanding in *The Professional Soldier* that seeks integration of the armed forces and society, not the separatist perspective offered by Samuel Huntington's *The Soldier and the State*[1] (whereby armed forces focus primarily on their own military purposes in service of national security objectives).

ASSESSING AMERICAN CIVIL-MILITARY SOCIETY

As we assess the US military in relation to this ideal type for a democratic civil-military society, we note some aspects close to the mark and others far from it.

1. Military members are full citizens. On the first element—that military members are full citizens completely integrated with other citizens in the society—citizens who merely happen to be in uniform, we find that they enjoy freedoms of speech and assembly, as with other citizens, so long as these do not become partisan or openly challenge military and political authorities to whom military members are subordinate. The American military norm is to remain aloof from partisan politics, but military members are encouraged to vote. Military personnel wishing to publish articles or books are subject not just to security, but also policy review—that they do not publish views critical of government policy, which remains a bone of contention, particularly among those who are academically or policy oriented.

On legal rights, efforts have been made in recent decades to improve due process for those facing disciplinary and administrative inquiries or hearings or, for criminal charges, courts martial. Critics sometimes cite World War I French prime minister (and also minister of war) Georges Clemenceau's "lock-step" interpretation that "military justice is to justice as military music [marches] is to music."[2] Using area defense counsel not subordinate to the commander is an attempt to compensate for the absence of separation of powers—the judiciary prosecutor, and jury (referred to as the "court martial board") all part of the military command.

In earlier centuries, global deployments far away from domestic courts made separate military courts martial a necessity. Although twenty-first-century worldwide communications and transportation make it possible for military personnel (as with civilians—fellow citizens not in the military) to be tried in civilian federal courts for alleged offenses, the likelihood of moving away from (much less eliminating) courts martial seems remote. Not only do the long-established tradition of using military courts created by legislative authority under Article I, Section 8,[3] of the US Constitution and rule-making authority of the Congress stand in the way, but so does strong resistance within the military because such a change would reduce the authority that commanders wield.

The line between systems of military discipline and justice is indeed a thin one—administrative, nonjudicial punishment in the former an alternative to legal action. Decisions to pursue legal actions against a military member are the prerogative of the commander. For disciplinary reasons or to maintain standards, the commander may decide to prosecute vigorously, even in less-serious cases that would not be pursued in civilian jurisdictions. At the same time, the commander's discretion can work to the advantage of the military member as when no, or lesser, charges are filed—a decision taken by the commander either because there is insufficient evidence or, due to the person's position or pattern of conduct, the commander elects not to bring the matter to court martial. This has become particularly problematic, however, in sexual assault or rape cases. Consequently, some members of Congress have favored taking the commander out of the loop on such matters, putting investigations and decisions to prosecute in legal channels.

A middle ground in statutory[4] and policy[5] reform expands rights of victims and puts military judges into the process of deciding whether to prosecute. Military judge advocates now have responsibility for both investigation of allegations and pre-trial hearings under Article 32, Uniform Code of Military Justice (UCMJ). The decision to prosecute remains with the commander at the 0-6 level (full colonel or navy captain) or higher, but except for "certain minor offenses" commanders are constrained from changing court martial outcomes based on such factors as the perpetrator's prior record. Military justice reform on such matters thus remains a work in progress—the attempt to provide justice to victims without, in DoD's view, unnecessarily undermining command authority.

2. The armed forces are representative of the people as a whole.
The second element—that the armed forces in a democratic society
are representative of the people as a whole, not drawn exclusively or
disproportionately from particular segments—is at odds demographically
with the all-volunteer force (AVF) as presently constituted. The AVF
tends to overrepresent southern, mountain west, and other rural areas
while underrepresenting northeast, west coast, and other urban areas.

In the absence of conscription, the demographic skewing away from
urban and suburban, northeast, and west coast populations likely will
persist. The net effect politically is to make the military decidedly more
rural than urban, as well as more Republican than Democratic. For those
concerned with sustaining a politically neutral civil-military balance,
having a military that is more demographically representative of the
entire American society remains an important objective.

Setting aside short-term cost considerations (which is never easy),
achieving greater representation across the society requires opening and
sustaining Reserve Officers' Training Corps (ROTC) units on college
campuses (to include state-supported, Ivy League, and other private
colleges and universities) in and around major cities throughout the
country, particularly in the northeast and on the west coast. Active
recruiting at the high-school level also can help draw more officers and
enlisted members from both underrepresented regions as well as some
from the more privileged strata of society. Finally, the army and air
National Guard units in each of the states provide a means for offsetting
regional and rural numbers in the active duty ranks as do reserve units
that, in principle, can draw more selectively from among volunteers
in their jurisdictions to achieve greater urban-rural and socioeconomic
balance.

Substantial progress has been made to integrate minorities, women,
and now people of gay or bisexual orientation as well as transgender
individuals, but doing so is an ongoing process that will take many decades
to accomplish fully, both in the military and in society as a whole. However

committed agents of change may be, cultural transformation does not come easily, much less quickly. The mission will be accomplished only when these distinctions—race or ethnicity, gender, or sexual orientation— no longer matter in daily military life. We take up this social-integration challenge in greater detail in three social studies later in the chapter.

3. The military is integrated within society. The military as corporate group—separated from others in society only to the extent that is functionally necessary to perform military tasks—is the third element of an ideal democratic civil-military society. To a substantial degree, the American AVF tends not to be closely integrated, but rather operates separately from the rest of society. Rather than conforming more closely to the pure type for democratic civil-military society, one finds military bases, forts, and posts constituting separate communities within society.

Allowing—even encouraging—military members to live in local communities rather than live on base or on post is one remedy. Postgraduate education programs for junior and mid-level military officers is another way to keep them connected to civil society. There is a "return" to civil society, of course, when leaving service, but even retirees usually maintain links to military associations. Some even spend their last decades in military retirement communities. Members of the National Guard and those in reserve units are the ones most integrated with civil society. Unless prolonged, their periods of active duty do not alter their societal links or identities as citizens merely performing military duties when called upon to do so.

4. The military is politically subordinated to civil authorities. Finally, on the fourth element—that in democratic societies the military is politically subordinated to civil authorities who represent the people in society as a whole—the American military gets high marks. Acceptance of civilian supremacy is the guiding principle. In a kind of participative democratic centralism, military personnel advise their civilian leaders, but readily shift to implementation when decisions finally are taken. Military subordination to civil authority—an extraordinarily important norm—is deeply embedded in the military cultures that define the active-duty all-volunteer force, National Guard units, and the reserves.

The Roots of the All-Volunteer Force (AVF)

More than four decades ago the AVF replaced post–World War II dependence on conscripts, itself an anomaly in an American experience that historically relied on volunteers in peacetime, draftees serving only in wartime. The AVF is now well into its "mid-40s" at the beginning of its "middle age."[6] We assess the AVF here in terms of both its capabilities and its relation to the society it serves. Put another way, how well does the AVF work as a strategic resource for the United States?

Although the US military may be the best-trained, well-equipped fighting force in the world, limits to its growth (or the speed by which it might expand) are critical factors that constrain US policymakers. When national objectives outstrip military capabilities, the strategic mismatch presents extraordinarily difficult challenges that force a trimming of objectives and acceptance of less-than-optimal decisions.

Technology only partially substitutes for troops—"boots on the ground"[7]—drawn from across American society. In this regard, we consider the American experience with respect to professional versus conscript armies, including the political unpopularity of selective service. For present and future policy makers, a central question is whether the AVF will continue to provide sufficient capacity to respond adequately to significant crises or other contingencies abroad.

Born in the crucible of societal conflict over the Vietnam War, the AVF effectively defused the antiwar movement, as secretary of defense Melvin Laird (1969–1973) and his successors, Elliot Richardson (1973), James Schlesinger (1973–1975), and Donald Rumsfeld (1975–1977), knew it would. Draft with deferments (draftees selected by local boards as part of the Selective Service System) had persisted after World War II in the post–Korean War, Cold War "peace" of the 1950s and 1960s. These deferments effectively gave those in the upper socioeconomic rungs of society a way to avoid military service altogether, with the burdens falling primarily on the middle, lower-middle, and working classes—much as they do now under the AVF.

In peacetime this was manageable. After all, defenders of the draft with deferments privileged the better off. Advocates of the AVF typically justified these arrangements as allowing those less fortunate an opportunity for upward social mobility. In wartime, of course, the unequal social distribution of the human cost of national service becomes more readily apparent.

This inequity of the draft with deferments was striking. Battlefield deaths, typically numbering almost 300 per week in the late 1960s at the height of the Vietnam War (in addition to the much larger numbers of those wounded in action), were borne primarily by those less privileged. It was a social inequity in want of a fix. In 1970, draft with deferments finally gave way to an annual lottery that, beginning in December 1969, rank-ordered draft-eligible men between eighteen and twenty-five years old. A random draw of 365 (or 366) birth dates for a given year established this rank-ordered list of dates and thus the likelihood of being called. This eliminated most deferments, many having worked to the advantage of young men of upper-middle and upper socioeconomic strata not wanting to serve in the battlefields of Southeast Asia.

With deferments made difficult, date of birth now mattered in this newly introduced, lottery-draft process. However greater the equity achieved, the lottery added fuel to the antiwar movement. Opposition to the war intensified as the draft now reached the sons of the more politically connected upper-middle and upper classes who could no longer readily obtain a deferment. There were also fewer opportunities to find the security provided in reserve and National Guard units then, with few exceptions, not subject to call-up. The lottery draft thus became combustible fuel for the growing antiwar movement. Society became extraordinarily turbulent and deeply divided. Campus protests, organized marches on the Pentagon, and horrific incidents occurred—perhaps the most volatile at Kent State University in Ohio in May 1970 when National Guard troops opened fire, killing four students and wounding nine more.

Consistent with the Nixon administration's "Vietnamization" policy (putting greater reliance on Vietnamese military and police and gradually winding down the commitment of US ground forces), the time was ripe for ending the draft and relying exclusively on volunteers—"professional" armed forces the historic American norm. No longer faced by draft calls, political opposition to the war continued, but at a much-reduced level of intensity. Progressive "Vietnamization" of the war—passing war fighting to the South Vietnamese armed forces, coupled with reduction in the number of American troops deployed in Southeast Asia, finally resulted in war termination in April 1975 when communist forces captured Saigon and established control throughout the country. To say the least, the South Vietnamese and American military defeat was extraordinarily hard for most Americans to accept. The widely held self-image of Americans never having lost a war until then resulted in a collective amnesia that lasted more than a decade until revisiting the war as an historical experience worthy of study became academically fashionable in the late 1980s.

After the defeat, healing such deep societal wounds became a high priority in both the Ford and Carter administrations with the AVF a cornerstone of a new national security policy. For many AVF supporters (including President Ford's secretary of defense, Donald Rumsfeld), the crisis was also an opportunity to return the United States to its historical reliance on volunteers when not engaged in major wars. It is a culturally based norm sustained to the present-time not just in the United States, but also in the United Kingdom and former British colonies or dominions within the Commonwealth. By contrast, continental European countries are just now moving away from traditions of citizen obligation established as the late eighteenth- and nineteenth-century legacy of the French Revolution—the *levée en masse*. Quite apart from preferences by many in the society to avoid mandatory military service, the principal rationale for ending conscription (shifting to a professional army) is both economic and reflective of the idea that a "zone of peace" has finally displaced the battlefield as Europe's historical mode. War among European states seems decidedly less likely now.

THREE SOCIAL CASE STUDIES: INTEGRATING AFRICAN AMERICAN AND OTHER MINORITIES, WOMEN, AND MILITARY MEMBERS OF DIVERSE SEXUAL ORIENTATION OR IDENTITY

The US military is a mirror of American society or, more precisely, the parts of society from which it is drawn. Substantial progress in American society as a whole toward greater acceptance of diversity in sexual orientation and identity, particularly among younger generations living in urban and suburban areas, has facilitated implementation of the "Don't Ask, Don't Tell" (DADT) repeal—much as changes in societal norms have facilitated (or constrained) the integration of women and minorities.

On race and ethnicity, gender, sexual orientation, and other identity issues, some critics complain about what they call social experimentation that they see undermining combat capabilities. These anti-integration opponents have always claimed that such diversity in the ranks would be prejudicial to good order and discipline and thus undermine unit cohesiveness and combat capabilities. Essentially this is the same argument made decades ago by those opposing inclusion of minorities and women—the claim more recently applied to gay, lesbian, bisexual, and transgender (LGBT) military members. However unfounded, the mantra has survived over the decades as an instrument intended to block such social progress.

Although there were well-publicized differences within the JCS on repeal, particularly while ground combat was still underway in Afghanistan, in fact the record shows that "since repeal [of DADT], within each service, there [were] isolated incidents, but almost no issues or negative effects associated with repeal on unit cohesion including

within war-fighting units."[8] The Commandant of the Marine Corps
testified before Congress that "he and his staff were careful to look for
issues during the training," adding "To be honest with you, we have
not seen it." From the front lines in Afghanistan, one Marine Corps
major general reported to the commandant, 'Sir, quite honestly they're
focused on the enemy.'"

While combat capabilities are the central focus in recruiting, organizing, training, and equipping armed forces, making militaries more
representative and compatible with the societies they defend is also
central to sustaining a democratic society in which civil-military relations
play so important a part. Applying combat-based standards of conduct
and realistic criteria for recruitment that are neutral in relation to race
and ethnicity, gender, sexual orientation or any other social criterion is
the approach recommended by those who see militaries as open to (and
broadly representative of) the citizenry as a whole.

Integrating African Americans and Other Minorities
In the first of the three social cases, the military was ahead of American
society in which segregation by race was still legal in the south and
other forms of discrimination against racial and ethnic minorities were
commonplace there and elsewhere in the country. By contrast, the armed
forces have been behind the pace set by more progressive forces in society
on integrating women—not to mention gay or bisexual and transgender
men and women.

However glacial the pace of change, substantial progress has been
made on integrating minority racial and ethnic groups in the decades
since President Harry Truman issued his executive order in 1948 directing
"equality of treatment and opportunity for all persons in the armed
services without regard to race, color, religion or national origin." It was
still a time of deep racial prejudice. After all, segregation by race was
legal in southern states until President Lyndon Johnson signed the Civil
Rights Act in 1964 sixteen years later.

African American soldiers fought in World War II (as in other wars going back to the American Revolution), but they did so typically in segregated units under command of white officers, many of whom were from the south and claimed (or were said to have) expertise in such matters. In fact, as one Inspector General (IG) Report (1944) indicates, the command was laced with prejudicial stereotypes then commonly held, particularly those alleging hypersexuality of African-American soldiers and an allegedly greater propensity to violence than white soldiers. The document is couched as an objective investigatory report but, taken as a whole, is more revealing of the IG 's own racism than of the several incidents the officer (a lieutenant colonel) addressed.[9]

Such deeply set, offensive understandings do not go away merely upon issuance of an executive order. The full integration of African American (and other ethnic minority) soldiers, sailors, and airmen would take decades to implement. Although as late as the Vietnam War, African Americans fought alongside other minority and white soldiers, in fact some slept in segregated barracks (allegedly their preference). Although there was no requirement to do so, individuals typically aggregated at tables in dining facilities by race.[10]

Mandatory racial-and-ethnic diversity training remained an essential part of the military experience in the 1970s and well into the 1980s. Although people of color registered socioeconomic gains from military service,[11] by 1979 the number of African American male enlistees in the army exceeded 36%, which constituted a disproportionate share of the burden of combat.[12] Reducing this imbalance somewhat were the rising numbers of Hispanics in the 1980s; the number of enlisting African Americans began declining in the 1990s.[13] African Americans also faced adverse "racial disparities" in the military justice system.[14] Retention and promotion rates (always indicators of how well accepted or integrated any group is) also lagged behind those of white soldiers and officers.[15] Such rates persist, notwithstanding ongoing DoD efforts to increase retention and promotion of minorities.

A congressionally sponsored Military Diversity Commission concluded that "the demographic composition of the officer corps is far from representative of the American population and . . . officers are much less demographically diverse than the enlisted troops they lead." Moreover, "with some exceptions, racial and ethnic minorities and women are underrepresented among senior noncommissioned officers."[16]

On ethnicity in the ranks: "While non-Hispanic whites make up 66 percent of the US population, they comprise 77 percent of active duty officers. Similarly, blacks account for 12 percent of the US population but represent just 8 percent of active duty officers. When it comes to Hispanic Americans, which make up 15 percent of the US population, they number only 5 percent of the officer corps." Finally, the data are most skewed in the flag ranks (generals and admirals): "The Army was the most diverse service, with minorities making up roughly 10 percent of its generals. In the other services, the minority general- or flag-officer population was 9 percent in the Marine Corps, 6 percent in the Navy and 5 percent in the Air Force."[17]

Militaries that reflect the degree of diversity of the countries of which they are a part contribute substantially to the viability of democratic civil-military society. The problem is not just one of proportional representation numbers, but also the opportunities to enter and advance within both enlisted and officer ranks. Discrimination thus continues to be a challenge, albeit not as severe as once was the case. Equal treatment in promotions as in other aspects of military life remains a core concern—much is still left to be done.

Integrating Women

In the second social case, if militaries are in fact representative of the societies they defend, then the challenge is to achieve greater integration and equal treatment of women. Modern technologies of warfare, which put greater emphasis on cognitive and motor skills than on brute strength, initially opened more avenues functionally to both men and women.

Whether for combat or noncombat tasks, *setting standards that are gender neutral* is the underlying social goal.

Women historically have played substantial roles in wartime duties (whether in battlefield medicine or clerical duties)[18] or, as in World War II, assigned to anti-aircraft batteries and tasked to ferry combat aircraft across oceans to the battlefront. Introducing women into the war effort challenged prevailing military-masculinist norms: "War (and the preparation for it)" was understood by many men as "'an entirely masculine activity' and the military experience as an initiation into manhood."[19] Given this well-established, socially constructed norm of war being an almost exclusively male preserve, formation in 1943 of the Women's Army Auxiliary Corps (WAAC) met substantial opposition by men in the military and in civilian life.

This was at the root of a slander campaign that alleged many of these women had loose morals, became pregnant, and had to return home. Following an FBI investigation, the allegations proved to be false, but the damage had been done. It was not until 1948 that the Integration Act finally gave women statutory legitimacy to serve in the military ranks— their numbers then constrained by a two percent ceiling, prohibitions on their engaging in combat, and denial by law of any chance for promotion to flag ranks. In succeeding decades these restrictions were gradually removed—the end of the draft and advent of the AVF in 1973 by necessity opening more opportunities for women.

In time, women were allowed to fly in combat-aircraft missions but were still barred from service in ground combat units.[20] This exclusion from combat positions also limited opportunities for promotion to command positions from which most flag officers (generals and admirals) are selected. Even in medical units, "military assignment policy" prohibited "the assignment of females to billets with high risk of combat exposure"—the consequence being lower promotion rates for enlisted women.[21]

These ground combat exclusions finally ended when Secretary of Defense Ashton Carter announced in December 2015 that DoD would open all "remaining occupations and positions to women" and that "there will be no exceptions."[22] A bold decision, but it likely will take years—probably decades—to effect full integration. Indeed, the integration of women in the armed forces has proven to be extraordinarily difficult for the women involved—harder even to achieve acceptance and coequality than the integration of gays, lesbians, bisexuals, and transgender which is now underway. Rape, sexual harassment, and sexism continue to challenge women in military units and offices.[23] Deeply set views among men (and many women) on proper male and female roles in the military pose major obstacles. In this regard, even as women in the air force and navy assumed pilot and other combat roles, their ground-force counterparts in army and marine units[24] were barred from even this opportunity. Excluding women from combat positions also reduced[25] their likelihood of promotion, particularly to colonel and flag-officer ranks.

One explanation for the difficulty women face lies in this "military masculinity" thesis argued by Aaron Belkin,[26] who draws as well from earlier work on gender and gender-related identities by Joshua Goldstein[27] and others. In the military ranks (as in societal understandings of the soldier's role), it still seems very much a man's world, particularly when it comes to ground combat.[28] The argument resonates with the work of Michel Foucault who wrote of the "relationship between a superior and a subordinate, an individual who dominates and one who is dominated, one who commands and one who complies, one who vanquishes and one who is vanquished."[29] Social constructions of military masculinity and the warrior ethic internalized by so many men—as well as the conflicting imperatives Belkin emphasizes in his account—pose formidable social and legal obstacles to women who seek to penetrate this male preserve, an inner sanctum of military masculinity.

For those women who do adopt (or adapt to) military-masculine expectations: "Their primary reference group is men (specifically military men), not women."[30] Indeed, as women "they may feel less opportunity and power" than when they identify with men.[31] At the same time, however, men may not reciprocate. Many may see themselves in male-dominant relationships with military women, which sometimes take the surface-level form of male-as-protector (often dominance in disguise) —"a clash between the traditional values of protecting women from the hardships and risks of direct combat versus the women's rights belief that men and women should be treated equally regardless of job difficulty or gender differences."[32]

Socially constructed, long-established martial values define this masculine space—strength, endurance, loyalty, bravery, honor, modesty, cleanliness, and rational control over one's impulses among those Belkin specifies.[33] In the displacement of emotions, he claims that repression of the "feminine" or nurturing side of men may result at times in outbursts of masculinist anger or aggressive acts in the field or with adverse effects on himself or family members at home. In this regard, domestic violence remains a significant problem in the military as are post-traumatic stress and suicide.

Complaints by men about women in the armed services often take the form of alleging that physical and other standards are lowered to accommodate them.[34] Pointing out that Olympic competitions divide men and women into separate competitive categories seems not to register. Nor does the claim that standards for a particular military function should be set independently of sex or gender—even if, as a practical matter, more men than women qualify in those requiring physical strength. Many also resent male commanders who are seen as protecting, paying deference to, or otherwise privileging women over men.

When we unpack these complaints, however, what we find is a military-masculinist bedrock held across the male ranks, particularly among soldiers and marines—the Marine Corps some years ago quite honestly seeking only "a few good *men*." It is against the backdrop of this embedded, masculinist-warrior culture that abuse of women occurs—sexism, sexual harassment, domestic (or workplace) violence and, in the extreme (though not uncommon), rape.

In a typical year, about 86% of sexual assaults in the army are women victimized by men; the navy 87%, marines 98%, and the air force 98%.[35] Incidents occur in all four services and across all officer, noncommissioned officer (NCO), and enlisted ranks, but most committed by enlisted men. Statistics by survey indicate about 26,000 cases of unwanted sexual contact, with only 3,600 actually reported. Failure to report indicates lack of trust in the system and fear of retaliation. Indeed, perpetrators are often in the victim's chain of command (25% of female victims and 27% of male victims were victimized by superiors), which underscores the lack of trust that victims have in the justice system and the fears they legitimately have of retaliation. The congressional response to this dilemma included inserting judge advocates general into the court martial process in sexual assault and rape cases, assigning professional military attorneys outside of the accused person's military chain of command.[36]

As with persons of color, promotion rates of women to senior positions also lags significantly behind men. The Military Leadership Diversity Commission found "very few females: only four percent of army generals, three percent of the marine generals, seven percent of navy admirals, and nine percent of the air force generals."[37] Dealing with promotions, adverse treatment of women, and working within the Department of Defense toward the goal of coequal treatment of women and men is the institutional domain of the Defense Advisory Committee on Women in the Services (DACOWITS) founded by Secretary of Defense (General) George C. Marshall in 1951.[38] The DACOWITS agenda still remains long more than six and a half decades later.

Numbers of women in the armed services make them a minority and, when their numbers drop below 20 percent, an even more defensive minority. There is a tendency, however, toward greater security in numbers,[39] particularly when any minority passes this empirical threshold.[40] Quite apart from gender-focused sensitivity and other forms of training, numbers matter.[41] Not only do women defend women more effectively when their numbers rise above 20–25 percent, but men are also more prone to join them to help counter untoward behavior directed against against women.

The issue of unequal treatment of women in general (including African American and other minorities in particular) has long been on the national (and, as noted earlier, the DACOWITS) agenda. Formidable obstacles challenge women; these seem even more difficult than those facing African American and other men of color who, once beyond the racial divide, can forge good working relationships with nonminority fellow soldiers through sharing the same military-masculinist culture, male bonding, and camaraderie. Indeed, the boundaries of military masculinity are pliable and can expand to include others not previously within the circle.

This military-masculinity construct—once largely confined to nonminorities—is not rigid. It can become more inclusive of others (including women who wish to adopt or practice these values). Short of changing the male-oriented warrior construct, Belkin notes how "both men and women can attain masculine status." In doing so, both "women and minorities have preserved military masculinity as an unproblematic identity that many Americans seek to emulate."[42]

Many women understandably resent having to adapt or alter their identities to comply with military-masculinist expectations as a prerequisite for successful careers in the armed forces. Over time (and with increasing numbers), women may succeed in redefining the construct to add more of the humane component associated with the feminine. Warriors can temper their masculinist toughness with greater degrees of understanding of human complexity without becoming "unmasculine," but such transformations are by no means assured. As with integrating African American and other minorities, the integration of women still leaves much to be done.

Integrating Military Members of Diverse Sexual Orientation or Identity

Governor William (Bill) Jefferson Clinton's campaign for president in 1992 included a commitment to follow President Truman's precedent by issuing an executive order to allow persons of diverse sexual orientation to serve in the armed forces. Soon after taking office in 1993, the new president's effort to deliver on his campaign promise ran into a firestorm on Capitol Hill.

Members of Congress, particularly on the Senate Armed Service Committee (chaired by Democratic Senator Sam Nunn) were joined in opposition to the policy change by the Joint Chiefs of Staff (then chaired by General Colin Powell). The claim that allowing gays to serve would be prejudicial to "unit cohesion"—good order and discipline[43] in the ranks —was essentially the same argument made against President Truman's 1948 decision to integrate African Americans and other minorities and efforts in the 1970s and 1980s to expand the roles open to women in the armed services.

Finding a middle course on the gay question was by no means easily accomplished.[44] The president's Article II constitutional authority as commander-in-chief to sign executive orders binding on the military was challenged directly by the congressional power in Article I, Section 8, of the Constitution to make rules for the armed services. That President Clinton and Senator Nunn were both southern Democrats made no difference; the two were at loggerheads.

Wisconsin Democrat Les Aspin, who had been chair of the House Armed Services Committee before becoming Clinton's secretary of defense, stepped into the breach in an effort to find a middle ground between the White House and the Congress. It was in this context that sociologist Charles Moskos (1934–2008), professor at Northwestern University and president (as well as chair) of the Inter-university Seminar on Armed Forces and Society (IUS), found a compromise in "Don't Ask, Don't Tell" (DADT) between the two deeply divided camps. To seal the compromise, it was passed into law, thus precluding any effort later to change the policy merely by executive order.

The intent of the new policy[45] may have been clear to those who crafted it, but implementation of "Don't Ask, Don't Tell" within the services was another matter. The "don't pursue" sentiment was quickly lost. Deeply held positions against homosexuality in the military culture led to interpretations of the law and policy that were at odds with original intent.[46] Discharge rates increased as aggressive pursuit of evidence became commonplace in many sectors of the armed services. Annual discharges of gay service members more than doubled in the first decade of DADT.[47] In essence, "Don't Ask, Don't Tell" had become worse for gay service members than before this compromise was put into law.

Nevertheless, the almost two decades of the DADT policy also witnessed substantial progress in American society as a whole toward greater tolerance and acceptance of openly gay men and women as well as those of bisexual orientation, particularly among younger generations living in urban and suburban areas. Not surprisingly, rural America in general and the south in particular have remained more socially conservative— less willing to tolerate (much less accept) homosexuals, often challenging their "alternative" life styles on religious and other grounds. Given the disproportionate numbers of those in the AVF that come from these areas, integration of openly gay or bisexual men and women has posed a greater challenge than if the armed services were more representative demographically of the society as a whole.

Former secretary of defense Robert M. Gates commented on this demographic asymmetry:

> The nearly four decades of all-volunteer force has reinforced a series of demographic, cultural, and institutional shifts affecting who is most likely to serve and from where. Studies have shown that one of the biggest factors in propensity to join the military is growing up near those who have or are serving. In this country, that propensity to serve is most pronounced in the South and the

Mountain West, and in rural areas and small towns nationwide—
a propensity that well exceeds these communities' portion of the
population as a whole. Concurrently, the percentage of the force
from the Northeast, the West Coast, and major cities continues
to decline.[48]

The military thus reflects the parts of society from which it is predominantly drawn—southern, mountain west, and other rural areas, not the urban and cosmopolitan centers and high-population states of the northeast and west coasts. An important exception to the general trend, of course, is recruitment from "inner-city" minority populations. Even with this asymmetry, however, the integration of men and women of gay and bisexual orientations and identities thus far has been easier to implement than many anticipated.[49] As in other countries,[50] unit cohesion and combat effectiveness apparently have not been adversely affected by the policy change as opponents had predicted.[51]

Militaries drawn from across society tend to reflect the same distribution of values and cleavages to be found in the society from which they are drawn. Not surprisingly, if they are drawn disproportionately from certain parts of society, the cultural values and social structures of these parts of society also will be represented disproportionately within a country's military. Rural, socially conservative values against same-sex relationships, for example, tend to be more prevalent among military personnel from rural areas than among those from more cosmopolitan, urban sectors where secular tolerance or live-and-let live values are more commonly held. Similarly, the less-than-equal roles and treatment of women in the military are due not only to traditional values that largely reserved military service to men (the military-masculinity construct discussed earlier), but also to socially conservative values toward women that reflect the social origins of military members holding these views.

Nevertheless, early findings indicate that integration of openly gay or bisexual men and women is easier to accomplish than the integration of women has proven to be. Research before the repeal of DADT had shown that 57.1% of military academy cadets favored the ban against admitting persons of same-sex orientation (compared to 46.5% of cadets in ROTC units and just 14.0% of undergraduates in civilian colleges and universities).[52]

However, my conversations with cadets and officers at the U.S Air Force Academy—on the fourth day after the repeal of "Don't Ask, Don't Tell" became effective—told a different story. To them, it was less of an issue than some expected, particularly among younger generations. Some cadets had already come out on Facebook—some surprises noted, but general acceptance by other cadets—even by those with strong religious convictions against homosexuality.[53]

The cadets (in their late teens and early twenties) for the most part were well beyond mere tolerance to varying degrees of acceptance—finding value in fully integrating people of diverse orientation. When asked why this was so, the respondents reflected on diversity-acceptance learning in school experiences, influences on their attitudes from movies; entertainers and sports figures who have come out; and messages in mass media, internet, and social networks. The positive effect of training sessions on accepting diversity in sexual orientation was also apparent.

At the US Naval Academy, same-sex couples were allowed to attend the May 2012 Ring Dance for rising seniors,[54] thus setting a significant precedent, to say the least a major departure from past practice at any of the service academies. The generational difference at the time was clear, however, when cadet attitudes were compared to Army officers and noncommissioned officers (NCOs), men in their thirties and forties with deeply held prejudices, some religiously based. All indicated, however, that they would comply with the new policy notwithstanding their own personal reservations.[55]

Indeed, the common thread articulated by members of the armed forces is their expressed commitment to following orders issued by the commander-in-chief and secretary of defense, whatever their personal views on homosexuality might be. Officers, NCOs, and cadets often cited the long-established norm of subordination to civil authority as instrumental in effecting this compliance. Moreover, DoD and the services implemented mandatory training for both military members and civilians, thereby systematically preparing the groundwork for the change in policy.[56]

Army training programs on the repeal of DADT, for example, specified ten principles designed to assure compliance:[57]

(1) Leaders have the task of implementing the new policy and thus are its "face."

(2) Standards of conduct apply to everyone regardless of sexual orientation. Among other things, this means that standards on public displays of affection will be not be different regardless of sexual orientation.

(3) Dignity and respect standards apply to everyone who wears the uniform regardless of sexual orientation.

(4) Rules and policies must be sexual-orientation neutral. This applies primarily to promotions and transfers.

(5) Given the professional commitment of soldiers, the order has been given and anyone who wears the uniform will carry it out.

(6) Anyone who wears the uniform is a soldier and should be treated as such regardless of sexual orientation.

(7) There is no expectation that soldiers will need to change their religious or moral views in order to accommodate the change in policy.

(8) There is no expectation that soldiers have to like the new policy; they merely need to carry out or comply with it.

(9) Army chaplains have "the right to serve and conduct religious services according to their faith and a duty to perform or provide religious support.

Finally, summing up the net effect of the previous nine principles:

(10) Soldiers should stay focused on their mission, which is to fight and win wars.

Comments made by Army officers on the change in policy indicated that there were likely far greater numbers of gays, lesbians, and bisexuals who would remain "closeted"—perhaps a latent support base for those who had come out. In this regard, "few gays or lesbians . . . come out of the closet in units where hostility and homophobia prevail."[58] Aware of the greater diversity than reported, cadets at the Air Force Academy indicated that they knew gay classmates who likely would not come out for their own personal reasons. They also suggested a greater propensity for women to come out than men—even among the entering class still in basic training.[59]

Conversational references to remaining "closeted" or "coming out" lead us to differentiate analytically between the underlying sexual orientation people have from their public and private identities. In an ideal circumstance orientations and identities would be the same but, as is well established, social pressures lead many gay and bisexual persons to adopt heterosexual ("straight") identities as their public face, sometime even denying to themselves the orientation they actually have (their private identities) in favor of the more socially accepted straight identities. As always, accurate numbers on sexual orientation and identity are elusive —more a matter of conjecture than anything more concrete. Bisexuality in particular remains an underreported orientation in society as a whole and the military in particular.

Addressing the need for a support group, in May 2012 the Air Force Academy officially recognized Spectrum, a cadet organization to "facilitate peer support, professional networking, and mentorship among gay, lesbian, bi-sexual, and questioning (GLBQ) cadets." It followed the Spectrum initiative at the US Coast Guard Academy—an organizational precedent set in December 2011,[60] subsequently in different stages of development at West Point, Annapolis,[61] and the Air Force Academy.

For its part, the Air Force Academy group promotes "respect, through education and advocacy, for GLBQ individuals" and will "maintain a framework of safety that protects the social well-being of each individual participant."[62]

Spectrum at the Air Force Academy is linked to the Blue Alliance —LGBT alumni affiliated with the Association of Graduates (AOG),[63] which also provides a path for reconnecting "many LGBT USAFA alumni who have over time been disassociated from the Academy and the AOG because of their sexuality or gender identity." The Blue Alliance is linked to its counterpart groups at West Point and Annapolis: Knights Out (US Military Academy alumni) and USNA Out (US Naval Academy alumni).[64] Among the other links the Blue Alliance identifies are Service Members United, *Gay Military Signal* (a prominent newsletter), and the Palm Center (the NGO that played a significant part in scholarly and politically connected work on Capitol Hill in the effort to repeal DADT and subsequently worked to legalize service by transgender military members).[65] Another widely read newsletter is *Outserve.*[66]

These grassroots efforts are buttressed by DoD, most notably in its first LGBT Pride Month event (June 27, 2012) addressed by President Obama, Defense Secretary Leon Panetta, and DoD General Counsel Jeh Johnson. In Johnson's keynote address, he provided assurance of the department's ongoing efforts to implement the repeal and address the remaining challenges under the Defense of Marriage Act (DOMA). The session concluded with a panel on "The Value of Open Service and Diversity."[67]

To put these positive findings in perspective, however, we also note problematic incidents that no doubt will continue to surface from time to time. For example, in 2013 the Air Force Academy hired a counselor in its character and leadership center who had previously worked as a conversion therapist in gay-to-straight transformation efforts. The man was also associated with the Focus on the Family organization that, on religious grounds, took positions against marriage equality and related same-sex social questions.[68]

After an inquiry into the hiring process, the Air Force Academy concluded that it was compliant with DoD procedures; thus there was no legal basis for the individual's termination. At the same time, however, the academy's superintendent indicated the academy would "continue to reinforce and foster a culture of dignity, respect and inclusion for all"—the aim "to eliminate negative sub-cultures, . . . illegal activities and sexual assault." She added: "As we develop lieutenants prepared to lead in our Air Force and in our nation, it is critical that we have a safe, non-threatening environment for every Airman—cadet, faculty and staff—regardless of sex, race, origin, orientation, ethnicity, religion, language, culture, or life experiences."[69]

Reading between the lines, the statement makes abundantly clear that implementing social change is hardly an overnight matter, but rather a decades-long process. Military posts and bases varied on same-sex married partner rights that also varied state-by-state until the Supreme Court finally legitimated same-sex marriage in its June 26, 2015 decision.[70] Prior to that decision, military members were allowed to use base or post chapels for this purpose only in states allowing such marriages even though Section 3 of DOMA that had prohibited same-sex marriage was overturned as a federal matter. Same-sex couples were permitted to travel to another state on leave or on permissive (self-funded) temporary duty (TDY) orders and, upon return to their post, base, or ship of assignment receive housing, medical, survivor, commissary and exchange, and other federal benefits to which opposite-sex spouses or family dependents were entitled.

Finally, as many as an estimated 15,500 transgender persons are now serving in the armed forces.[71] Given the success in repealing DADT, those seeking to end prohibitions on military service across the LGBT spectrum[72] turned their focus to allowing transgender members to serve openly. In July 2015, Secretary of Defense Ashton Carter responded by initiating a six-month study designed to effect integration of transgender members. In fact, it took a year of work across the services before

Secretary Carter announced his decision to open without exception all military and civilian positions in DoD to transgender persons.[73]

Not just in society as a whole but also in the military, transgender persons often feel marginalized even by lesbians, gays, and bisexuals. As one transgender retired officer put it: "LGB" refers to sexual orientation or identity, "T" alone to gender identity. Thus, the LGBT designation really refers to two very different categories of identity.

As with the other two social cases on women and minorities, much remains to be done to achieve a degree of social integration that mirrors progress on the same issues in the American society from which the armed forces are drawn.

AFTERWORD

A military that mirrors the diversity of the society it is pledged to defend is what one expects in a democratic society. Achieving coequality of military members from these groups with others in the majority is more than a mere declaration of intent. It is an important part of a decades-long project in society as a whole, the military in particular.

NOTES

1. Samuel Huntington, *The Soldier and the State* (New York: Vintage Books, 1964).

2. See Robert Sherrill, *Military Justice is to Justice as Military Music is to Music* (New York: Harper Colophon Books/Harper & Row, 1969, 1970), 2. By contrast, there is the saying: "If you're guilty, opt if you can for a civil trial; if innocent, a military trial."

3. "To make rules for the government and regulation of the land and naval forces."

4. National Defense Authorization Act for Fiscal Years 2014 and 2015.

5. Department of Defense, Office of the General Counsel, "The Military Justice System's Response to Unrestricted Reports of Sexual Assault," October 30, 2014. Source: http://www.sapr.mil/public/docs/reports/FY1 4_POTUS/FY14_DoD_Report_to_POTUS_Annex_4_OGC.pdf, accessed June 10, 2016.

6. For an excellent, comprehensive history of the AVF, see Bernard Rostker, *I Want You: The Evolution of the All-Volunteer Force* (Santa Monica, CA: RAND Corporation, 2006).

7. Although the metaphor "boots on the ground" is in common use, the author prefers "troops on the ground." The word "troops" puts emphasis on the human dimension of citizens in uniform called upon to serve and make sacrifices. Boots are easily replaced. The men and women who bear the wounds and loss of life in combat are not.

8. DoD General Counsel Jeh Johnson (June 27, 2012). The same conclusion about the relative ease of GLBT integration is reported in Aaron Belkin *et al.*, "Readiness and DADT Repeal: Has the New Policy of Open Service Undermined the Military?" *Armed Forces & Society* 39 (October 2013): 587–601.

9. I have accessed this unpublished IG Report of incidents related to soldiers in the North African theater in World War II.

10. Conversation and what I observed at an air force billeting facility at Tan Son Nhut air base in Saigon, 1968–1969.

11. See Roger D. Little and J. Eric Fredland, "Veteran Status, Earnings and Race," *Armed Forces and Society* 5, no. 2 (February 1979): 244–260.

12. See Charles C. Moskos in "Symposium: Race in the United States Military," *Armed Forces and Society* 6, no. 4 (Summer 1980): 589.

13. David J. Armor and Curtis L. Gilroy, "Changing Minority Representation in the U.S. Military," *Armed Forces and Society* 36, no. 2 (January 2010): 223–246.; cf. Armor's earlier "Race and Gender in the U.S. Military," *Armed Forces and Society* 23, no. 1 (Fall 1996): 7–27 and 2.

14. Dan Landis, Mickey R. Dansby, and Michael Hoyle, "The Effects of Race on Procedural Justice," *Armed Forces and Society* 24, no. 2 (Winter 1997): 183–220, the quote from p. 206.

15. On challenges the civilian and military leadership faced on racial integration during this period, see Moskos in "Symposium: Race in the United States Military," op. cit., 586–613.

16. Ibid.

17. Daniel Sagalyn, "Report: U.S. Military Leadership Lacks Diversity at Top," PBS NewsHour summary at http://www.pbs.org/newshour/rundown/20 11/03/military-report.html, accessed August 18, 2012. For the full Military Leadership Diversity Commission (MLDC) Report (2011): https://www. hsdl.org/?abstract&did=11390.

18. Linda Grant De Pauw, "Women in Combat: The Revolutionary War Experience," *Armed Forces and Society* 7, no. 2 (Winter 1981): 209–226.

19. Regina F. Titunik, "The First Wave: Gender Integration and Military Culture," *Armed Forces and Society* 26, no. 2 (Winter 2000): 240. Titunik's quote on the military as masculine activity is from John Keegan, *A History of Warfare* (New York: Alfred A. Knopf, 1993), 8–9.

20. Ibid., 241–243.

21. Lawrence V. Fulton *et al.*, "Policy Implications for Female Combat Medic Assignment: A Study of Deployment and Promotion Risk," *Armed Forces and Society* 38, no. 3 (July 2012): 500–512, the quote from p. 500.

22. Department of Defense, Press Briefing by Secretary of Defense Ashton Carter, December 3, 2015.

23. The problem has persisted over decades to the present. See, for example, Juanita M. Firestone and Richard J. Harris, "Sexual Harassment in the U.S. Military: Individualized and Environmental Contexts," *Armed Forces and Society* 21, no. 1 (Fall 1994): 25–43; Leora N. Rosen and Lee Martin, "Sexual Harassment, Cohesion, and Combat Readiness in U.S Army Support Units," 24, no. 2 (Winter 1997): 221–244; and Juanita M. Firestone and Richard J. Harris, "Sexual Harassment in the U.S. Military Reserve Component: A Preliminary Analysis," *Armed Forces and Society* 36, no. 1 (October 2009): 86–102.

24. On gender discrimination, see Emerald M. Archer, "The Power of Gendered Stereotypes in the US Marine Corps, *Armed Forces and Society* 39, no. 2 (April 2013): 359–391.

25. Ibid., 80.

26. Aaron Belkin, *Bring Me Men, Military Masculinity and the Benign Façade of American Empire* (New York: Columbia University Press, 2012). See also his earlier "'Don't Ask, Don't Tell,': Does the Gay Ban Undermine the Military's Reputation," *Armed Forces and Society* 34, no. 2 (January 2008): 276–291.

27. Joshua Goldstein, *War and Gender: How Gender Shapes the War System and Vice Versa* (Cambridge, UK: Cambridge University Press, 2001).

28. Male bonding in units linked to hypermasculine understandings are a substantial challenge to women in military units. See Leora N. Rosen, Kathryn H. Knudson, and Peggy Francher, "Cohesion and the Culture of Hypermasculinity in U.S. Army Units," *Armed Forces and Society* 29, no. 1 (Spring 2003): 325–349.

29. Michel Foucault, *The History of Sexuality*, trans. Robert Hurley, vol. 2 (New York: Vintage Books, 1984, 1990), 215.

30. Karen O. Dunivin, "Gender and Perceptions of the Job Environment in the Air Force," *Armed Forces and Society* 15, no. 1 (Fall 1988): 86.

31. Whether in the military, the corporate world, or the professions, not all women adopt a masculinist approach when dealing with male counterparts. Sociologist Wilford Scott observed the work of Rosabeth Moss Kanter, *Men and Women of the Corporation*. 2nd ed. (New York: Basic Books, 1977, 1993), in which she identified five different or alternative coping strategies in "gendered" organizations in which women comprised less than 30%, particularly in which they were a distinct minority on the order of 10–15 or 20% or fewer: (1) "honorary male" exhibiting a more masculine mode of conduct and interaction with men, (2) the "tough" female role, (3) motherly or nurturing, (4) flirtatious, and (5) passive.

32. Armor, 24. See also Iris Marion Young, "The Logic of Masculinist Protection: Reflections on the Current Security State," *Journal of Women in Culture and Society* 29, no. 1 (2003).

33. Belkin, 4. See also Sabine T. Koeszegi, Eva Zedlacher, and René Hudribusch, "The War Against the Female Soldier? The Effects of Masculine Culture on Workplace Aggression," *Armed Forces and Society* 40, no. 2 (April 2014): 226–251.

34. This complaint is a repetitive theme in the interviews that my research associate and I conducted in 2011 and 2012.

35. See DoD's *Annual Report on Sexual Assault in the Military* (FY12): http://www.sapr.mil/index.php/annual-reports. I owe thanks to Research Associate Eric de Campos for his study of this extensive report.

36. The National Defense Authorization Act (December 2013) thus amended the *Uniform Code of Military Justice* (UCMJ): Articles 32 (investigation), 60 (action by the convening authority), 120 (rape and carnal knowledge) and 125 (sodomy). See David Vergun, "New Law Brings Changes to Uniform Code of Military Justice," *Army News Service*, January 8, 2014.

37. MLDC Report, *op. cit*; cf. http://www.pbs.org/newshour/rundown/201 1/03/military-report.html.

38. For its website, see http://dacowits.defense.gov.

39. In one study "a higher percentage of females was associated with greater acceptance of women and less sexual harassment." See Rosen and Martin, 236.

40. Conversation I had with a sociologist, a civilian woman, took place during a student conference on U.S. affairs (SCUSA) held at the U.S. Military Academy (West Point) in 1990.

41. As one study notes: "Women make up half of the United States population but a mere 15 percent of the military." See David E. Rohall, Morten G. Ender, and Michael J. Matthews, "The Effects of Military Affiliation, Gender, and Political Ideology on Attitudes Toward the Wars in Afghanistan and Iraq," *Armed Forces and Society* 33, no. 1 (October 2006): 75; cf. Armor, 24. On the other hand, some observed a decline in unit cohesion when the proportion of women in a unit increases substantially. See Leora N. Rosen *et al.*, Gender Composition and Group Cohesion in U.S. Army Units: A Comparison across Five Studies, *Armed Forces and Society* 25, no. 3 (Spring 1999): 382.

42. Belkin, 6.

43. The language was institutionalized by statute (10 USC 654). In fact, "DADT repeal has had no overall negative impact on military readiness...." See "Readiness and DADT Repeal: Has the New Policy of Open Service Undermined the Military?" in *Armed Forces and Society* 30, no. 4 (October 2013): 587.

44. Formal prohibition against same-sex relationships while in military service were put in place as the United States mobilized for World War I in 1916 and later strengthened in World War II—those of gay or bisexual orientation subject to discharge.

45. "Don't Pursue" gay service members who "Don't Tell" was the apparent intent; however, the "Don't Pursue" phrase was omitted in the final legislation.

46. The now-classic discussion of these prejudices is Randy Shilts, *Conduct Unbecoming: Gays and Lesbians in the U.S. Military* (New York: St. Martin's Press, 1993); cf. Mary Ann Humphrey, *My Country, My Right to Serve: Experiences of Gay Men and Women in the Military, World War II to the Present* (New York: Harper Collins, 1988).

47. The rate increased from 40 per 100,000 in 1993 to about 88 per 100,000 in 2002. By 2010 the discharge rate had declined to 35 per 100,000, but enforcement had become very uneven both across the services and among units within a particular service. See U.S. Department of Defense, *Report of the Comprehensive Review of the Issues Associated with the Repeal of 'Don't Ask, Don't Tell,'"* 23 at http://www.defense.gov/home/features/20 10/0610_dadt/DADTReport_FINAL_20101130(secure-hires).pdf

48. Lecture at Duke University (September 29, 2010).

49. For diverse attitudes on homosexuality in the military, see James E. Parco and David A. Levy (eds.), *Attitudes Aren't Free: Thinking Deeply About Diversity in the U.S. Armed Forces* (Montgomery, AL: Air University Press, 2010), 139–298; cf. Wilbur J. Scott and Sandra Carson Stanley (eds.), *Gays and Lesbians in the Military* (New York: Aldine de Gruyter, 1994).

50. For example, Israel ended its ban on gay soldiers in 1993 apparently without undermining "operational effectiveness, combat readiness, unit cohesion, or morale." See Aaron Belkin and Melissa Levitt, "Homosexuality and the Israel Defense Forces: Did Lifting the Gay Ban Undermine Military Performance?" in *Armed Forces and Society* 27, no. 4 (Summer 2001): 544 and 558. The same has been true in Canada (1992), the UK (2000), Australia (1992), New Zealand (1993), continental Europe, and other high-income countries. Leader of the pack was the Netherlands (1974)!

51. See Bonnie Moradi and Laura Miller, "Attitudes of Iraq and Afghanistan War Veterans Toward Gay and Lesbian Service Members," *Armed Forces and Society* 36, no. 3 (April 2010): 397–419.

52. See Morton G. Ender *et al.*, "Civilian, ROTC, and Military Academy Undergraduate Attitudes toward Homosexuals in the U.S. Military," *Armed Forces and Society* 38, no. 1 (January 2012): 164–172. The data is on p. 167.

53. The conversations took place on September 23, 2011. Subsequent conversations in July and August 2012 sustained these findings.

54. See the report and photos at http://usnaout.org/120520-ring-dance. Alumni were an important support group for the effort—in their words a "'link in the chain' to fulfill the USNA Out mission of 'changing lives and minds of alumni and midshipmen.'"

55. Conversations reported by a research associate in July and August 2011 at Fort Carson in Colorado Springs, Colorado.

56. See the U.S. Department of Defense study "Report of the Comprehensive Review of the Issues Associated with the Repeal of 'Don't Ask, Don't Tell'" and the "Support Plan for Implementation" (November 30, 2010), which were the bases for the service departments to develop their own implementation plans and training packages.

57. My research associate represented these principles as they were understood by those tasked with their implementation at Fort Carson.

58. Aaron Belkin and Melissa Levitt cite this observation by Laura Miller. See Belkin and Levitt, 558.

59. This finding, reaffirmed in conversations with LGB cadets in October 2013, supports Aaron Belkin's view that women in the military are more likely than men to come out. He also observes that the proportion of lesbians in the military is likely higher than in society as a whole, the proportion of gay men in the military is likely lower than in the overall population (conversation with Belkin, May 2013).

60. See http://coastguard.dodlive.mil/2012/03/spectrum-helps-cga-produce-leaders-of-character (March 14, 2012 post on the official blog of the U.S. Coast Guard: "Coast Guard Compass") and http://thinkprogress.org/lgbt/2012/03/27/452385/gay-and-lesbian-cadets-find-acceptance-in-wake-of-dont-ask-dont-tell-repeal.

61. Source http://usnaout.org/spectrum subsequently taken offline.

62. The group initially had a website, https://sites.google.com/site/spectrumusafa, (a rainbow part of its logo) where its mission and objectives were posted, also information on LGBT history, culture, and the "straight perspective."

63. For more on its work, see http://blue-alliance.org.

64. See KnightsOut.org and USNAOut.org; for the latter, see http://usnaout.org/spectrum.

65. See http://www.servicemembers.org, http://www.gaymilitarysignal.com, and http://www.palmcenter.org.

66. See http://outservemag.com. Issues can be found electronically at http://outservemag.magcloud.com.

67. For video of speeches at the first DoD LGBT Pride Month event (June 27, 2012) by President Obama, Defense Secretary Panetta, and DoD General Counsel Jeb Johnson's keynote address, which provides a summary of the government's work implementing the repeal of DADT legislation followed by a panel discussing "The Value of Open Service and Diversity" on YouTube.

68. See Lila Shapiro, "Gay Cadet Lashes Out At Air Force Press Release Claiming Gays Are Welcome," *Huffington Post*, November 21, 2013.

69. See "Media Advisory: Statement from U.S. Air Force Academy Superintendent, Lt. General Michelle D. Johnson, on Dr. Mike Rosebush's employment at USAFA," posted December 21, 2013.

70. *Obergefell v. Hodges*.

71. The estimate is based on research for society as a whole indicating about 0.3% are transgender.

72. Aaron Belkin's Palm Center, for example, has transgender integration in the armed forces as a top priority.

73. U.S. Department of Defense, "Secretary of Defense Ash Carter Announces Policy for Transgender Service Members," news release, June 30, 2016, http://www.defense.gov/News/News-Releases/News-Release-View/Article/821675/secretary-of-defense-ash-carter-announces-policy-for-transgender-service-members.

CHAPTER 9

ORGANIZATION AND BUDGET

Strategy connects means to ends—objectives or purposes like security of a state and its people—organzation and budget core to implementing any strategy.

National unity—organizing thirteen, now fifty, states and territories into a single political entity, a federation—was the late-eighteenth century strategic formula for security both at home and abroad. Organization of the US military establishment developed over time in relation to very subjective understandings of both threats and opportunities facing the country. Organized globally, the US military now operates abroad under a regional, unified command structure that encompasses countries in Europe, North and South America, Africa, the Middle East, Asia, and the Pacific.

Sustaining this military establishment brings us to finance, the defense budget-as-policy. In this regard, the United States has a capital- and technology-intensive comparative advantage in relation to adversaries and other competitors that directly affects the way decision makers construct American defense policy. That the US dollar is a globally accepted mode of payment for financing US foreign and national security outlays is an instrumental privilege that facilitates implementation or conduct of American policy abroad. This currency or "dollar" advantage is jeopardized by those on Capitol Hill who threaten default on US obligations, thus undermining not only the credit worthiness of the United States but also its national security.

EARLY US STRATEGIC THINKING ABOUT ORGANIZING AND FUNDING SECURITY

To the constitutional framers, dealing with domestic (state-against-state) and international threats (mainly from Britain and Spain) was their primary concern. The first nine *Federalist papers* by John Jay and Alexander Hamilton were allocated to the security to be realized by the unity of the thirteen states.

Strategy specifies means and links them to desired ends or objectives. Securing the new republic in relation to both internal and external threats was the clear objective. Unity of the thirteen states, developing and sustaining adequate defenses, maintaining trade and other forms of commerce, and avoiding unnecessary entanglement in European politics were important planks in what became a grand strategy for American national security.

Principal architects of this grand strategy were writers of the *Federalist Papers*—John Jay, Alexander Hamilton, and James Madison (1788–1789), their construction receiving endorsement in George Washington's farewell address (1796) drafted by Hamilton and Madison. The opening lines of the *Federalist Papers* speak to their understanding of how security of the union was so important. As Hamilton wrote:

> AFTER an unequivocal experience of the inefficiency of the subsisting federal government, you are called upon to deliberate on a new Constitution for the United States of America. The subject speaks its own importance; comprehending in its consequences

nothing less than the existence of the UNION, the safety and welfare of the parts of which it is composed....

In Federalist No. 2, Hamilton's fellow New Yorker, John Jay, observed how "ample security ... could only be found in a national government more wisely framed." He adds in *Federalist* No. 3: "Among the many objects to which a wise and free people find it necessary to direct their attention, that of providing for their SAFETY seems to be the first." To Jay in *Federalist* No. 3: "One good national government affords vastly more security against dangers." More specifically, Jay identified "the neighborhood of Spanish and British territories, bordering on some States" as problematic, but less so for a "united nation" with a "national government" that would "proceed with moderation and candor to consider and decide on the means most proper to extricate them from the difficulties which threaten them."

Jay is concerned in *Federalist* No. 4 lest the states "split into three or four independent and probably discordant republics or confederacies, one inclining to Britain, another to France, and a third to Spain, and perhaps played off against each other by the three. What a poor, pitiful figure will America make in their eyes!" He is explicit in specifying unity and a strong national defense as the remedy: "Union and a good national government . . . instead of INVITING war, will tend to repress and discourage it. That situation consists in the best possible state of defense, and necessarily depends on the government, the arms, and the resources of the country."

He adds that "the safety of the whole is the interest of the whole, and cannot be provided for without government" given that "one government can collect and avail itself of the talents and experience of the ablest men." Moreover, "it can apply the resources and power of the whole to the defense of any particular part, and that more easily and expeditiously than State governments or separate confederacies can possibly do."

Jay concluded by asking: "Leave America divided into thirteen or . . . into three or four independent governments—what armies could they raise and pay—what fleets could they ever hope to have? If one was attacked, would the others fly to its succor, and spend their blood and money in its defense?" His decisive answer in *Federalist* No. 5 is that "weakness and divisions at home would invite dangers from abroad; and that nothing would tend more to secure us from them than union, strength, and good government within ourselves."

Quite apart from external threats to national security, in *Federalist* No. 6 Alexander Hamilton addressed domestic threats that would occur in the absence of union—those that "flow from dissensions between the States themselves, and from domestic factions and convulsions." These dissensions, he argued in *Federalist* No. 7 likely would lead to "alliances between the different States or confederacies and different foreign nations." Accordingly, the country "gradually" would become "entangled in all the pernicious labyrinths of European politics and wars." Hamilton continues this line of argument in *Federalist* No. 8: "If we should be disunited . . . we should be, in a short course of time, in the predicament of the continental powers of Europe."

Finally, Hamilton stated in *Federalist* No. 9 that "a FIRM Union will be . . . a barrier against domestic faction and insurrection." He underscored the "utility" for national security through unity is both domestic ("to suppress faction and to guard the internal tranquility [sic] of States") and international, ("to increase their external force and security").

Both Hamilton and James Madison assisted Washington in drafting his Farewell Address (1796). Not surprisingly, the same themes developed in the *Federalist Papers* find their way into this address. As Washington declared: "The unity of government which constitutes you one people . . . is a main pillar in the edifice of your real independence, the support of your tranquility at home, your peace abroad; of your safety; of your prosperity; of that very liberty which you so highly prize." Acknowledging regional differences between north and south extending to new territories further west, he observed how "no alliance, however strict, between the parts can be an adequate substitute [for unity]; they must inevitably experience the infractions and interruptions which all alliances in all times have experienced."

Unity is also his preferred means for dealing with external threats to national security: "If we remain one people under an efficient government, ...the period is not far off when we may defy material injury from external annoyance." Thus, "belligerent nations, under the impossibility of making acquisitions upon us, will not lightly hazard the giving us provocation." Given the American distance across the Atlantic, a central plank in the grand strategy he outlined is detachment—the avoidance of unnecessary entanglement in European politics: "Why, by interweaving our destiny with that of any part of Europe, entangle our peace and prosperity in the toils of European ambition, rivalship, interest, humor or caprice?" Maintaining "a respectable defensive posture, we may safely trust to temporary alliances for extraordinary emergencies."

The similarity of this prescription for security to the plan by Machiavelli (1469–1527) for Italian security is striking. Security would be achieved by unifying its city-states, thus ending armed conflict among them and enhancing their capabilities against French, Spanish, or any other external interventions in Italian affairs. Following the Florentine's prescription, they put in place in the late eighteenth century what would take another century to achieve in Italy, some 300 years after Machiavelli had written *The Prince*.

Benjamin Franklin, John Adams, Thomas Jefferson, and likely his protégé, James Madison, understood this Machiavellian formula for security in the country they were constructing.[1] It was directly applicable to the American coalition of what had been thirteen British colonies that could easily divide along north-south lines (as did occur in 1860). They saw external threats as coming principally from Britain and Spain. In the War of 1812, Britain challenged the assertion of American independence established three decades earlier in the Treaty of Paris (1783) that formally ended the American Revolutionary War, with fighting having terminated two years earlier.

Security Against Threats and the Pursuit of Opportunities

What is a threat?—the core security question—and *what is an opportunity?* are highly subjective calculations. We enter the realm of psychology, perception and misperception, and the sense we make and retain of such observations. The understandings that emerge are a function not just of "facts"—as if they were objective truths knowable in themselves, but also of the interpretive lenses worn by decision makers who identify them. These "lenses" are informed by prior (often very personal) experiences, understandings, and orientations. Like imprints on the brain, these idiosyncratic perspectives filter what is observed and color the interpretations of what is at issue.

Intersubjective exchanges among decision makers are a social psychology of group dynamics central to decision-making processes. There is a back and forth in further developing mental understandings that may bring the parties together cognitively. Alternatively, they may remain set in their ways, sometimes holding very different positions. In these circumstances, authoritative choice becomes more difficult.

Some of these positions may be a function of bureaucratic position. Foreign service officers in the State Department may see things differently than military or civilian officials in the Department of Defense (DoD). For its part, the DoD is constituted as a complex set of different bureaucracies with diverse understandings or points of view on security matters, those of the Office of Secretary of Defense (OSD) sometimes at odds with the Joint Chiefs of Staff (JCS) or particular service departments. Politics enters the process explicitly when give and take, pulling and hauling, and the forming of coalitions and countercoalitions among the players occur.

The Pentagon as a whole and its component parts are social constructions institutionalized over time. Within the many interconnected halls of the "building," the five-sided, five-story principal residence of the Department of Defense (DoD), there always seems to be a hurricane of activity—people going to and fro, walking up and down ramps, and around or across ten corridors and rings of hallways and that circle the eye of the storm. Notwithstanding the complexity of interactions within, the neat lines of the Pentagon are a metaphor for the relative order that emerges. Like the eye of a hurricane, the inner court is a place of relative calm—a park-like atmosphere in a place for social gathering where trees grow, flowers bloom, no military hats are worn, and people buy ice-cream cones. The contrast between the pacific eye and the turmoil outside of it within corridors and hallway rings is striking.

The Pentagon is also a puzzle palace to outsiders trying to fathom the workings of the world's largest corporation, whether measured by budget or by numbers of people engaged in a global network of agencies, bases, military units, and other subsidiary entities that collectively constitute the DoD. Bewildering in its complexity, the "building" (as insiders often call the Pentagon) has three main components or constellations of actors: the Office of the Secretary of Defense (OSD), the Joint Chiefs of Staff (JCS), and the military service departments—army, navy (which includes the marine corps), and the air force.

The United States has military installations worldwide, particularly in Europe, the Middle East, East Asia and the Pacific. Domestically, one present-day legacy of the post-civil war occupation and reconstruction years is the disproportionate number of military installations (including military headquarters) located in southern states. Concentrating military installations in the south is a social construction that emerged largely as an unintended consequence of these events. The warmer climate south of the Mason-Dixon Line facilitates the conducting of training and other operations; this no doubt contributed to keeping army posts there. Twentieth-century army air fields associated with established army posts later became air force bases. Southern representation on Armed Services committees in both houses helped solidify the political base to keep and expand these installations.

Expansion of the United States across the continent during the nineteenth century, particularly after the Civil War ended (1865), was accompanied by construction of a large number of army posts to provide security to the settlers. The Indian wars that ensued left a tragic legacy of destruction—surviving Native Americans put on reservations or assimilated within the US population as a whole. When this "pacification" of native tribes was complete, most of these forts or other posts were closed—their memory captured by the names of cities and towns that had grown up around them.

Prior to 1947 when the DoD came into existence as part of the post–World War II National Security Act, the locus of power and authority resided in separate, cabinet-level War (Army) and Navy Departments. To say the least, fighting World War II (1941–1945) in two "theaters"—Europe and the Pacific—posed major organizational challenges. Civilian control under the president was vested in a secretary of war and a secretary of the navy, as had been the arrangement since the early days of the republic.

Washington's four-person cabinet (1789) in rank order included Secretary of State Thomas Jefferson, Secretary of the Treasury Alexander Hamilton, Secretary of War Henry Knox, and Attorney General Edmund Randolph. The Continental Army had been founded on the eve of the revolution in 1775. Although the US Navy and Marine Corps also trace their origins to that year, it was not until 1798 when President John Adams appointed its first secretary, Benjamin Stoddert, that the Navy Department attained cabinet status. As the Navy's "army," the Marine Corps famously saw action in Tripoli (1801–1805) as part of the Jefferson administration's campaign against piracy in the Mediterranean directed against American merchant ships.

For the most part, the army, the navy and its marine corps operated independently throughout their histories. Battles on land were the province of the army, those at sea or along coastlines the responsibility of the navy and marines. But those were simpler times.

World War I, fought primarily in Europe, also had its "side show" in the Middle East, principally the responsibility of European allies. Moving troops and supplies to the battlefield required naval support. New technologies also challenged the neat land-and-sea dichotomy that delineated roles and missions between the army and navy. The air over the battlefield and at sea became a combat zone in its own right. Invention of the airplane found military application in use for reconnaissance, primitive bombing (sometimes merely dropping ordnance from the cockpit), and fighter-pilot dogfights as defenders tried to shoot down enemy aircraft from the sky.

Originally assigned to the army's Signal Corps (1914), in the interwar period the new air arm would become its own Army Air Corps, the Army Air Forces in World War II and, after World War II, the US Air Force (1947)—decidedly separate from the US Army. Naval aviation took off in the interwar period as the US Navy followed the British Royal Navy in the development, production, and deployment of aircraft carriers. Submarines were also added to the fleet in the years before World War I. In the buildup to World War II, the US Navy had become organizationally much more complex with both surface (including battleships, aircraft carriers, cruisers, destroyers, and other ships), subsurface units, and the marine corps (itself later developing its own air arm).

Invention of the tank, able to move rapidly across the battlefield, expanded not only the size of the battlefield but also the speed of combat operations. This led organizationally to armor becoming an army branch alongside the infantry (foot soldiers still elevated collectively as the "queen of battle") and artillery ("the king of battle").

The relations among branches or divisions within and between the army and navy were becoming far more complex. In 1921, General Billy Mitchell (later dubbed 'father" of the air force) famously conducted a demonstration of the army's air power against surface ships—the easy sinking of a destroyer that humiliated the admiralty and undermined any claim to invincibility at sea from air attack. The surface fleet was obviously vulnerable to attacks not only from submarines but, as it became clear after World War I, also from the air.

Naval aviation developed separately from anything happening in the army. The navy simply adapted technologies for carrier-based operations also developed by the British Royal Navy. In some respects, the navy had become its own unified command with both surface ships and submarines —its amphibious ground force in the marines, and naval aviation as its own air force. From the navy's perspective, there was little need to coordinate with the army other than to move troops and supplies in both world wars to European and, in World War II, to Pacific and Asian battlefields. Similarly, the army ran its own show in whatever theater it was deployed.

Given this historically based organization structure, World War II in Europe became primarily a responsibility of the War Department; in the Pacific, the navy. Thus, General Dwight D. Eisenhower became Supreme Allied Commander in Europe for conducting the D-Day landings in Normandy and subsequent campaigns against the German Wehrmacht on the European continent. In the Pacific Fleet, Admirals Chester Nimitz (Pacific Fleet Commander) and William "Bull" Halsey (South Pacific Commander) had the principal responsibilities in theater except for ground campaigns led by General Douglas MacArthur (Far East Army Commander) in islands occupied by Japan. The then markedly underdeveloped concept of jointness between the services found its organizational manifestation in a newly constructed, Washington-based, wartime Joint Chiefs of Staff (JCS).

To say the least, fighting World War II in two geographically separated theaters—Europe–North Africa and the Pacific—posed major organizational challenges. Reflecting on the World War II experience, it fell to President Harry Truman's administration to formalize integration of the ground, naval, and air arms organizationally in the JCS. At the same time, however, was fear on Capitol Hill of creating a general staff so strong that it would threaten civilian control of the armed services. Instead of a free-standing general staff, each service department (army, navy, and air force) would retain its identity with the task of organizing, training, and equipping respectively ground, naval, and air forces for prompt and sustained combat operations.[2]

In this and subsequent reorganizations, existing administrative structures were left in place, and new structures placed on top of them. The resulting bureaucratic layering of multiple headquarters increased overhead or "tail" compared to "tooth"—those who conduct operations and actually do the fighting.

Figure 5. Major DoD Organizational Constellations.

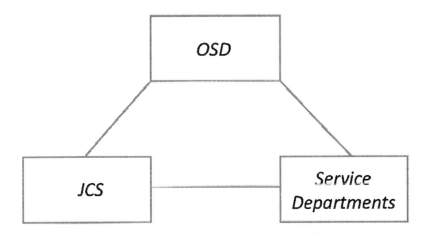

Within the newly created DoD, the locus of authority under the secretary of defense initially remained with the three service departments—not the JCS. A reorganization act in 1958 gave important budgetary tools to OSD that would not be exercised fully until the Kennedy administration took office in January 1961. Setting spending priorities, a task previously left primarily with the services, now became the prerogative of Secretary of Defense Robert S. McNamara and his staff within OSD. The locus of authority on this important issue had shifted from the services to OSD. In many respects, the budget—the allocation of dollars, where they go—*is* policy.

Assertion of these new OSD prerogatives in the Kennedy and Johnson administrations aroused the ire of many generals and admirals who resented what they saw as civilian intrusion into matters best understood by military professionals. Further strengthening of OSD and enhancing the position of the JCS—all at the expense of the service departments— would have to wait some three decades.

The two most important power levers for controlling any large organization are controls on budget and human resources. Passage of the Goldwater-Nichols Act (1986) added personnel (including military promotions) to budgetary authority already in the OSD tool chest. Encouraging greater "jointness" across the services, Goldwater-Nichols established a JCS chair and vice chair with an independent voice separate from (and sometimes at odds with one or more of) the service departments. Commanders of the unified combatant commands in Europe, the Pacific, and elsewhere report directly to the secretary of defense, usually on a day-to-day basis through the JCS. They also provide their input to DoD's budgetary process—a direct communication of combatant command needs unfiltered by separate service department preferences.

DIVIDING UP THE GLOBE:
THE UNIFIED COMBATANT COMMANDS

The service departments retain responsibility for organizing, training, and equipping the army, navy, marine corps, and air force, but commanders of the unified combatant commands and their service components (not the service chiefs of staff) are the agents for combat and other operations worldwide. The sheer size of the world's largest bureaucracy becomes clearer in the following paragraphs.[3]

As institutionalized social constructions, organizations have histories that legitimate their existence by the functions they have performed over time. Not surprisingly, they resist efforts to alter them—the ways they are structured or perform their tasks and the authoritative positions they hold. Thus, DoD reform efforts (including those of Goldwater-Nichols in 1986) tend to leave existing bureaucratic elements in place, superimposing on them new organizational structures designed to streamline command lines and consolidate control of task performance.

The added cost of this bureaucratic layering in personnel, headquarters infrastructure, communications, and transportation among organizational elements (dispersed not only globally but also across the United States) is enormous. As indicated in the following section, creation of two new unified combatant commands for the Middle East and Africa to perform functions originally performed by the European Command followed the same pattern of a unified command with separate service components on top of commands within each service. Accommodating US Marine Corps interest in its own voice meant adding a fourth service component to the unified command structure (previously the navy component provided voice for both navy and marine corps commanders).

Although the Pacific Command (Hawaii) and Southern (Latin America) Command (Florida) have remained intact over the decades, the European Command in Germany lost most of the Middle East and Africa as its areas of responsibility, the former becoming Central Command in Florida in the Reagan years (1983), Africa becoming its own command in the George W. Bush administration (2008) colocating it with the European Command in Stuttgart, Germany. Nevertheless, overseas deployments of ground and air force units and equipment remain primarily in the Pacific and Europe—the Central and African commands drawing combat and support assets from the latter and continental US-based forces.

Finally, the responsibility of Colorado-based Northern Command (NORTHCOM) is homeland defense for the United States[4] in particular, but also collaborating with both Canada and Mexico on terrorism directed toward North America. Alongside these regionally focused organizations are three functional commands with worldwide scope. Two have deterrence or combat missions, one focused on combat support in war and peace. Strategic Command (STRATCOM) in Nebraska consolidates both offensive and defensive capabilities vis-à-vis nuclear and other weapons of mass destruction—deterrence its principal objective. (Part of STRATCOM is its Cyber Command, CYBERCOM, which is colocated with the National Security Agency (NSA) at Ft. Meade, Maryland.) The Special Operations Command (SOCOM) in Florida oversees clandestine military missions of one kind or another. DoD refers to these as special operations that fall under the secretary of defense; when CIA performs similar tasks they are called covert actions subject to presidential approval. Finally, all-service and commercially contracted air-, sea- and land-based transportation falls under a single Transportation Command (TRANSCOM) in Illinois.

Consolidating functions previously performed exclusively by the service departments is another dimension of increasing jointness. Staffed by civilian and military professionals are seventeen separate DoD agencies and ten "field activities" responsible to the secretary of defense and monitored by OSD. For example, the services have retained their own intelligence units in addition to those in the unified combatant commands and, in turn, their components. Lest the Central Intelligence Agency be the only single (and often competing) voice on such matters, the Kennedy administration in 1961 established the DoD's own Defense Intelligence Agency (DIA).. Robert McNamara was then the new secretary of defense.

As noted earlier, the vast DoD bureaucracy or, perhaps more accurately, *set of overlapping bureaucracies* is an historically grounded, institutionalized social construction resistant to change. This ever-pervasive inertia is also a backdrop for competition among the organizational units for authority—there is not just interservice rivalry among service departments, but also competition for voice and position with JCS, OSD, and its DOD agencies. Cutting bureaucracy means budget cuts that reduce established organizational roles that also have important congressional and industrial bases of support—the military-industrial-congressional complex identified publicly by President Dwight Eisenhower in his farewell address in 1961.[5] It is an iron triangle: military interests in DoD; members of Congress, particularly those on Armed Services as well as Appropriations and Budget committees in both houses; and private-sector lobbyists (referred to generically as "K Street," given that most of them occupy offices there in downtown Washington, DC).

The great difficulty, of course, lies in the bureaucratic overhead that at times obstructs effective operations. Metaphorically it is a large ship difficult (at times seemingly impossible) to steer. The extensive, often-duplicative layers of bureaucracy between those in authority and those who are assigned to carry out operational tasks often requires innovative leaders willing to use novel approaches, particularly when combat missions are at hand.

If decision makers are serious about defense-cost reductions that do not adversely impact combat capabilities (and may even enhance them), these economies can be found in the duplicative command headquarters that fall around and between the lines that connect commanders to the military units whose job it is to fight and win the wars and armed interventions they are directed to conduct. Streamlining the route between command and those who bear the burdens of combat is not a bad thing.

STRATEGY, FORCE POSTURE, AND BUDGET

Mandated by Congress in 1997 is a Quadrennial Defense Review (QDR) conducted by the Defense Department specifying its national security strategic goals, assessing military capabilities in relation to these strategic objectives, and determining budget needs to fund these efforts. The 2014 QDR, for example, identifies three broad strategic objectives—"defending the homeland; building security globally by projecting US influence and deterring aggression; and remaining prepared to win decisively against any adversary should deterrence fail."

To achieve these ends, measures "include reducing force structure in order to protect and expand critical capabilities, modernizing the forces, and investing in readiness." Investments will sustain the country's "technological edge over potential adversaries," particularly focusing on innovation. The document calls for "reducing overhead and streamlining activities" along with reforming military compensation to sustain the all-volunteer force.

Indeed, combat capability—the operational component of strategy by which commanders organize, train and lead soldiers, sailors, or airmen to battle on land, sea, or air—is directly affected by (1) military-related technologies; (2) logistical capacity to support battlefield operations; and (3) the degree to which the people in American society not only provide educated and skilled, service-committed military personnel, but also stand behind its soldiers, sailors, and airmen and thus contribute to their morale in the contingencies in which they are engaged.

This formulation is consistent with Clausewitz's understandings of warfare—adding technology to the mix, as depicted in the causal schematic in figure 2.1 (see chapter 2). The industrial revolution occurred subsequent to Clausewitz's experience in the Napoleonic wars; technological developments were then less significant and thus less prominent in his writings.

Major titles in the US defense budget (in upper-lower case and italicized here) relate directly to this causal schematic. *Operations & Maintenance* (O&M) and *Procurement* outlays directly affect operations on the battlefield as well as logistics—bringing supplies essential to conducting combat and supporting those so engaged. Technology is reflected in *Research, Development, Test and Evaluation* (RDT&E) of weapons systems followed by *Procurement* and subsequent deployment of them. Finally, efforts to maximize the social dimension of strategy fall mainly in the *Personnel* budget title.

More than $10 billion a year for research, development, and maintenance of nuclear weapons are part of the Department of Energy's budget, thus not counted in the DoD annual budget. DoD's budget includes outlays for pension and other benefits for both civilian and military retired personnel, but the Department of Veterans Affairs covers all veterans entitled to benefits at an annual budget just under $80 billion, another outlay off of DoD's books. DoD dollars do support defense-related space programs, but the Defense Department also benefits from just under $20 billion of NASA's spending on space programs. Finally, the military intelligence program of just under $20 billion is funded under DoD, but the national intelligence program of more than an additional $50 billion also benefits DoD. Putting these figures together, substantially more than $150 billion in defense-related spending is on the books of other government agencies.

The defense budget is an ongoing political process both within the DoD and the executive branch (OMB, the Office and Management and Budget within the Executive Office of the President, also a key player) and Capitol Hill that holds the purse strings. Article I, Section 7, of the US Constitution makes clear that "all bills for raising revenue shall originate in the House of Representatives; but the Senate may propose or concur with amendments as on other Bills."

With respect to the DoD budget, Section 8 specifies Congressional authority "to raise and support armies, but no appropriation of money to that use shall be for a longer term than two years"—the two-year limitation reflecting concerns that a standing army might threaten liberties much as the British Royal Army had in the events prior to, and during, the Revolutionary War. Also, provision was made for Congress "to provide and maintain a navy" and, by application of the Constitutional elastic clause, a twentieth- and twenty-first-century air force.[6]

As a practical matter, Executive-Congressional relations on the budget were socially constructed since the founding of the republic, institutionally taking present form over the decades of the twentieth and twenty-first centuries—landmark milestones the Budget and Accounting Act of 1921 and the Congressional Budget Act of 1974. The latter was passed at a time of executive weakness relative to the Legislative branch due to the Nixon administration's Watergate scandal and increasing unpopularity of the Vietnam War. The net effect was to strengthen the Congressional role in budget and spending matters. This edge was sustained in incremental amendments in 1985, 1990, and 1997 and in actual practice in the more than four decades since the 1974 Act was passed.

President Nixon had used executive authority to refuse spending moneys appropriated by Congress for reducing deficit spending or, more precisely, for projects he opposed. Actual practice—impounding some $12 billion of appropriated funds—gave momentum to a "zero-sum" Congressional effort to curb executive authority, expanding its own in the process. Reacting to Nixon's impoundment, the Budget Reform Act required presidents to spend funds appropriated for purposes specified by legislation.

At the same time, however, the executive office still was expected to avoid waste that comes from spending needlessly in spite of changed circumstances, expired contracts, and other exceptions. Required to report deviations (deferrals or rescissions) subject to Congressional approval, OMB effectively has carved out the presidential role—legitimizing over time the exercise of executive authority in certain, previously ambiguous, circumstances.

The 1974 Act changed the fiscal year from July 1st through June 30 the following calendar year to October 1 through September 30—the intent being to give Congress the time it needed to complete the multiple-committee process specified in legislation. As a practical matter, of course, passing budget authorization and appropriations bills is less a function of the time it takes to craft legislation through committees in two houses of Congress than it is of the tactical politics of delay and blockage that can confound any calendar of deadlines that might be constructed. Given political polarization and partisan gridlock, continuing resolutions that allow government agencies to spend at existing appropriations levels (or, in the absence of such permission, to shut down) have become more common in recent years, as have "rescissions" or cancellations of planned spending.

Under the same 1974 legislation, the president's Bureau of the Budget (Bubud) became the Office of Management and Budget (OMB). In addition to existing appropriations committees, the Act also created budget committees in both houses supported by a Congressional Budget Office (CBO) responsible to the Congress. No longer would the executive office's OMB be the only budget authority in town. Congress would now have its own budget office in addition to its long-standing Government Accountability Office (GAO) that, among other functions, investigates and studies the ways and means of government spending, thus exercising Congressional oversight on diverse government programs.

Congressional budget parameters due annually in mid-May were to be a basis for actions by Appropriations Committees in both houses, which were in principle subject to these caps on spending set by the Budget Committees. Passage of the budget—the appropriations bills—is due by the beginning of the new fiscal year, October 1. Because of mostly partisan politics, we're not surprised when the deadline passes, hopefully with a continuing resolution in place. To the contrary, the surprise comes when the deadline is met and government operations proceed in accordance with an agreed budget. Partisan politics, always part of the process, have been extraordinarily intense since the turn of the century.

As with most other social constructions, the budgetary process remains a work in progress—the norms and agreed rules of actual practice being as significant as, or even more so, than the original legislation that framed its main lines. As a practical matter, the deeply divided, polarized politics and the consequent failure to meet budget and appropriations deadlines— continuing resolution spending at the same levels of the previous year's budget—has given the executive branch somewhat more discretion in the allocation of funds than it might otherwise have. Still under constraints, however, DoD and the armed services find that funding programs at desired levels to be highly problematic in the absence of an agreed budget with the authority that legislation conveys.

Finally, the United States enjoys an extraordinary advantage in that the dollar is still the world's most accepted currency for payment of both government and private-sector obligations both at home and abroad. Indeed, the US government pays for the enormous costs of conducting American foreign and national security policy with US dollars, the national currency it produces.

Particularly troubling, however, are politics on Capitol Hill that threaten US default on its obligations. When opponents of deficit spending threaten to vote against raising the national debt ceiling to cover outlays for programs already authorized and appropriated by Congress, their actions disturb financial markets and tend to undermine national credit worthiness. Doing so also threatens the unquestioned acceptance of the dollar as payment for US foreign policy and national security obligations. Securitizing the dollar—explicitly recognizing its ongoing global role as an American national security asset—is the subject of another volume.[7]

THE FORMAL PROCESS

At the beginning of the calendar year, DoD provides Congress a proposed budget for the fiscal year that begins October 1 and ends on September 30 the following year. This DoD budgetary process is highly proceduralized, with meetings and exchange of papers detailing requests within each and among its three major DoD constellations that have decided stakes in the outcome—OSD (to include its DoD-wide agencies), the JCS (to include its unified combat commands), and the three armed services departments (army, navy, and air force).

Reviews of spending—reconciling budget authority with actual outlays —in the current fiscal year occur at the same time that budget targets are negotiated for the forthcoming as well as future fiscal years. It is a multiring political circus. The stakes are real. Whatever may be said in Washington, follow the money. The budget *is* policy—all the rest merely rhetoric.

The armed services, budget, and appropriations committees in both houses are principal actors in the defense budgetary process. The Congressional Budget Office (CBO) and the Government Accountability Office (GAO) are the two, presumptively nonpartisan, Congress-wide agencies that provide budget-related data analysis and other studies.

DoD first seeks "authorization" from Congress each year for Operations and Maintenance (O&M), personnel, Research, Development, Test and Evaluation (RDT&E) of weapons systems, procurement, and other programs. The annual National Defense Authorization Act emerges after hearings, other behind-the-scenes work by House and Senate armed services committees (and, importantly, their staffs), drafting separate bills subject to amendment and passage on the floor by each house as a whole, differences reconciled, and bills passed into law by both houses.

Authorization is not enough, of course, as moneys also still need to be "budgeted" (consistent with ceilings set by the Budget Committees) and finally "appropriated"—the latter principally the domain of defense subcommittees and staffs of Appropriations Committees in both houses. Overlapping memberships and developing other close ties between members of the Armed Services and Appropriations committees, particularly their defense subcommittees, are politics that facilitate final agreement.

Table 12. DoD Budget in Typical Year.*

By Service Department

24.3% Army
29.8% Navy (including Marines)
27.8% Air Force 18.1% Defense Wide
(Total= $495,604,183 in FY15 Budget)

By Title: Category of Defense Spending

27.3% Military Personnel
40.1% Operations and Maintenance (O&M)
18.5% Procurement
12.8% Research, Development, Test and Evaluation (RDT&E)
 0.2% Revolving and Management Funds
 1.1% Military Construction
 0.2% Family Housing
(Total= $495,604,183 in FY15 Budget)

Source. Office of the Undersecretary of Defense (Comptroller)/Chief Financial Officer, *United States Department of Defense, Fiscal Year 2015 Budget Request: Overview* (March 2014), p. A-3.

ORDER OF BATTLE: UNITS, MILITARY PERSONNEL, AND THEIR WEAPONS

Compiled and published annually by the International Institute for Strategic Studies, *The Military Balance* remains the best unclassified source for order of battle data on the United States and other military establishments worldwide. Almost one and a half million men and women are on active duty (just under 0.5% of the US population as a whole).

Table 13. An Overview: US Military Order of Battle at a Glance.

	Active Duty	Reserves	National Guard
Army			
Brigade Combat Teams (BCTs)	32		28
Combat Aviation Brigades (CABs)	11		8
Navy			
Ships	283		
Carrier Strike Groups	10		
Marine Corps			
Marine Expeditionary Forces	3	-	
Infantry Battalions	23	8	
Air Force			
Combat Squadrons	36	3	20
Aircraft	3563	337	1056

Source. Office of the Undersecretary of Defense (Comptroller)/Chief Financial Officer, *United States Department of Defense, Fiscal Year 2015 Budget Request: Overview* (March 2014), p. A-1.

Plans are to reduce those numbers unless unanticipated contingencies arise that compel their retention or expansion. Cuts are taking place predominantly in the ground forces that were substantially increased to fight wars in Iraq and Afghanistan following the 9/11 attacks on the United States by al Qaeda. Reaching a peak of some 570,000 in this period, the US Army is gradually downsizing to some 450,000—a 21% overall reduction to slightly above the pre–World War II size in 1940.[8] Contingency plans also have been made should the budget require army officials to reduce force size even further to 420,000.

In addition to the overhead associated with these layers of command is the "tail" of noncombat personnel required to support those actually engaged in combat operations—the "tooth" or "tip of the spear" commonly used metaphors. At the "other end of the spear" are the logistics of getting troops, weaponry, ammunition, equipment, and other supplies to the battlefield and maintaining them that relies both on military personnel and civil servants assigned to these mission-essential tasks or outsourced private contractors. Reducing the military "tail" also means relying on civil servants or contractors for the welfare and security of military members and their families. This includes housing, dining halls, medical and physical exercise or athletic facilities, police, postal and other communications, entertainment, and other morale-boosting activities.

Since the end of World War II in 1945, more "tail" has been used to support fewer troops. As one Army study puts it: "Combat elements have progressively declined as a proportion of the total force since 1945."[9] For the army as a whole: "Combat troops have formed a range between a quarter and slightly over a third of all general purpose forces deployed by the United States since World War II."[10] In combat contingencies since the end of World War II, however, the proportion of total army personnel allocated to headquarters has doubled to 40% from 20% while, at the same time, combat troops in the field have declined to around 25% from about 38% at the end of World War II.[11] By contrast, combat troops numbered over 50% in the American Expeditionary Forces (AEF) in World War I.[12]

Outsourcing noncombat functions—logistics, feeding the troops, civil engineering and other tasks previously assigned to military personnel —is one approach to reducing the support tail, albeit at an increased budgetary cost. More controversial is the assignment of security and even some combat-related tasks to civilian contractors—so-called corporate warriors.[13] Increased private-sector contracts and jobs are bases of Congressional support for outsourcing military functions. Estimates are that such civilianizing of military tasks in the long run also saves DoD budget dollars, particularly for pension and health-care entitlements military personnel receive after twenty or more years of service.

Beyond food and other service-related functions, combat units now depend heavily on civilians to maintain equipment. Where to draw the lines and how far DoD can civilianize such operations without undermining combat capability and reliability of forces are problematic. One can order soldiers into dangerous combat zones, but the same may not always be true for civilian contractors.

Like other advanced, capital-rich, economically developed countries, the United States enjoys a strategic advantage in applied military technologies. Given the size of its technologically oriented economy and the world role the United States plays, more emphasis has been placed on developing advanced weapons systems than in most other countries. Because of these circumstances, defense planners understand the economic logic of comparative advantage and thus tend to see US strategic advantage by substituting technology (capital) for labor to the maximum extent possible.

Thus, the capital-intensive naval and air forces (that now also resort to use of unmanned vehicles for many dangerous missions) are more in the American comparative advantage than are its technologically advanced but more labor-intensive army and marine corps. Nevertheless, soldiers on the ground[14] remain an indispensable part of US military capability.

The tendency across both Republican and Democratic administrations is to downsize to smaller numbers of regular, increasingly mobile, ground-force units, with their argument being that this is more affordable than sustaining much larger standing armies.[15] Developing Special Forces units trained and equipped for customized missions, particularly against insurgent or other groups, is also consistent with a strategy of force development that, to the extent possible, maximizes capital or technological advantage, minimizing reliance on labor-intensive, ground-force units. Such thinking is at the root of this "revolution in military affairs" (RMA).

National Security's Interagency Players

DoD and its worldwide deployment of combat-ready military forces is not the only security-related organization. The Department of Homeland Security (DHS) constructed in the aftermath of the 9/11 al Qaeda attacks on the Pentagon and the World Trade Center, has primary responsibility for the "home game"—*homeland security* for people and property in fifty states and territories.

To do so, Congress consolidated some twenty-two agencies under DHS. The reconstruction was extraordinarily ambitious. Whether in the private or public sector, merging organizational units with diverse corporate cultures is always problematic. Soon after DHS came into existence, one senior-level employee working for then DHS secretary Tom Ridge quipped that coordinating all of these agencies within DHS made the hunt for Osama bin Laden look simple by comparison.

Table 14. The Department of Homeland Security at a Glance.

- The Coast Guard
- The Transportation Security Agency (TSA)
- Federal Emergency Management Agency (FEMA)
- The Secret Service
- Customs and Border Protection
- Immigration and Customs Enforcement
- Citizenship and Immigration Services
- Federal Law Enforcement Training Center
- Science & Technology Directorate
- Office of cybersecurity and Communications, National Protection and Programs Directorate
- Office of Operations Coordination
- Office of Infrastructure Protection

DoD remains a key player for the military component of the home game—its responsibility dubbed homeland *defense* to differentiate it bureaucratically from homeland *security* that belongs to DHS. Present at the creation of DHS in 2002, then secretary of defense Donald Rumsfeld assured DoD's responsibilities and prerogatives would be preserved and kept separate from those of the new cabinet department then under construction. The only DoD losses to DHS were its National Biological Warfare Defense Analysis Center and its National Communications System, although the latter's focus on cybersecurity is amply covered by DoD's own National Security Agency, headquartered at Fort Meade in Maryland.

Northern Command in Colorado Springs has responsibility for the forty-nine states and Caribbean territories (Puerto Rico and US Virgin Islands). The state of Hawaii and Pacific territories (Guam, American Samoa, and the Northern Marianna Islands) come under the Pacific Command in Honolulu.

DoD retains primacy in the military "away game" abroad. The State Department, CIA, FBI, Treasury Department, and other agencies work their parts of the home and away games, ideally in tandem with both DHS and DoD. Of course, such coordination across bureaucratic boundaries is never easy.

THE INTERAGENCY PROCESS—THE NATIONAL AND HOMELAND SECURITY COUNCILS

Created in 1947, the National Security Council (NSC) is part of the president's executive office. Statutory members are the president, vice president, secretary of state, secretary of defense, and secretary of energy who has nuclear weapons responsibilities. Other participants (and their staffs) include the chairman of the Joint Chiefs of Staff (JCS) and the director of national intelligence (DNI). Other cabinet and agency officers participate to a greater or lesser degree depending on the issues at hand.

These principals are often represented by members of their staffs who participate in the interagency process.

Newer to the scene is the Homeland Security Council, constructed by executive order a month after the 9/11 attacks. Congress gave it statutory standing in 2002. The Homeland Security Council brings together those cabinet officers and other agencies that have a more domestic focus. Thus, its statutory members include the president, vice president, attorney general, and secretaries of defense, health and human services, transportation, homeland security, and directors of the Federal Emergency Management Agency (FEMA) and FBI. As statutory participants, the Homeland Security Advisor to the president and the chairman of the JCS are also part of the Homeland Security Council process. Although this formal structure remains in place, the Obama administration set a precedent by combining the National and Homeland Security staffs. For its part, the NSC remains the principal player in national security matters.

Each administration has used the NSC structure to meet the preferences of very different presidents. President Dwight D. Eisenhower, for example, used it much as he had used staffs as a military commander. President John F. Kennedy, by contrast, was more prone to use it less formally, bringing diverse voices in to deliberations as famously occurred in the executive committee that he and his brother, Attorney General Robert Kennedy, assembled during the Cuban missile crisis in October 1962.

In the 1980s, by contrast, President Ronald Reagan allowed the NSC structure to be used to carry out covert actions vis-à-vis Nicaragua and Iran opposed by Democrats—then the majority in the Congress. Arms (including spare parts) needed by Iran were channeled from Israeli to Iranian inventories—the former replenished from US stocks. Arms transfers to Iran as means to secure release of American embassy personnel held as hostages in Tehran opened the channel. Later Tehran's payments for arms were used to finance the counter-left, anti-Sandinista policies favored by the president, but opposed by the Democratic majority in congress. Legal restraint on CIA from engaging in such actions resulted in the NSC stepping into the breach. National Security Adviser Robert McFarlane and staff member, marine Lt Colonel Oliver North, became embroiled in what became known as the Iran-Contra scandal.

In the aftermath, Texas Republican Senator John Tower chaired a commission on Iran-Contra. Brent Scowcroft, principal member and former president Gerald Ford's national security adviser (an air force retired three-star General), quickly became the intellectual (and moral) force that oversaw drafting the commission's findings and recommendations. In the future, the NSC was not to be engaged in carrying out policy, as had occurred in Iran-Contra.

It was instead to be the means by which a given president would understand the diverse views expressed and alternative policy actions proposed by NSC participants. In the Scowcroft pattern, national security advisers would assemble and give fair hearing to alternative views of cabinet officers, principally the secretary of state and the secretary of defense or their representatives. Although the national security adviser could express his or her own view, it would not displace the views of the cabinet secretaries or their staffs. Being the beneficiary of diverse counsel, the president would thus be in a better position to make informed decisions.

This national security adviser "as honest broker" was the role Scowcroft had played for both presidents Gerald Ford and George H. W. Bush. This was in sharp contrast to both Republican Henry Kissinger (for whom Scowcroft had served as deputy in the Nixon administration) and Democrat Zbigniew Brzezinski in the Carter administration. As national security advisers with the president's ear, Kissinger and Brzezinski were both quite willing (and able) to challenge the views of secretaries of state and defense and other cabinet officers.

For the most part, the Scowcroft model of national security adviser as honest broker has been followed in the Bill Clinton, George W. Bush, and Barack Obama administrations. Doing so has not always been easy. For her part, National Security Adviser Condoleezza Rice facilitated a one-on-one dinner meeting between President Bush and secretary of state Colin Powell on the eve of finalizing the 2003 decision to invade Iraq and depose the Saddam Hussein regime. Vice President Dick Cheney and Secretary of Defense Donald Rumsfeld were agitated by Rice's move, which they feared would turn the president against the intervention they advocated.

Theirs was a decades-long friendship and policy partnership. Both had served in the Ford administration when Rumsfeld displaced Elliot Richardson as secretary of defense with the assistance of Cheney, then the president's chief of staff, who also influenced President Ford to make other changes in his post-Nixon administration.[16] The Cheney-Rumsfeld advocacy of invading Iraq traced back to Cheney's role as secretary of defense in the George H. W. Bush administration when the president, supported by Scowcroft, opposed going on to Baghdad after forcing the Iraquis to withdraw from their occupation of Kuwait.

Apart from keeping the coalition of some forty states together, Bush and Scowcroft reasoned that weakening Iraq would open the door to increased Iranian influence in Iraq, particularly among fellow Shia who had suffered under the Sunni regime under Saddam. Keeping a balance of power between Iran and Iraq was more important to them than any attempt to overthrow the regime.

Finishing the job George H. W. Bush had allegedly left undone gained support among a cadre of policy intellectuals and others, later dubbed "neoconservatives." The election of George W. Bush, followed by al Qaeda's 9/11 attack on New York and Washington, provided the convenient occasion for finally "finishing the job." That the 9/11 attacks had originated from al Qaeda sanctuaries in Afghanistan that had nothing to do with Iraq was beside the point.

Taking down the Iraqi regime and establishing an American strategic presence was the two-fold purpose. Iraq's use of chemical weapons against Iran in the Iraq-Iran war as well as against Iraqi Kurds and Shia was used to buttress unfounded claims that the Iraqi regime was also bent on acquiring nuclear weapons. Added to these, the rhetoric became hyperbolic. Indeed, the United States was to help build a democracy in Iraq as a model for all of Araby!

In fact, the intervention, the under-resourced way in which it was conducted, and tragic errors during the occupation (dismantling the Iraqi army and removing Baathists from positions of civil authority) not only destabilized Iraq, but also led to the chaos spilling over to Syria and thus contributed directly to the rise of ISIL. Moreover, diverting resources to Iraq undermined the effort by the United States and its coalition partners in Afghanistan where the al Qaeda threat had originated in the first place.

AFTERWORD

Whatever the discourse in defense politics on the Potomac, in the final analysis the budget *is* policy. The way US forces are structured reflects the capital and technological comparative advantage that the United States enjoys relative to its adversaries or other competitors. Continuing resolutions in lieu of agreed, statutory budgets undermine efforts to link force posture to agreed national strategic objectives.

Pursuit of US foreign and national security objectives depends upon the continual acceptance of the dollar in payment of US obligations, particularly for defense-related outlays. Threatening to default on US obligations unnecessarily puts US use of its currency for payments abroad at risk.

NOTES

1. Machiavelli's writings were found in Adams' library, both Franklin and Jefferson claiming to have read his work in the original Italian.
2. On organizational politics leading to the construction of the DoD, see John C. Ries *The Management of DEFENSE: Organization and Control of the U.S. Armed Services* (Baltimore, MD: The Johns Hopkins University Press, 1964).
3. Mentioned in the text are the unified combatant commands and their army, navy, marine corps, and air force components. Not discussed or detailed are operations and support commands within each of the services.
4. *Homeland "defense"* is, in effect, the military part of *homeland "security"*— the latter term used to refer to the Department of Homeland Security (DHS). NORTHCOM has responsibility for homeland defense except for Hawaii and other Pacific territories where PACOM has the task.
5. Although reference to the Congress was in the original draft, Eisenhower dropped it in the final version.
6. Article I, the final clause in Section 8: Congress has authority "to make all laws which shall be necessary and proper for carrying into execution the foregoing powers, and all other powers vested by this Constitution in the government of the United States, or in any department or officer thereof."
7. Paul R. Viotti, Viotti, *The Dollar and National Security: The Monetary Component of Hard Power* (Stanford, CA: Stanford University Press, 2014).
8. Thom Shanker and Helene Cooper, "Pentagon Plans to Shrink Army to Pre-World War II Levels," *New York Times*, February 23, 2014.
9. See John J. McGrath, "The Other End of the Spear: The Tooth-to-Tail Ratio (T3R) in Modern Military Operations," Occasional Paper 23, Long War Series (Fort Leavenworth, KS: Combat Studies Institute Press, n.d.), 77.
10. Ibid., 86.
11. Ibid., 82.
12. Ibid., 65–66.
13. For example, see P.W. Singer. *Corporate Warriors: The Rise of the Privatized Military Industry.* (Ithaca, NY: Cornell University Press, 2003, 2008).

14. I prefer to refer to *soldiers* or *troops* rather than the more impersonal "*boots* on the ground" precisely because the latter gives relatively short shrift to the human sacrifice military personnel make.
15. On the ongoing need for ground forces, see Michael E. O'Hanlon, *The Future of Land Warfare* (Washington, DC: Brookings, 2015).
16. Pundits at the time dubbed it the midnight massacre.

RECONSTRUCTING REALISM

The new issues (cyber security, global climate change, natural incidents, pollution, resource depletion, pandemics, and mass murders) that challenge us in our brave new world do not displace conventional defense-related concerns on the US national security agenda. Indeed, the anarchy of world politics—the absence of any central authority over the sovereignty of states (much less one with means to enforce its will)—likely will persist throughout the twenty-first century.

Creating such an authority that would alter international politics, even if it were possible, likely would not be desirable. A central authority of that kind poses risks to the liberal understandings that define the American republic and those of US allies, as well as coalition partners and other countries sharing this vision of how social and political life ought to be constituted. Displacing democratic ideals with one or another form of authoritarian governance is a risk likely not worth taking.

If this is so, then coping with this anarchic condition in which states in this brave new world (as in previous centuries) means that we can expect the use of force—wars (and "rumors of wars"), armed interventions, and military influence on the course of events—still to be the order of the day.

Thus, we are not surprised when Russia uses force or military-backed influence to secure its objectives in Syria, Georgia, Crimea, and the Ukraine.

Given the economic growth of China and the expanded capabilities of its armed forces, Beijing has more forcefully asserted its claims to disputed islands while building new, man-made islands with the backing of its navy in the South China Sea. Response to such actions has taken diplomatic form bolstered by strengthening US military or naval presence as a signal of American and allied resolve. Fortunately, what the parties tend to avoid is war between or among great powers that would result from direct military confrontation between or among them.

Claims that the sovereign state is in decline or will in time defer to corporations or other nonstate actors are much exaggerated. The more threatening the brave new world becomes, the more resilient the state becomes. Challenges posed by Sunni-led ISIL that claims it is establishing a caliphate, in lieu of the state as we know it, only tend to draw diverse state actors into loose coalitions in efforts to defeat what is essentially a revolutionary challenge to the state-centric *status quo*. Thus, diverse regimes in Damascus, Baghdad, and Tehran find common cause against ISIL (or *Daesh*, as they prefer to call it).

Cooperative security requires a highly sophisticated balancing of interests by the United States as it works openly with Iraq and tacitly with Syria and Iran against ISIL, but also collaborates with Turkish, Arab, and European partners who may oppose dealing with one or another of these players. Saudi Arabia and its relation to Iran is a case in point. Expansion of Iranian influence through its ties to Shia groups it has spawned or now supports elsewhere in the region is a direct challenge to the Saudi Kingdom which, not surprisingly, tends to champion what the regime sees as Sunni causes. In this regard, one even finds bases of support for ISIL within the kingdom and elsewhere among the emirates so long as ISIL does not challenge these regimes. Direct or tacit support by Saudis and Emirati for ISIL is also a way of pushing back against Iran and its fellow Shia in Iraq and Syria.

Once again, this persisting absence of central authority above the sovereign state—much less one with the capabilities to enforce international law and generally agreed norms—means that the use of force and other forms of political violence by both state and nonstate actors will continue to pose substantial threats to American national security and that of US allies and coalition partners. Diplomacy that avoids interstate wars, ends those that have broken out, and forges cooperative or collaborative state-to-state linkages may facilitate relations among states, but have little or no effect on nonstate actors that fall outside the normal state-to-state discourse that has become routine. Collective efforts to challenge or block nonstate actors prone to use violence in support of their causes do depend on diplomatic efforts to put these state coalitions together.

Multilateralism that results in agreed rules among state players is at least a partial remedy that can help them manage their relations. Constructing consultative or regulatory regimes to apply collective governance to selected issues is one approach. Given that certain regions (e.g., Northeast Asia, Central and South Asia, and the Persian or Arab Gulf) are at present undermultilateralized, then constructing regimes and institutional mechanisms to manage conflicts or foster greater cooperation or even collaboration is one way to impose structure on otherwise anarchic relations in these regions.

The payoff to national security that can emerge from establishing bases for enhanced regional and global governance of this kind has substantial promise. American leadership toward such ends is an essential ingredient. An anarchic world calls for such efforts, but success in taming the challenges of this brave new world is by no means assured.

The broad US interest is stability—maintaining its power and influence in the world it has been constructing in cooperation with others, particularly since the end of World War II. Not surprisingly, it is a world that reflects the liberal values that are at the core of the American experience.

The rule of law and freedoms to transit across borders, express ideas, form associations, import and export, invest and reap returns (or suffer losses) in a global economy are among the values prized among the fifty US states that have been exported globally in cooperation with the leaders of similarly constituted republics.

Stability is what is needed to maintain these values, enhance human rights, and provide security. It is a conservative commitment to gradualism best served by a reconstructed realism[1] (in many ways akin to tenets of classical realism) that also emphasizes the ways and means of cooperative security. Given the preeminent position it enjoys in the global order of relations, the United States is a conservative, not a revolutionary power that tries to alter radically the *status quo*.[2] It is a posture inherently opposed to rash, ill-thought-out uses of force that destabilize countries and regions.

What policy makers need as part of their operational code in this brave new world is *virtù*, the enlightened boldness that avoids or limits the use of force to what may be necessary (*necessità*), capitalizing instead on what can be gained through both bilateral and multilateral diplomacy befitting a great power with the enormous economic, military, and other capabilities of the United States. It is an adept use of its power to influence, persuade, and achieve its cooperative security objectives in relation to allies, coalition partners, and even adversaries that will sustain the US position in this brave new world.

CONCLUDING REFLECTIONS ON POLICY

The national security agenda in a still-anarchic, globalized world is daunting. Added to the "old realities" of interstate wars, armed interventions, insurgencies, terrorism, and other forms of political violence, national security decision makers also have to deal with the "brave new world" of cyber warfare, criminal networks, mass murders, natural threats from asteroids to climate change, water shortages, food shortages and resource competition, pandemics, weaponization of space, and proliferation of weapons of mass destruction. Policy-relevant conclusions include:

(1) Intelligence remains an important asset that policymakers need as they grapple with these new threats and old realities.

(2) Security will require cooperative action across the US government and private sector as well as with allies, coalition partners, other states, and both international and nongovernmental organizations.

(3) US defense spending—more than a third of what the entire world allocates to defense—is clear indication of consensus among policy elites in both political parties that the use of force likely will continue to be an important dimension of American national security policy.

(4) The way policymakers structure US forces reflects the capital and technological comparative advantage that the United States enjoys relative to its adversaries or other competitors.

(5) Pursuit of US foreign and national security objectives depends upon the continual acceptance of the dollar in payment of US obligations, particularly for defense-related outlays.

(6) Insurgencies, the turbulence they cause (and from which they are spawned) and the political violence they employ within and outside their regions likely will remain a major challenge on the American national security agenda for decades to come. Success in counterinsurgencies that attempt to transform a society abroad is usually beyond available means—not to mention knowhow.

(7) Military members fully integrated with—not apart from—American society not only aid national purposes, but also provide a check (buttressed by strongly held military norms) against any military intervention in domestic politics. A military that mirrors in diversity the society it is pledged to defend is what one expects in a democratic society. Successfully integrating minorities, women, and LGBT military members

is an important part of a decades-long project in society as a whole, the military in particular.

NOTES

1. On constructivism and realism, see Samuel Barkin, *Realist Constructivism: Rethinking International Relations Theory* (Cambridge, UK: Cambridge University Press, 2010).
2. For this distinction between conservative and revolutionary power in a different historical context, see Henry Kissinger, *A World Restored* (London: Phoenix Press, 1957).

ABOUT THE AUTHOR

Paul R. Viotti is Executive Director of the Institute on Globalization and Security at the University of Denver, where he is also a professor in the Josef Korbel School of International Studies. Professor Viotti holds a PhD in Political Science from the University of California, Berkeley, an MS from The George Washington University, an MA from Georgetown University, and a BS from the US Air Force Academy. His previous publications include *The Dollar and National Security, American Foreign Policy*, five editions of *International Relations Theory*, five editions of *International Relations and World Politics*, and three editions of *The Defense Policies of Nations*. He has served as President (1993–2003) and Vice Chair of the Board (2003–2016) for the Denver Council on Foreign Relations.

INDEX

CPSIA information can be obtained
at www.ICGtesting.com
Printed in the USA
FFOW02n0306261117
43680536-42527FF